Performers' Rights and Recording Rights

INTELLECTUAL PROPERTY LAW MONOGRAPHS

Performers' Rights and Recording Rights

UK Law Under the Performers' Protection Acts 1958–72 and the Copyright, Designs and Patents Act 1988

Richard Arnold

Barrister

ESC Publishing Limited
Oxford 1990

Published by ESC Publishing Limited
Mill Street
Oxford OX2 0JU
United Kingdom

Typeset by VAP Publishing Services
Printed by Billings Ltd

ISBN 0 906214 60 2

Contents

Part II The New Law of Performers' Rights and Recording Rights

Appendices

Preface

There was a period during the 1970s when it was said that the performances of the pop group Abba were Sweden's highest-earning export after Volvo cars. During the course of the twentieth century entertainment has become one of the largest and most profitable sectors of the world economy. Fundamental to this industry are the activities of two groups of people: creative artists and interpretative artists.

Though there are art forms that do not require any third party to mediate between the creator and the audience, there are also many forms that do require this. The largest subsectors of the entertainment industry are the record and the film and television industries. These could not exist without musicians, actors and other artists to interpret the works of composers and writers.

The United Kingdom can claim to have been among the first countries by its law to recognise that the fruits of creative artists' imagination deserve to be treated as their property, their 'copyright'. It is a remarkable fact that until 1988 this recognition was denied to interpretative artists. Until 1988 no performer had any statutory civil right to prevent the unauthorised exploitation of his performance.

With the enactment of the Copyright, Designs and Patents Act 1988 it is only a slight exaggeration to say that a new era has begun. Although the legislature for reasons best known to itself has declined to use the word 'copyright', the 'performer's rights' conferred by Part II of the Act are in effect the long-awaited performer's copyright (albeit not a full copyright since the rights are not assignable and imitation is not an infringement).

This change had to some extent been anticipated by the courts in the *Peter Sellers* case. In that case the estate of the actor Peter Sellers was awarded a million dollars damages together with 4.51 per cent of the gross receipts of the film *The Trail of the Pink Panther* for United Artists' unauthorised use in that film of clips and out-takes from previous films in the Pink Panther series featuring performances by Sellers. That decision was partly based upon a somewhat questionable interpretation of a criminal statute, the Dramatic and Musical Performers' Protection Act 1958. The 1988 Act puts the matter beyond doubt.

This book has two main purposes. The first is to state the law as it was before the coming into force of the 1988 Act on 1 August 1989: that is to say, under the Performers' Protection Acts 1958–72. It may be asked why space should be devoted to law that has been superseded. There are two answers. First, the earlier law applies to all acts done before commencement of the 1988 Act on 1 August 1989. These will remain actionable (unless the decision of the Court of Appeal in the *Peter Sellers* case is subsequently overruled by the House of Lords) until 1995. At present there is no text dealing with the subject. It is only dealt with in works on copyright, and due to pressure of space the treatments are inadequate. Secondly, the statute is largely based on the earlier law as it has evolved. It is the author's view that an understanding of the earlier law is at least of assistance in interpreting the new.

The second main purpose is, of course, to provide a guide to the new legislation. Part II of the 1988 Act provides litigants with new weapons, and poses others new problems (particularly in the drafting of performers' contracts). Although those experienced in copyright law will be better prepared than others for dealing with the new provisions, even they will find that unfamiliar concepts lie in wait. There will in due course be decisions of the courts interpreting the new provisions. Until then a degree of speculation is inevitable. It is hoped, however, that the book will be of assistance to practitioners and others by providing some signposts to the new territory.

I have endeavoured to state the law as at 31 July 1989 in Part I of the book and as at 1 August 1989 in Part II.

I would like to acknowledge my debt to Hugh Laddie, Peter Prescott and Mary Vitoria for the assistance I have gained from their indispensable work *The Modern Law of Copyright* (Butterworths 1980; referred to in this book as 'Laddie *et al.*'). I have attempted, in a very small way, to follow their example.

I have also benefited from Professor Cornish's *Intellectual Property: Patents, Copyright, Trade Marks and Allied Rights* (Sweet & Maxwell 1981 and 1989; referred to as 'Cornish').

My thanks are due to John Lane for considerable assistance with checking and proofreading. The errors that remain are entirely my own.

Above all, I am grateful to my wife Mary Elford for her support.

Richard Arnold

11 South Square
Gray's Inn
London WC1

Table of Cases

Table of Statutes and Statutory Instruments

Statutes

Statutory Instruments

1 Introduction

1.01   The title of this book refers to two new species of the genus *copyright*.[1] It may therefore be of assistance to some readers briefly to describe what copyright is, its history and how it has come to be extended to performers.

What is Copyright?

1.02   Copyright is first and foremost the right to control copying of a work. The owner of copyright has the right to copy the copyright work, while others do not. By extension, the copyright owner can control the way in which copies are dealt with. As new ways have been found to exploit copyright works by reproduction and dissemination, so the scope of copyright has progressively been enlarged. Copyright may thus conveniently be viewed as a bundle of rights in a work: the right to copy it, the right to adapt it, the right to perform it in public, the right to sell copies, the right to rent out copies and so on.

1.03   Copyright is a member of the family *intellectual property*. This family, which also includes patents, registered designs, trade marks and confidential information, is so called because it consists of rights of property in intellectual creations. All of these rights are intangible, but it is fundamental that they are regarded as property just as much as tangible property. Thus copyright is capable of being owned by one or more persons and of being bought and sold or otherwise dealt in.

1.04   It is a truism that, unlike some other intellectual property rights such as patents, copyright is not a monopoly. Copyright does not inhibit independent creation. The owner of the copyright in a photograph of St Paul's Cathedral

---

1   It should be made clear that this is an assertion, not an unequivocal statement of legal fact. Part II of the Copyright, Designs and Patents Act 1988, which creates the rights in question, deliberately eschews the word 'copyright'. Nevertheless, it is argued elsewhere, the effect is to create two new copyrights (albeit not full copyrights): see Ch. 4, paras. 4.02–03. See also Cornish, 1st edn, pp. 448–9; cf. 2nd edn, pp. 358–61.

cannot complain if another person independently takes an identical photograph of St Paul's Cathedral. It will be appreciated, however, that in many contexts a right to prevent copying is as good as a true monopoly. The high degree of improbability that two persons will independently write the same song means that having copyright in a song is virtually the same as having a monopoly in that song. Nevertheless, there is a difference.

1.05   It is an interesting question whether this is true of performances, with which this book is concerned. The Oxford English Dictionary definition is suggestive:

> **performance** . . . 3. *spec.* a. The action of performing a ceremony, play, part in a play, piece of music, etc.; formal or set execution. . . . c. The performing of a play, of music, of gymnastic or conjuring feats, or the like, as a definite act or series of acts done at an appointed place and time; a public exhibition or entertainment.[2]

What this omits, however, is that the act or series of acts is done by an appointed individual or individuals. Thus a performance is a something done by a particular individual at a particular place and at a particular time.[3]

1.06   It follows from this that it is impossible to create the same performance twice. Even if the same individual were to give a subsequent performance that was indistinguishable from the first, it would still be a different performance merely by virtue of taking place at a different time. Still less is it possible for a different performer to produce the same performance. In short, it is inherent in the concept of performance that each performance is unique. This is the distinction between creative artistry and interpretative artistry: the creative artist produces an artefact, an object separate from himself, whereas the interpretative artist produces a performance that is inseparable from himself. It is therefore the author's view that copyright in a performance (meaning at least the exclusive right to record, broadcast and exploit recordings of that performance) is, contrary to the general rule, a genuine monopoly.

The History of Copyright[4]

1.07   Although it is sometimes said that the first copyright case was that of St Columba,[5] it is generally accepted that there was no copyright or anything similar prior to the invention of printing. Printing in itself may not have led to

---

2   2nd edn.
3   See Ch. 4, para. 4.05 for the present statutory definition.
4   See generally Birrell, *The Law and History of Copyright in Books* (1899); Scrutton, *Law of Copyright* (4th edn, 1903); Feather, 'The History of Copyright and the Book Trade' [1988] EIPR 377.
5   St Columba is supposed to have copied Abbott Fenian's Psalter. The Abbott complained to King Diarmed, who gave judgment for the Abbott, saying 'to every cow her calf, and accordingly to every book its copy'.

any demand for copyright, but it seems that over the following three centuries, a combination of commercial pressure by booksellers and a desire for censorship by Church and State led to rigorous controls on printing.

1.08　The first form of copyright consisted of the prerogative claim by the Crown to the exclusive right to print books such as the Bible, statutes and in due course common law books. This privilege was naturally exercised by the King's Printer. Other printers, however, were able to petition the Crown for the grant of letters patent giving them a monopoly over the printing of particular books, in some cases for a period of years.

1.09　Needless to say, a system that depended on petitions to the Crown was rather haphazard. Much more effective was the control that came to be exercised over the printing of books by the printers' and stationers' guilds. This was formalised by the grant of a charter to the Stationers' Company in 1556. The charter created a system with three main elements. Lawfully printed books were those entered on the Stationers' Register; only Company members could enter a book on the Register; and the Company was empowered to search for and destroy unlawfully printed books. The significance of the second element was that Company members could be expected not to copy each others' books for fear of expulsion or other penalty.[6] In other words, the system was based on restrictive practice.

1.10　Originally, the Stationers' Register was a record of who owned the manuscript which had been approved by censors such as the Archbishop of Canterbury. State control over the printing of subversive or heretical material was enforced by the Court of the Star Chamber. Decrees issued by the the Star Chamber in 1586 and 1637 codifying the law as to printing may be regarded as the first attempts at a copyright statute (the 1637 decree later formed the basis for the Licensing Act of 1676).

1.11　Under this system, control over printing was vested in the stationer, and not the author. The author's only property was in his manuscript: he could not even print it himself, but had to contract with a member of the Stationer's Company. As registration came to be regarded as giving an exclusive right, the stationers got into the habit of purchasing from authors the right to print a book 'for ever'. Ownership of 'copies' came to be treated as property, being inherited by sons or widows and also bought and sold. This became commercially very significant in the book trade, and gave rise to the argument that there was at common law a perpetual copyright.

1.12　After the abolition of the Star Chamber, this system was preserved first by orders of Parliament and then by statute, with a brief lapse from 1679 to 1685, until Parliament refused to renew it in 1694. After this, piracy (that is to

---

6　A by-law of the Company made in 1681 imposed a fine of 12 pence per copy for copying another member's book. ,

say, unauthorised copying of published editions) of books, particularly by Scottish publishers after the Act of Union,[7] became so common that authors and booksellers were moved to agitate for a statutory copyright. Legend has it that the resulting Copyright Act of 1709, known as the Statute of Anne, was originally drafted by Swift.[8]

1.13   This Act for the first time conferred rights on authors and through them their assigns. Under it the author and his assigns had the sole right of printing books for a term of 14 years from the date of publication, and if the author was still alive at the expiry of this period there was a second term of 14 years. Books published before the Act were protected for 21 years from the date of commencement. The titles of books still had to be registered at Stationers' Hall, but it was no longer a stationers' monopoly.

1.14   Nevertheless, the book trade seems to have regarded the Act as little more than providing statutory penalties for infringement of their property rights. After the expiry of the 21-year transitional period a number of cases were brought, particularly against Scots and country booksellers, in which it was argued that notwithstanding the expiry of the statutory protection booksellers had property rights in copies which were perpetual like any other form of property. This question was not settled until 1774, when the House of Lords in *Donaldson v Becket*[9] held that the Statute of Anne had abolished common law copyright in published works.

1.15   After the Statute of Anne, copyright developed in four ways. First, the term of protection was successively extended by amending Acts of 1801 and 1814 and by the Copyright Act 1842 (Talfourd's Act), which repealed the Statute of Anne. Under the 1842 Act, copyright in published works lasted for the life of the author plus seven years or 42 years, whichever was the longer.

1.16   Secondly, the protection afforded by copyright was enlarged to include 'use rights'. Thus the Dramatic Copyright Act 1833 (Bulwer Lytton's Act) created the performing right for dramatic works, and this was extended by the 1842 Act to musical works.

1.17   Thirdly, copyright was accorded to other classes of work. Engravings were first protected by the Engraving Copyright Act of 1734 (succeeded by statutes of 1766, 1777 and 1836). Sculptures followed in 1798 (and 1814), and drawings, paintings and photographs were brought into the fold by the Fine Arts Copyright Act 1862.

1.18   Fourthly, copyright became international. The Statute of Anne only protected books by British authors. In 1838 the first International Copyright Act was passed which enabled copyright to be conferred on foreign authors by

---

7   See Prescott, 'The Origins of Copyright: A Debunking View' [1989] EIPR 453.
8   Birrell, Note 4 above, pp. 20, 93.
9   (1774) 4 Burr. 2408.

Order in Council; a wider Act was passed in 1844. In 1851 Britain entered into the first bilateral copyright convention. This was succeeded by a number of others until in 1886 a muiltilateral convention was agreed at Berne. This provided for reciprocal protection to be accorded by contracting States to each others' authors. It was given effect to by the International Copyright Act 1886. At the Berlin revision of the Berne Convention in 1908, two important matters were agreed: that copyright should arise automatically on making the work, without any need for registration or other formality; and that the minimum term should be author's life plus 50 years.

1.19 All these developments were brought together in the Copyright Act 1911, the first modern copyright statute. This brought all the different copyrights under one piece of legislation, including giving statutory protection to unpublished works for the first time.[10] In addition, the first 'neighbouring right'[11] was established, namely the copyright in sound recordings.

1.20 The 1911 Act was succeeded by the Copyright Act 1956. This again established a number of new rights, in this case copyright in cinematograph films, broadcasts and the typographical format of published editions. Technological change meant that the 1956 Act was out of date very soon after it arrived on the statute book: it made little or no allowance for either new subject matter for copyright, such as computer programs,[12] or for new means of copying, such as photocopiers and cassette recorders. Nevertheless a new statute had to wait until 1988, and the creation of yet further new rights by the Copyright, Designs and Patents Act 1988. It is with two of these new rights that this book is primarily concerned.

The Evolution of a Performers' Copyright

1.21 To begin with, copyright was concerned with artefacts, with books and then engravings. Bulwer Lytton's Act arose from a recognition that certain classes of work were principally exploited through performance, and accordingly rights in performances were required. At this time no thought was given to the performers involved, merely to the author of the work performed. The reason for this was obvious enough, namely that performers did not need protection, for the only way in which their performance could be exploited was by the public paying for admission to a performance. Performers might be

---

10 Section 31 abolished common law copyright in unpublished works.
11 The term 'neighbouring rights' is used in a narrow sense (meaning rights of performers, phonogram producers and broadcasters) and in a broad sense (meaning rights similar to but less than full copyright). The latter sense, which is used here, derives from the reluctance of civil law systems based on the concept of *droit d'auteur* to accord full copyright where the 'author' is a corporation. See Appendix 2, para. A2.13 and Note 44.
12 These were not specifically provided for by statute until the passing of the Copyright (Computer Software) Amendment Act 1985.

unfairly exploited by impresarios, but that was simply a matter of contract between the performer and the impresario.

1.22   As ever with copyright, it was technology which changed the position. Once performances could be fixed, it was possible to exploit them other than by simply charging the public admission to a show. A new artefact came into being which could be reproduced and disseminated.

1.23   Although both sound recordings and cinematograph films were both well-established technologies by 1911 (indeed, the 1911 Act accorded copyright to producers of sound recordings), the position of performers was neglected. Not until 1925 was any attempt made to protect performers from the unauthorised exploitation of their performances that the new technologies made possible. The Dramatic and Musical Performers' Protection Act 1925 prohibited the recording of performances without consent and dealing in recordings so made. Even then, however, the only remedy provided was criminal. During the passage of the Act through Parliament, the Labour Opposition of the day pointed out that an injunction and damages would be a more appropriate remedy, but this was rejected.[13]

1.24   After this the story was one of incremental extension of the criminal law by successive statutes and of intermitent attempts by performers to claim civil remedies in the courts.[14] In 1930, the first unsuccessful attempt was made in the *Blackmail* case.[15] In 1952 the Gregory Committee in its Report on the reform of copyright law rejected a proposal by the Musicians' Union, Equity and the Variety Artistes Federation (it is not entirely clear who the latter represented) that performers should be given a 'performers' right' in the nature of copyright.[16] The Copyright Act 1956 amended the 1925 Act belatedly to extend it to films. In 1958, a consolidating Act was passed, which remained the principal statute until the passing of the Copyright, Designs and Patents Act 1988.

1.25   In 1961 a considerable step forward was taken with the signing in Rome of a multilateral convention for the protection of performers, phonogram producers and broadcasting organisations.[17] This laid down minimum levels for protection to be accorded by contracting States. It was given effect to by the Performers' Protection Act 1963. The principal change effected by this statute was to enlarge the categories of performers able to claim protection under the 1958 Act. On the face of it, the remedies provided were still only criminal. A further statute in 1972 merely increased the penalties.

---

13   See Appendix 1, paras. A1.03–04.
14   See Appendix 2 for full details.
15   *Musical Performers Protection Association Ltd v British International Pictures Ltd* (1930) 46 TLR 485. See Appendix 2, para. A2.02.
16   Cmnd 8662 at para. 180. See Appendix 2, para. A2.03.
17   Cmnd 2425. See Appendix 2, paras. A2.12–15.

1.26   Between 1977 until 1983, however, there were a series of cases in which performers and those with whom they had exclusive contracts (particularly record companies) argued that they had civil rights of action under the Performers' Protection Acts. Some temporary successes were achieved, notably in the *island Records* case,[18] but these were effectively reversed by the decision of the Court of Appeal in *RCA v Pollard*.[19] The state of the authorities remained uncertain, however, until another decision of the Court of Appeal in the *Peter Sellers* case[20] in 1987, in which it was held that performers did have a civil right of action after all (though not record companies and the like).

1.27   In the meantime, the process of legislative reform was underway. The Whitford Committee was appointed in 1972 to review the law of copyright and reported in 1977. The Committee, rather oddly, recommended against giving performers a copyright in their performances, but in favour of making civil remedies such as an injunction and damages available.[21] It was this compromise recommendation that ultimately led to Part II of the Copyright, Designs and Patents Act 1988.

1.28   The Whitford Committee Report was followed by Green Papers in 1981[22] and 1983,[23] a White Paper in 1986[24] and finally by legislation in the shape of the Copyright, Designs and Patents Act 1988. This statute finally places it beyond doubt that performers have civil remedies by granting them 'performers' rights' which are in effect the long-awaited performers' copyright. In addition, 'recording rights' are granted to those who have exclusive recording contracts with performers.

Proposals for Reform

1.29   With the 1988 Act so recently on the statute book, it may seem somewhat premature to look ahead to possible future developments. Part II of the Act was long overdue, however, and in a number of respects is not everything it could be. In any event, it is to be anticipated that technological change will require further amendment or overhaul of the Copyright Act in due course, and this may provide the opportunity for a further look at the position of performers.

---

18   *Ex Parte Island Records Ltd* [1978] Ch 122. See Appendix 2, para. A2.07.
19   [1983] Ch 135. See Appendix 2, para. A2.09.
20   *Rickless v United Artists Corp.* [1988] QB 40. See Appendix 2, paras. A2.10–16.
21   Cmnd 6723 at para. 412.
22   Cmnd 8302.
23   Cmnd 9445.
24   Cmnd 9712.

1.30   The following points deserve consideration:

(1) The first and most obvious task is to bring performers into the copyright fold proper, rather than to continue to pretend that performers' rights are in some way different to other copyrights. This should be done by bringing performers' rights under what is now Part I of the Act, rather than in a separate Part. This would have the advantage of eliminating unnecessary duplication in drafting (for example, Schedule 2) and ensuring consistency of interpretation. It may be objected that performers' rights *are* different to copyright at least[25] to the extent that they are not infringed by copying or reproduction of the performance itself.[26] This is a point that in itself deserves consideration (see sub-paragraph (5) below), but even if this limitation were retained, it is not on its own a sufficient reason to treat performers' rights as so different to other copyrights that they need to be exiled to a separate Part.

(2) Turning to substance rather than form, performers' rights should be upgraded to a full property right so as to be assignable and otherwise transmissible to the same extent as other copyrights, rather than to the limited extent provided at present.[27] It is hard to see why performers and their heirs should be prejudiced by comparison with other copyright owners in this way.

(3) Next, performers' rights should be extended to sportsmen and women. As is argued elsewhere in this book,[28] no theoretical distinction can be drawn between sportsmen and other performers. Nor is there any economic justification for so doing. On the contrary, the economic arguments for granting performers' rights to sportsmen can only gain in force, for example with the introduction of satellite television channels devoted solely to sport. It is only snobbery that says that an opera singer should be accorded rights in his or her performance and not a boxer or tennis player.

(4) Consideration should also be given to the duration of the rights. The fixed term of 50 years adopted in the 1988 Act has the advantage of being the same term as for films and sound recordings.[29] It may, however, reasonably be questioned why a playwright should be entitled to life plus 50 years but an actor or director only to 50 years. The principal reason

---

25   Purists may also protest at the erosion of the distinction between a 'neighbouring right' and a copyright, but the true distinction, which is between a 'neighbouring right' and an 'author's right' (see Note 11 above), is not one recognised by the Copyright, Designs and Patents Act 1988: Part I contains common provisions for copyrights which are 'author's rights' and for those which are not.
26   See Ch. 5, para. 5.08.
27   See Ch. 4, paras. 4.57–61.
28   Ch. 4, paras. 4.21–22.
29   Copyright, Designs and Patents Act 1988, section 13.

why copyright in films and sound recordings is a fixed term is that the 'author' for the purpose of these species of copyright is likely to be a corporation, and so it is not possible to set a term *post mortem auctoris*. This difficulty does not apply to performers. On the other hand, the same difficulty does arise in relation to recording rights. It would be quite possible to have different terms for performers' rights and recording rights, but it is not clear whether this would be acceptable. This may be easier to gauge when a body of experience with these new rights has been built up.

(5) Finally, there is the difficult question of copying of performances themselves (as opposed to recordings or broadcasts of them). If the protection afforded to a playwright includes preventing another person from copying the whole or a substantial part of his play, is there any reason of principle why an actor should not be accorded the same right? Identical copying is, of course, an impossibility in the case of performances.[30] Copying of a substantial part is quite possible, however. The difficulty then lies in deciding where to draw the line between the permissible and the impermissible. Most people, one suspects, would say that impersonators should be permitted to continue their acts. But what about less frivolous copying of performances? An example of this is 'sound alike' advertising.[31] Another is 'sound alike music', music intended primarily for public performance (particularly as background music in shops and the like) in which the performers deliberately strive to imitate an existing performance as closely as possible. Since activities of this nature are economically damaging to the original performers and would seem to have little 'artistic' justification, it may be justifiable to give performers the right to prevent them.

---

30 See para. 1.05–06.
31 See Ch. 5, para. 5.08.

PART I

The Old Law of
Performers' Protection

2 Criminal Law

Introduction

2.01 Part II of the Copyright, Designs and Patents Act 1988 is partially retrospective.[1] Section 180(3) of the Act provides that the rights conferred by Part II apply in relation to performances taking place before commencement (1 August 1989[2]). No act done before commencement, or pursuant to 'arrangements made' before commencement, is to be an infringement, however. In contrast to Part I, there are no transitional provisions. The law to be applied to acts done before 1 August 1989 is therefore that contained in the Performers' Protection Acts 1958 to 1972 as amended.[3] As from 1 August 1989, the Performers' Protection Acts 1958–72 are repealed in their entirety.[4] It would therefore appear that acts done after 1 August 1989, but pursuant to arrangements made before that date, are not caught by either the Performers' Protection Acts 1958–72 or Part II of the Copyright, Designs and Patents 1988.[5]

2.02 The Performers' Protection Acts 1958–72 protect performers by making certain acts done in relation to their performances criminal offences. They

---

1 In the sense that it affects, albeit for the future only, the consequences of past conduct. See *Halsbury's Laws*, 4th edn, vol. 44, para. 921.
2 Copyright, Designs and Patents Act 1988 (Commencement No. 1) Order 1989, S.I. 1989 No. 816.
3 The Interpretation Act 1978, section 16(1)(c) provides that, unless the contrary intention appears, the repeal of an enactment does not affect any right, privilege, obligation or liability acquired, accrued or incurred under that enactment, and subsubsection (d) that it does not affect any penalty, forfeiture or punishment incurred in respect of any offence committed against that enactment. See for example, *Free Lanka Insurance Co. Ltd v Ranasinghe* [1964] AC 541. In the absence of transitional provisions, there is nothing in the 1988 Act to show a contrary intention.
4 Copyright, Designs and Patents Act 1988, section 303(2) and Schedule 8; Copyright, Designs and Patents Act 1988 (Commencement No. 1) Order 1989, Note 2 above.
5 See Ch. 6, para 6.51. In *Grower v BBC* (*The Times*, 6 July 1990) it was conceded that the plaintiffs had no cause of action under the 1988 Act in relation to acts done pursuant to a copyright licence granted in July 1988.

do not confer any copyright on performers. It has been argued in a number of cases that performers may nevertheless obtain civil relief under the Acts, and the Court of Appeal so held in the *Peter Sellers* case.[6] For the reasons discussed in Appendix 2, that decision is open to some doubt. The 1988 Act, however, effectively gives legislative confirmation to the decision. Therefore, although Part II constitutes an entirely new code (the long title states that it is 'to make fresh provision'), an understanding of the old law may be necessary to interpretation of the new.[7]

Protected Performances

2.03   The performances protected are those

of any actors, singers, musicians, dancers or other persons who act, sing, deliver, declaim, play in or otherwise perform literary, dramatic, musical or artistic works.[8]

This could be interpreted in two ways. First, that the performance must be of either (a) an actor, singer, musician or dancer or (b) any other person who acts, sings, delivers, declaims, plays in or otherwise performs a literary, dramatic, musical or artistic work. Second, that the performance must be of (a) an actor, singer, musician, dancer or other person who (b) acts, sings, delivers, declaims, plays in or performs a literary, dramatic, musical or artistic work. The difference is that under the first interpretation the performance of an actor, singer, musician or dancer would be protected even if he or she were not performing a literary, dramatic, musical or artistic work (ignoring, for the moment, the question of improvisation[9]). It is not easy to think of instances where this might be the case. If, for example, the performance were a display of juggling, could it be said that the performer was an actor, singer, musician or dancer? It seems clear that the performer must be categorised by the nature of his performance.[10] The second interpretation is therefore to be preferred.

Definition of works

2.04   The Acts contain no definition of 'literary, dramatic, musical or artistic

---

6   *Rickless v United Artists Corp.* [1988] QB 40.
7   In general, a codifying statute should be construed by first asking what is the natural meaning of the words used. Recourse may be had to the previous law, however, when construing provisions of doubtful import or words which have acquired a technical meaning. See *Halsbury's Laws*, 4th edn, vol. 44, para. 892. Note, however, that Part II does not contain any provision corresponding to section 172(2) of Part I, namely that the law shall not be construed as having changed merely because of a change of expression.
8   Dramatic and Musical Performers' Protection Act 1958, section 8(1) as amended by the Performers' Protection Act 1963, section 1(1).
9   As to which see para 2.05.
10   See also para. 2.13.

works'. The obvious assumption is that these words are used as terms of art, in other words that they bear the same meaning as in the Copyright Act 1956.[11] This is not necessarily correct – many terms are given different definitions to those in the 1956 Act – but it is difficult to see any other basis on which to proceed. Nevertheless, it will be submitted that where necessary these words should be given a slightly broader construction in the Performers' Protection Acts than in the Copyright Act.[12]

Improvised performances

2.05 Applying the Copyright Act definitions raises the question of fixation. What if the performance is extempore? For simplicity, let us suppose that the performance is entirely extempore, in the limited sense that no part of what is performed has been reduced to writing or other material form prior to the performance. Under the Copyright Act 1956 no copyright subsists in Part I works unless and until they are 'made' that is, reduced to writing or other material form[13] (or at least published).[14] Thus, although the work may exist in its author's mind, copyright does not subsist until it (or a reproduction of it) is fixed in material form.[15] Once the work exists, albeit unfixed, however, it can be performed and the performance will, it is submitted, be protected. Thus performers' protection is independent of copyright.

2.06 The difficulty with this is the definition of 'dramatic work' in section 48(1) of the 1956 Act,[16] which

> includes a choreographic work or entertainment in dumb show if reduced to writing in the form in which the work or entertainment is to be presented, but does not include a cinematograph film, as distinct from a scenario or script for a cinematograph film.

This suggests that a choreographic work or dumb show is not a 'dramatic work' if not committed to paper before performance. There does not appear to be any reason why the performance of such a work should not be protected,

---

11   It should be noted that throughout this chapter and Ch. 3 reference is made to the Copyright Act 1956 rather than to the Copyright, Designs and Patents Act 1988 unless the contrary is expressly stated.
12   See para. 2.06 for an example.
13   Copyright Act 1956, section 49(4).
14   *Ibid.*, section 2(1),(2). By section 49(2)(c) a literary, dramatic, musical or artistic work is only published if reproductions of the work have been issued to the public, and by sub-subsection (a) performance does not constitute publication.
15   See the discussion in Laddie *et al.*, paras. 2.12–2.17. Note that there may be a copyright in the fixation separate from the copyright in the work: *Walters v Lane* [1900] AC 539, 554–5 (per Lord James of Hereford), distinguishing between *mere* fixation (for example, writing down dictation verbatim) and fixation involving skill and labour (for example, recording ordinary speech in shorthand, transcribing, punctuating and correcting). This is expressly stated in the Copyright, Designs and Patents Act 1988: see section 3(2),(3).
16   Derived from Article 2(1) of the Berne Convention (Brussels text). The condition was abolished in the 1967 Stockholm revision of the Convention.

however; on contrary, if it cannot be the subject of copyright. It may be, therefore, that the courts would accept that 'dramatic work' is to be given a broader construction in the Performers' Protection Acts than in the Copyright Act.

2.07   What if the performance is entirely extempore? In other words, nothing exists even in the performers' mind prior to the moment of performance?[17] It may be objected that there cannot be a 'work' until it is complete, that is, until the improvisation is finished. This cannot be right, however, for a work in progress or an unfinished or unrevised work is still a 'work'. It is therefore submitted that a pure improvisation is a 'work' so that the performance is protected.[18]

Interviews

2.08   An interview is a particular form of improvisation. It is submitted that just as a jazz performance is an improvised collective musical work, so an interview is an improvised collective literary work.[19]

Aleatoric works

2.09   An aleatoric (or aleatory) work is a work which is 'dependent on uncertain contingencies',[20] for example one in which the author gives the performer (or even the audience) a number of options to choose between or one in which options are selected by some random means. Again, it is submitted that such pieces are works within the meaning of the Performers' Protection Acts.[21]

Artistic works

2.10   The oddity of protecting performances of 'artistic works' appears to originate from a misunderstanding of the Rome Convention. Article 3(a) of the Convention defines 'performers' as

> actors, singers, musicians, dancers, and other persons who act, sing, deliver, declaim, play in, or otherwise perform literary or artistic works.

The term 'literary and artistic works' here includes dramatic and musical works, being derived from Article 2(1) of the Berne Convention. It has been

---

17   Assuming for the sake of the argument that this is possible. In practice a large part of, say, a jazz musician's improvisation is likely to have been thought of in advance, if only momentarily. That being the case, it can be said with some degree of truth that the work comes into existence before it is performed.

18   If fixed it may also be the subject of copyright.

19   See the discussion in Ch. 4, paras. 4.24–25.

20   *Oxford English Dictionary*, 2nd edn. The word is derived from *aleator*, a dice player, from *alea*, a die.

21   See also the discussion in Ch. 4, para. 4.26.

suggested[22] that the inclusion of artistic works in the 1963 Act may give protection to the performers of a tableau vivant, but this would seem to be a species of dramatic work (specifically, a dumb show) and so covered in any event. The same is the case with most forms of 'performance art'. On the other hand, certain forms of 'conceptual art' may be protected.[23] Another possibility is that persons such as lighting technicians are protected. The basis for this is that the lighting design for a play or opera is, typically, a part literary and part artistic work which is in a real sense 'performed' by a technician each night.[24] It is difficult to see in what sense a costume or production design, on the other hand, might be said to be 'performed'.

Borderline cases

2.11   In areas of doubt, it would appear justified to construe the class of protected performances widely. If the criterion of originality for copyright purposes, namely the exercise of skill and labour,[25] were taken as the yardstick for judging whether or not to grant protection, the likely result would be that almost all performances were protected.[26] It is precisely in those situations where copyright is for whatever reason unavailable that protection is most needed. This may mean interpreting 'literary, dramatic, musical or artistic works' slightly more broadly in the context of the Performers' Protection Acts than under the 1956 Act.[27]

Circus performers and sportsmen

2.12   Doubts have been expressed as to whether performances of figure skating and ballroom dancing are protected.[28] It is submitted that (subject to the question of fixation) these are choreographic (that is, danced) works within section 48(1) of the 1956 Act and therefore protected. Synchronised swimming might be regarded as being in the same category. It is not clear whether performances such as those of magicians, clowns, jugglers, acrobats and other circus performers are protected.[29] The definition of 'dramatic work' could be

---

22   Laddie *et al.*, para. 18.8, referring to *Hanfstaengl v H.R. Baines & Co. Ltd* [1895] AC 20.
23   For example, some of the works of the American artist Sol LeWitt. Each of these works consists only of its title, which is a series of instructions for a drawing. All the purchaser of the work receives is a certificate. In order to exhibit the work, the instructions are carried out. This is usually done by persons other than LeWitt himself. These persons thus do 'perform' the work.
24   Although lighting desks are increasingly computerised. The lighting design itself (and the computer program) will be protected by copyright.
25   See Laddie *et al.*, paras. 2.30–44.
26   Originality is not, of course, a requirement under the Performers' Protection Acts.
27   See para. 2.06 for an example.
28   Cornish, 1st edn, page 446; Laddie *et al.*, para. 18.8.
29   The Whitford Committee thought that they were not, and recommended that they should be: Cmnd 6732 at para. 407. The recommendation has been implemented in the Copyright, Designs and Patents Act 1988. See Ch. 4, paras. 4.18–20.

stretched to cover some of these: clowning is surely 'dumb show' or mime, for example, while juggling and acrobatics could be so regarded.[30] Other circus performances are probably not protected, while sporting activities other than those mentioned are almost certainly not.[31]

Interpreters and executants

2.13   The English text of the Rome Convention only uses the word 'performer'. In the French text[32] the expression *'artiste interprète ou executant'* is used. The French text is to be preferred, for it makes it clear that both *artiste interprètes* and *artistes executants* are protected.[33] Thus performers who merely interpret, such as conductors and directors, are included as well those who execute the interpretation of another, such as musicians and actors. It is debatable whether the Performers' Protection Acts cover merely interpretative artists. If the construction of section 1(1) of the 1963 Act advanced in paragraph 2.03 of this work is correct, it is arguable that the 'other persons' whose performances are protected must be construed *ejusdem generis* with 'actors, singers, musicians, dancers'. This might be taken to mean that the persons in question must be executive artists. Similarly with 'act, sing, deliver, declaim, play in or otherwise perform'. It is submitted, however, that this would be to adopt a much too legalistic approach. The word 'musician', after all, is ambiguous: is not the conductor of an orchestra a 'musician'?[34] For this reason, and in order to comply with the Rome Convention,[35] it is submitted that the Acts should be construed as protecting interpretative artists. On the other hand, the line is likely to be drawn at collaborating artists such as costume designers.[36]

Performance or adaptation

2.14   Some interpretative artists – particularly some theatre directors – alter a work to such an extent that their contribution must be categorised as adaptation rather than mere performance, though it will qualify as performance as well.[37] This is discussed in Chapter 4.[38]

---

30   They formed part of *commedia dell 'arte*, after all.
31   The Gregory Committee was urged to extend copyright to sportsmen by the Association for the Protection of Copyright in Sport, but rejected the proposal: Cmnd 8662 at para. 180. As the examples quoted show, however, it is not easy to draw the line between 'artists' and 'sportsmen'. See Ch. 4, para. 4.22 for a theoretical discussion.
32   The English, French and Spanish texts of the Convention are equally authentic: Article 33(1).
33   See 'Preparatory Document for and Report of the WIPO/Unesco Committee of Governmental Experts on Dramatic, Choreographic and Musical Works', para. 62 in [1987] *Copyright* 185, 199.
34   See also the discussion in Ch. 4, para. 4.29.
35   This being the express purpose of the Performers' Protection Act 1963.
36   See para. 2.10. Costume designs and the like are protected by copyright.
37   Assuming the argument advanced in para. 2.13 is correct.
38   See paras. 4.31–33.

Mechanical or electrical means

2.15 'Performance' includes

> any performance, mechanical or otherwise, of any such work, being a performance rendered or intended to be rendered audible by mechanical or electrical means.[39]

The effect of this provision, which derives from the 1925 Act, is unclear. It cannot be concerned with the mere amplification of voices or musical instruments, for no one could suppose that a performance ceases to be a performance merely because it is amplified. The original purpose appears to have been to extend protection to broadcast performances, in order to prevent members of the public recording them from the radio.[40] This possibility would seem to be adequately covered, however, by the inclusion in section 1(a) of the 1925 Act (and now sections 1 and 2 of the 1958 Act) of the words 'directly or indirectly'.[41]

2.16 The words are apt, on the other hand, to include recorded performances (although it might be queried why the draughtsman did not just say so if this was intended). It may be that the intention was to extend protection to performances of recordings (that is, playing them back),[42] but the inclusion of the words 'or intended to be rendered' spreads the net wider than this. A more likely alternative is that the intention was to ensure that a performance recorded by a broadcasting organisation for later broadcast would be protected as well as a live[43] broadcast performance. The provision does not distinguish between such ephemeral recordings and other records, however. Thus the effect of the provision appears simply to be that performances do not have to be live to be protected under the Performers' Protection Acts.[44] This is supported by the stipulation that the 'performer' in the case of a mechanical performance means the person whose performance is mechanically reproduced (and not the person who does the reproducing).[45]

2.17 If this interpretation is correct, every copying of a record without consent will constitute a breach of the Acts as well as an infringement of any copyright that may subsist. Even if it is not, however, it is probable that the same result follows from the use of the words 'directly or indirectly' — at least

---

39 Dramatic and Musical Performers' Protection Act 1958, section 8(1).
40 See Appendix 1, para. A1.02.
41 See para. 2.26.
42 Cf. the definition of 'performance' (in the context of perform*ing* rights) in the Copyright Act 1911, section 35(1):

> 'performance' means any acoustic representation of a work and any visual representation of any dramatic action in a work, *including such a representation made by means of any mechanical instrument* [emphasis added].

43 In the sense of not pre-recorded. See Ch. 4 paras. 4.35–36.
44 Cf. the position under the Copyright, Designs and Patents Act 1988. See Ch. 4, paras. 4.35–36.
45 Dramatic and Musical Performers' Protection Act 1958, section 8(1).

so far as section 1 and 2 offences are concerned. The Acts do not extend to a performance rendered or intended to be rendered *visible* by mechanical or electrical means.[46] The interpretation discussed in the preceding paragraph is thus not applicable to films and videos; but an offence may still be committed by copying a film and thus indirectly making a film from the performance(s) embodied in the film which has been copied.[47]

Venue of performance

2.18   Section 1(2) of the 1963 Act provides that the 1958 Act applies

> as respects anything done in relation to a performance notwithstanding that the performance took place out of the United Kingdom.

The venue of the performance is therefore irrelevant.[48] It is submitted that this is not affected by section 2 of the 1963 Act. Although this section is exceptionally difficult to construe,[49] it seems clear that, whatever else it may mean, the section is not concerned with the venue of the *performance* as opposed to that of the *making of the record*.[50] Either way, the section does not apply to films.

No qualification or formalities

2.19   Just as the venue of the performance is irrelevant, so too, it would appear, is the nationality, domicile or residence of the performer. There is nothing in the Performers' Protection Acts which requires the performer to have any connection with the United Kingdom, or with any other country. Similarly, there is no requirement for any formalities to be observed as a precondition of protection.

Duration of Protection

2.20   The Performers' Protection Acts do not contain any stipulation as to the duration of the protection which they provide. It had been suggested that this was because the necessity for consent died with the performer, thereby providing a natural limit to the protection.[51] In the *Peter Sellers* case both Hobhouse J and the Court of Appeal held that liability under the Acts did not

---

46   Cf. Copyright Act 1956, section 48(1).
47   See para. 2.34.
48   The venue of an act done in relation to a performance is important, however. See paras. 2.24, 2.42 and 2.75–79.
49   See paras. 2.76–78.
50   A contrary suggestion is discussed in Laddie *et al.*, at para. 18.4.
51   Phillips, *Introduction to Intellectual Property* (1986), para. 17.3.

cease with the death of the performer, with the consequence that performers were protected in perpetuity.[52] Their reasons differed, however.

2.21 Hobhouse J noted that the 1958 Act nowhere referred to the death of the performer and took the view that *prima facie* if the performer had died without giving his consent an offence could still be committed. He proceeded to reject the submission that the statute should be narrowly construed, relying on two principal considerations as reinforcing his interpretation. The first was that section 7 of the 1958 Act envisaged that consent might be given on behalf of a performer, and this could include consent given by someone authorised to give it after the performer's death. The second was that in the judge's view the Act was passed primarily to protect the economic interests of performers, and so it would be to frustrate rather than to fulfil the purpose of the Act to construe it as ceasing to apply after the performer's death.[53] He was not perturbed that there would thus be no point in time at which performances would fall into the public domain, commenting that Parliament would no doubt act if and when it considered that a problem had arisen.[54]

2.22 In the Court of Appeal, the Vice-Chancellor disagreed with Hobhouse J's views on section 7 (which, it may be pointed out, primarily exists to provide someone who obtains consent from a person who represents that he has authority to give it with a *defence*[55]):

> Section 7 is dealing with the ostensible authority of an agent to give consent on behalf of a performer; it depends on a representation that the agent is authorised by the performer to give such consent on his behalf. If the performer has died, no such authority to consent as agent could exist: such authority dies with the performer. Personal representatives are not the agents of the deceased; their powers rest not on the authority given to them by the deceased, but on a quite separate authority given to them by law to stand in the place of the deceased.[56]

The Vice-Chancellor held, however, applying *Dean v Wiesengrund*,[57] that *prima facie* a right conferred on a man by statute survived his death and that clear words were required if it was to be held that the right was purely personal so as to die with him. There were no such words in the 1958 Act, and so the right to give or withhold consent survived the death of the performer to vest in his personal representatives. The Vice-Chancellor agreed with Hobhouse J as to the purpose of the Act.[58]

2.23 *Dean v Wiesengrund* was a case where, as all the three members of the Court of Appeal that heard it pointed out,[59] the statute under consideration

---

52 [1986] FSR 502, [1988] QB 40.
53 [1986] FSR 502, 508–9.
54 As it now has in the Copyright, Designs and Patents Act 1988. See Ch. 4, para. 4.56.
55 See paras. 2.82–86.
56 [1988] QB 40, 57.
57 [1955] 2 QB 120.
58 [1988] QB 40, 56–7.
59 [1955] 2 QB 120, 124, 129, 137.

created a *debt*. The conclusion that it was enforceable by the creditor's personal representatives after his death was therefore inescapable. It is doubtful whether it is authority for the proposition for which the Vice-Chancellor relied upon it. The general rule is that all property, whether real or personal, to which a deceased person was entitled for an interest not ceasing on his death devolves upon his personal representative.[60] It is submitted that the question whether the right to give or withhold consent under the Performers' Protection Acts survives the death of the performer involves a two-stage inquiry. Firstly, does the right qualify as personal property? Second, if it does, is the performer's interest such as not to cease upon death? As to the first, it is submitted that, being a statutory right, it is personal property. As to the second, it is submitted that this depends upon the true construction of the statute and not upon any presumption. The absence of any provision for a term of protection would seem to suggest that the legislature thought that the right would cease upon death.[61]

Prohibited Acts

2.24   The Performers' Protection Acts make it an offence knowingly to do the following acts in the United Kingdom:

(i) making a record directly or indirectly from or by means of a protected performance without the consent in writing of the performer(s);[62]

(ii) making a cinematograph film directly or indirectly from or by means of a protected performance without the consent in writing of the performer(s);[63]

(iii) selling, letting for hire, distributing for the purposes of trade or by way of trade exposing or offering for sale or hire a record or film made in contravention of the Acts;[64]

(iv) using for the purposes of public performance or exhibition a record or film made in contravention of the Acts;[65]

(v) otherwise than by use of a record or film broadcasting the whole or part of a protected performance without the consent in writing of the performer(s);[66]

(vi) otherwise than by use of a record or film or the reception and immediate re-transmission of a broadcast including the whole or part of a

---

60   See *Halsbury's Laws*, 4th edn, vol. 17, para. 1071.
61   Cf. the question of whether rights under the Performers' Protection Acts are assignable, discussed in Ch. 3, paras. 3.02–08.
62   Dramatic and Musical Performers' Protection Act 1958, section 1(a). See paras. 2.26–2.33.
63   *Ibid.*, section 2(a). See paras. 2.34–37.
64   *Ibid.*, sections 1(b), 2(b). See paras. 2.38–42.
65   *Ibid.*, sections 1(c), 2(c). See paras. 2.43–47.
66   *Ibid.*, section 3. See paras. 2.48–50.

protected performance in a cable programme without the consent in writing of the performer(s);[67] or

(vii) making or having in one's possession a plate or similar contrivance for the purposes of making records in contravention of the Acts.[68]

Consent

2.25 Although absence of consent is part of the *actus reus* of a number of the offences, it is convenient to deal with this topic when considering the requirement of *mens rea*.[69]

1. Making a record

2.26 By section 1(a) of the Dramatic and Musical Performers' Protection Act 1958, it is an offence for a person knowingly to make a record directly or indirectly from or by means of a protected performance without the consent in writing of the performer(s). The requirement of knowledge is in contrast to the position under the Copyright Act 1956, where making a record is a primary infringement.[70]

Record

2.27 'Record' is defined as meaning

> any record or similar contrivance for reproducing sound, including the soundtrack of a cinematograph film.[71]

The wording of this is different to the definition contained in section 48(1) of the 1956 Act, but the effect seems to be the same. Thus although the soundtrack of a film is not expressly covered by the latter, the definition is wide enough to do so.[72]

Directly or indirectly

2.28 The inclusion of the words 'or indirectly or by means of' has the effect that copying a record – thus indirectly making a (new) record from the (previously-recorded) performance – amounts to a breach of the Acts, in addition to an infringement of any copyright that may subsist. It is doubtful that this was intended,[73] but such is the natural meaning of the words. In the

---

67 Performers' Protection Act 1963, section 3(1) as amended by the Cable and Broadcasting Act 1984, section 57(1) and Schedule 5, para. 13(1). See paras. 2.51–2.54.
68 Dramatic and Musical Performers' Protection Act 1958, section 4. See paras. 2.55–56.
69 See paras. 2.60–79. See also the section on defences, paras. 2.80–93.
70 Copyright Act 1956, section 12(5)(a).
71 Dramatic and Musical Performers' Protection Act 1958, section 8(1).
72 See, however, the provisions of section 13(9) of the Copyright Act 1956.
73 It appears that the intention was to prevent recording of broadcast performances. See para. 2.15 and Appendix 1, para. A1.02.

Peter Sellers case the defendants conceded[74] that they had made a film 'directly or indirectly' from Sellers' previously recorded performances in out-takes and clips from earlier films. Although this concession was strictly unnecessary, to have argued otherwise would have been difficult.

More than one work

2.29   It is clear from the wording of section 1(a) of the 1958 Act that each work must be considered separately. In other words, each time a record is made from a performance of a work, there may be an offence, even if more than one work is included in a single performance or a single record.

Part of a work

2.30   The converse does not follow: it is still an offence to make a record from a performance of part only of a work. Although it is a principle of statutory construction that penal statutes are to be construed strictly,[75] and it might be said that an entire work must be recorded before there is an offence,[76] a person still makes a record 'from' a work even if he only records part. The rule of construction means no more than that if, after the ordinary rules of statutory construction have been applied, there remains any doubt or ambiguity, the defendant is entitled to the benefit of the doubt.[77] It is submitted that the Performers' Protection Acts are not ambiguous in this respect, and that it cannot have been the intention of the draughtsman to make only the recording of an entire work an offence.

2.31   It might be argued that a contrary conclusion follows by comparison of the respective definitions in the 1958 Act of 'record' and 'cinematograph film': the latter[78] expressly includes a film of part of work, the former does not. Apart from the difficulty of seeing why records and films should be treated differently, however, the distinction is illusory. 'Record' is not defined by reference to works at all, but merely to 'sound'. This must include part of a work. Nor is this construction affected by the fact that section 3 of the 1958 Act expressly prohibits the broadcast of any part of a performance of a work.[79] The difference in wording is sufficiently accounted for, it is submitted, by the absence of a preposition from section 3. If section 3 merely read 'broadcasts a performance of a work', broadcast of the entire work would be necessary before there was an offence. As has been just been argued, this is not so with making a record 'from the performance of a work'.

---

74   *Rickless v United Artists Corp.* [1986] FSR 502, 507.
75   See *Halsbury's Laws*, 4th edn, vol. 44, para. 910 and cases cited in note 1.
76   As is suggested by Cornish, 1st edn, p. 447.
77   See *Halsbury's Laws*, 4th edn, vol. 44, para. 910 and cases cited in note 5.
78   Dramatic and Musical Performers' Protection Act 1958, section 8(1). See para. 2.35.
79   See paras. 2.48–50.

2.32   The construction will nevertheless be subject to the *de minimis* principle, so that it will not be an offence to record a negligible part of a work. This may result in the courts effectively requiring that a substantial part be taken.

Part of a performance

2.33   It follows from the considerations advanced in the preceding paragraphs that the position is not affected if only part of a particular performance is recorded. Again, a more than negligible – possibly, a substantial – part must be taken.

2.   Making a film

2.34   By section 2(a) of the 1958 Act, it is an offence for a person knowingly to make a cinematograph film directly or indirectly from or by means of a protected performance without the consent in writing of the performer(s). It would appear that copying an existing film amounts to making a film indirectly from performances embodied in the copied film.[80] Again the need for knowledge differs from the corresponding Copyright Act provision.[81]

Cinematograph film

2.35   A 'cinematograph film' is defined as

> any print, negative, tape or other article on which a peformance of [a work] or part thereof is recorded for the purposes of visual reproduction.[82]

This definition is significantly different to that contained in section 13(10) of the Copyright Act 1956. Whereas under the 1956 Act 'cinematograph film' includes any soundtrack,[83] under the Performers' Protection Acts the soundtrack is excluded and treated as a record.[84] Thus making a soundtrack from a protected performance is an offence under section 1(a) and not under section 2(a) of the 1958 Act.[85] The definition is wide enough to encompass videos, laser discs and other technologies.

2.36   Note that it is expressly provided that a film of a performance of *part* of a work is within the Acts.[86] If more than one work is filmed there may be more than one offence.[87]

---

80   See para. 2.26.
81   Copyright Act 1956, section 13(5)(a).
82   Dramatic and Musical Performers' Protection Act 1958, section 8(1).
83   Copyright Act 1956, section 13(9).
84   See para. 2.27.
85   For other effects of this see paras. 2.38 and 2.43.
86   Cf. paras. 2.30–32.
87   See para. 2.29.

Making

2.37   Section 8(2) of the 1958 Act defines the 'making' of a film as

the carrying out of any process whereby a performance . . . or part thereof is recorded for the purposes of visual reproduction.

Again, the definition is wide enough to encompass all technologies.

3. Dealing in contraband records or films

2.38   Sections 1(b) and 2(b) respectively of the 1958 Act make it an offence knowingly to sell, let for hire, distribute for the purposes of trade or by way of trade expose or offer for sale or hire a record or film made in contravention of the Acts. It should be noted that under the Performers' Protection Acts the soundtrack of a film is treated as a record,[88] so that dealing in a non-silent film may involve an offence under section 1(b) as well under section 2(b). Other than that, these provisions are substantially similar to the secondary infringement provisions contained in section 5(3) and (4) of the Copyright Act 1956. Presumably they are to be construed in the same way as the copyright provisions, and authorities on the latter are applicable to the former.

Sale or return

2.39   Where a person supplies goods to another on sale or return and subsequently receives notice that the goods infringe a third party's copyright he is not liable for secondary infringement if he fails to demand the return of the goods.[89]

Exposure for sale

2.40   Showing a sample to a potential customer and asking for orders is apparently not an exposure for sale and so cannot be an infringement of copyright.[90]

Distribution for the purposes of trade

2.41   It is possible for a trader to handle goods without distributing them. For example, a bookbinder who bound infringing copies of trade lists did not distribute them because his only intention was to return them to the printer after binding.[91] It is not clear, however, whether a carrier or warehouseman who does no more than carry or store goods for a consignor or consignee could

---

88   See paras. 2.27.
89   *Schofield & Sims Ltd v Robert Gibson & Sons Ltd* [1928–35] MCC 64. See the discussion in Ch. 5, paras. 5.40–41.
90   *Britain v Kennedy* (1903) 19 TLR 122.
91   *J. Whitaker & Sons Ltd v Publishers Circular Ltd* [1946–49] MCC 10.

be said to be distributing the goods so as to be liable if given the requisite knowledge. It is submitted that a person who merely holds goods to someone else's order in this way should not be regarded as a distributor.[92]

Importation

2.42 In contrast to section 5(2) of the Copyright Act 1956, importation *per se* is not a prohibited dealing under the Performers' Protection Acts. Dealing within the United Kingdom in a record (but not a film) made abroad may, however, be prohibited by virtue of section 2 of the 1963 Act. This topic is dealt with separately.[93]

4. Using contraband records or films for public performance or exhibition

2.43 Sections 1(c) and 2(c) respectively of the 1958 Act make it an offence knowingly to use for the purposes of public performance a record made in contravention of the Acts or knowingly to use for the purposes of exhibition to the public a film so made. The requirement of knowledge is in contrast to Part II of the Copyright Act 1956, where causing a record to be heard in public and causing a film to be seen or heard in public both constitute primary infringements.[94] Again, the fact that under the Performers' Protection Acts the soundtrack of a film is treated as a record,[95] means that public screening of a non-silent film may involve an offence under section 1(c) as well under section 2(c).[96]

Public

2.44 The meaning of 'in public' has been considered in a number of copyright cases[97] in relation to infringements of copyright in films and sound recordings. While the wording of the provisions in the 1958 Act are slightly different, it would seem that the copyright authorities are applicable. These indicate that the decisive factor is the *nature* of the audience, rather than its size or whether it paid for the pleasure or the nature of the venue. A public performance or exhibition is one for which the audience is not a domestic or quasi-domestic one. It seems that a domestic or quasi-domestic audience is one that lives under one roof.[98] Thus a performance of a play by members of the

---

92 Cf. *Smith Kline & French Laboratories Ltd v R.D. Harbottle (Mercantile) Ltd* [1979] FSR 555.
93 See paras. 2.76–79.
94 Copyright Act 1956, sections 13(5) and 12(5) respectively.
95 See para. 2.27.
96 As with the offences of dealing in contraband records and films: see para. 2.38.
97 See Laddie *et al.*, para. 7.46 and the cases cited there.
98 *Jennings v Stephens* [1936] 1 Ch 469 explaining *Duck v Bates* (1884) 13 QBD 843.

Womens' Instititute of one village to an audience of members of the Institute of another village was held to have been 'in public' even though non-members had not been admitted and no charge had been made.[99]

2.45   Applying this construction of 'public' in sections 1(c) and 2(c) of the 1958 Act achieves a result parallel to that effected by the provisos to sections 1 and 2, namely that in relation to the offences under sections 1(a) and 2(a), it is a defence to prove that the record or film was made for 'private and domestic use only'.[100] The offences under sections 1(b) and 2(b) are different because the acts concerned are of *trading* in records and films and so cannot involve private enjoyment of them.

Broadcasting

2.46   An interesting question is whether a broadcast of a record or film made in contravention of the Acts is a 'performance' or 'exhibition' so as to be capable of constituting an offence. This is expressly excluded from section 3 of the 1958 Act.[101] Unless, therefore, such broadcasting is an offence under sections 1(c) and 2(c), it is not prohibited by the Acts at all. It is odd that broadcasting organisations (which are, after all, commercial entities) should be the only persons so privileged with respect to their dealings in records and films.[102] It is nevertheless submitted that to hold otherwise would involve a strained construction of 'performance' and 'exhibition'. In addition, it would subvert what was surely the intended effect of including the qualification in section 3.

Records made abroad

2.47   Using a record (but not a film) made abroad for public performance in the United Kingdom may be prohibited by virtue of section 2 of the Performers' Protection Act 1963. This is dealt with separately below.[103]

5.   Broadcasting a performance

2.48   Under section 3 of the 1958 Act it is an offence, otherwise than by use of a record or cinematograph film, knowingly to broadcast the whole or part of a protected performance without the consent in writing of the performer(s).

---

99   *Ibid.*
100   See paras. 2.88–89.
101   See paras. 2.48–50.
102   Section 3 was originally introduced by the Copyright Act 1956 (see section 45 and Schedule 6) and so the qualification anticipates the exception contained in Article 7 clause 1(a) of the Rome Convention.
103   See paras. 2.76–79.

Broadcast

2.49 'Broadcast' is defined as

broadcast by wireless telegraphy (within the meaning of the Wireless Telegraphy Act 1949), whether by way of sound broadcasting or of television.[104]

It is possible that this means that broadcast by wireless telegraphy within the meaning of the 1949 Act[105] other than sound broadcasting or television – for example, morse code – is not covered. Television broadcast by satellite is included.

Otherwise than by use of a record or film

2.50 At first sight, it might be thought that the purpose of this qualification was simply to ensure that an offence under section 1(c) or 2(c) was not also an offence under section 3, so that, for example, a public screening of a film made in contravention of the Acts would not also constitute an illegal broadcast. That is already achieved, however, by the definition of 'broadcast' quoted above. It is therefore clear that the qualification must exclude broadcasts of records and films. In other words, the performance must be live (in the sense of not pre-recorded) for a broadcast of it to be an offence under this section.[106]

6. Including a performance in a cable programme service

2.51 By section 3(1) of the Performers' Protection Act 1963,[107] it is an offence, otherwise than by the use of a record or film or the reception and immediate re-transmission of a broadcast, knowingly to include a protected performance or a part thereof in a cable programme without the consent in writing of the performer(s).

Cable programme

2.52 'Cable programme' means a programme[108] included in a 'cable programme service'.[109] 'Cable programme service' means either (a) a cable programme service within the meaning of the Cable and Broadcasting Act 1984 or (b) a service provided outside the United Kingdom which would be

---

104 Dramatic and Musical Performers' Protection Act 1958, section 8(1).
105 See Wireless Telegraphy Act 1949, section 19(1),(3),(6).
106 See also para. 2.46.
107 As amended by the Cable and Broadcasting Act 1984, section 57(1) and Schedule 5, para. 13(1).
108 Which includes any item included in the service: Dramatic and Musical Performers' Protection Act 1958, as amended by the Cable and Broadcasting Act 1984, section 57(1) and Schedule 5, para. 7(4).
109 Dramatic and Musical Performers' Protection Act 1958, section 8(1), as amended by the Cable and Broadcasting Act 1984, section 57(1) and Schedule 5, para. 7(3).

such a service if section 2(7) and references to the United Kingdom in section 2(1) of the 1984 Act were omitted.[110]

Cable programme service

2.53 'Cable programme service' is defined in section 2(1) of the Cable and Broadcasting Act 1984 as:

> a service which consists wholly or mainly in the sending by any person, by means of a telecommunications system[111] (whether run by him or by any other person), of sounds or visual images or both either

> (a) for reception, otherwise than by wireless telegraphy, at two or more places in the United Kingdom, whether they are so sent for simultaneous reception or at different times in response to requests made by different users of the service; or

> (b) for reception, by whatever means, at a place in the United Kingdom for the purpose of their being presented there either to members of the public or to any group of persons.

Interactive services are excluded, however.[112] Section 2(7) excludes telecommunications systems the running of which do not require to be licensed under Part II of the Telecommunications Act 1984.

Inclusion of a programme in a cable programme service

2.54   Inclusion of a programme in a cable programme service means inclusion by the person providing the service.[113]

7.   Making or possessing plates for making contravening records

2.55   Section 4 of the 1958 Act makes it an offence to make or have in one's possession a plate or similar contrivance for the purpose of making records in contravention of the Acts. 'Possession' may be wider than actual physical possession: it may include, for example, the situation where goods are in the custody of a bailee from whom the defendant has a right to recover them on demand.[114] Knowledge is not expressly required; but the purpose for which a plate is made or possessed will be a question of *mens rea*.[115]

---

110   *Ibid.*
111   Within the meaning of the Telecommunications Act 1984 (see section 2(1)): Cable and Broadcasting Act 1984, section 56(2).
112   Cable and Broadcasting Act 1984, section 2(4).
113   Dramatic and Musical Performers' Protection Act 1958, section 8(3), added by the Cable and Broadcasting Act 1984, section 57(1) and Schedule 5, para. 7(5), to import section 48(3) of the Copyright Act 1956 as amended by the Cable and Broadcasting Act, section 57(1) and Schedule 5.
114   See *Tower & Co. Ltd v Gray* [1961] 2 QB 351.
115   See *Warner v Metropolitan Police Commissioner* [1969] 2 AC 256.

Plate

2.56 'Plate' is not defined. In section 18(3) of the Copyright Act 1956 it is defined to include

> any stereotype, stone, block, mould, matrix, transfer, negative or other appliance.

Some of these, like 'plate' itself, are inappropriate to the technology of record production. Nevertheless, it seems clear that 'plate' is intended to bear a comparably wide meaning. It does not extend to a record itself, however.[116]

Other Offences

1. Giving of consent without authority

2.57 By section 4 of the Performers' Protection Act 1963,[117] it is an offence for a person giving consent to the making of a record, film or broadcast or inclusion in a cable programme to represent that he was authorised by the performers to give it on their behalf when to his knowledge he was not so authorised *provided* that his consent would afford the person to whom it was given a defence under section 7 of the 1958 Act.

Authorised

2.58 It is arguable that the construction placed upon section 7 by the Court of Appeal in the *Peter Sellers* case[118] means that a person who represents, contrary to the fact, that he is a deceased performer's personal representative and as such purports to give consent does not commit an offence under this section. The argument would be that such a person does not represent that he is 'authorised *by the performers* to give it *on their behalf*' (emphasis added), which would require a representation of agency, but that he is authorised *by law* to give it on his own behalf standing in the performer's shoes. It is submitted, however, that this is to adopt too legalistic an approach to the section. Assuming that both representor and representee are ignorant of the niceties of the law as to executors, it is likely that the representor will represent – and, more importantly, be understood by the representee to represent – that he is authorised to consent on the performer's behalf, notwithstanding that it is as a matter of law impossible for the representation to be true. It is consistent with the purpose of the section for the representor in those circumstances to be guilty of an offence.

---

116 *CBS Songs Ltd v Amstrad Consumer Electronics plc* [1988] AC 1013.
117 As amended by the Cable and Broadcasting Act 1984, section 57(1) and Schedule 5, para. 13(2).
118 [1988] QB 40. See para. 2.22.

2.   Connivance or neglect of director etc. of body corporate

2.59   Section 4A of the 1963 Act, which was inserted by section 3 of the Performers' Protection Act 1972, provides that where an offence under the Acts committed by a body corporate is proved to have been committed with the consent or connivance, or to be attributable to any neglect on the part of, any director, manager, secretary or similar officer of the body corporate, or any person purporting to act in any such capacity, that person too is guilty of the offence. 'Connivance' would seem to imply knowledge of, and acquiesence in, the commission of the offence but not necessarily any active participation. 'Neglect' implies failure to perform a duty of which a person knows or ought to know.[119] Section 4A thus goes further than the common law position as to joint tortfeasorship or procuring the commission of a tort.[120]

Mens rea[121]

Knowingly

2.60   Corresponding to the common law maxim *actus non facit reum nisi mens sit rea*[122] is the rebuttable presumption that statutory offences require proof of *mens rea*.[123] The appearance of the word 'knowingly' in a criminal statute makes the requirement of *mens rea* explicit. In such cases it is necessary to prove knowledge on the part of the defendant of all the elements of the *actus reus*. Thus to establish liability for any of the seven offences discussed in paragraphs 2.25 to 2.57 above, the prosecution must show that the defendant had knowledge of all constituents of the prohibited act.[124]

2.61   In the *Gaumont* case[125] the appellants had made a sound film of the band of which the respondent was a member in performance at a dance hall. The respondent had not consented to this and preferred an information. The evidence of the appellants' manager was that he had obtained written consent to the filming from the dance hall's owners and had thought everything necessary had been done when he sent the film crew to the performance. He did not know that he required the consent of each performer in writing. The magistrate held that there was no *mens rea*, but that *mens rea* was not an essential ingredient of the offence. Accordingly he found the appellants guilty.

---

119   Per Simonds J in *Re Hughes, Rea v Black* [1943] Ch 296, 298. As to circumstances in which a director may or may not be held liable for neglect see *Crickitt v Kursaal Casino Ltd (No. 2)* [1968] 1 All ER 139 and *Huckerby v Elliott* [1970] 1 All ER 189.
120   See *C. Evans & Sons Ltd v Spritebrand Ltd* [1985] 1 WLR 317, *CBS Songs Ltd v Amstrad Consumer Electronics plc* above, Note 116 and *Unilever plc v Gillette (UK) Ltd* [1989] RPC 583.
121   See generally Archbold, *Pleading, Evidence and Practice in Criminal Cases*, 43rd edn, (Sweet & Maxwell 1988) vol. 2, ch. 17.
122   The deed does not make the man guilty unless his mind be guilty.
123   See for example, *Sweet v Parsley* [1970] AC 132 and *Gammon (Hong Kong) Ltd v Attorney-General of Hong Kong* [1984] 2 All ER 503.
124   *Gaumont British Distributors Ltd v Henry* [1939] 2 KB 711.
125   *Ibid.*

2.62   On appeal by way of case stated, the appellants argued that *mens rea* was required, and that since the magistrate had found that they lacked it, they were entitled to be acquitted. The respondent argued that 'knowingly' applied only to 'making a record' in section 1(a) of the 1925 Act and not to 'without the consent in writing of the performers', relying upon *Brooks v Mason*.[126] The Divisional Court remitted the case to the magistrate to find whether the appellants knew that the respondent's consent had not been obtained. The magistrate's response was that the appellants had never applied their minds to the question.

2.63   The appeal was allowed. The Divisional Court distinguished *Brooks v Mason* on the basis that that decision turned upon the absence of the word 'knowingly' from the exception clause of the provision in question. In the case of the Dramatic and Musical Performers' Protection Act, knowledge was an essential ingredient and that included knowledge of the absence of consent on the part of the performers. As to the question of fact, the Court expressed its dissatisfaction with the magistrate's reply to its question, indicating that it would have preferred a yes or no answer. Since, however, the magistrate had not found that the appellants *had* known, the appellants were not guilty.

Wilful blindness

2.64   It is possible that the decision in *Gaumont v Henry* would have been different had the magistrate found that the appellants had known of the requirement for consent but, although not positively knowing that consent had not been given, had suspected the truth but deliberately avoided making any inquiries to confirm their suspicions. There is authority for the view that 'knowingly' includes this state of mind (sometimes referred to as 'wilful blindness'), which it could be said borders on recklessness.[127] Recent decisions of the courts, however, have adopted the view that this is only a matter of evidence. Thus the jury may consider whether the defendant had a strong suspicion which he avoided confirming in order to decide whether in fact he knew; but suspicion without knowledge does not suffice for guilt.[128]

2.65   It may, on the other hand, be significant that all the recent decisions

---

126   [1902] 2 KB 743. In that case it was held that a licensee who 'knowingly' sold intoxicating liquor in vessels which were in fact unsealed could not rely upon the words 'excepting such intoxicating liquors as are sold or delivered in corked or sealed vessels' as providing a defence even though he honestly believed that the vessels were sealed.
127   See *Evans v Dell* [1937] 1 All ER 349, per Devlin J in *Roper v Taylors Central Garages Ltd* [1951] 2 TLR 284, 288–9, per Lord Reid in *Warner v Metropolitan Police Commissioner* (1968) 52 Cr App R 373, 389 and *Atwal v Massey* (1972) 56 Cr App R 6.
128   See *R v Grainge* (1974) 59 Cr App R 3, *R v Griffiths* (1974) 60 Cr App R 14, *R v Ismail* [1977] Crim LR 577, *R v Smith* (1977) 61 Cr App R 217 and *R v Pethick* [1980] Crim LR 242. It is submitted that this is (*pace* the headnote) the correct interpretation of Lord Bridge of Harwich's brief and somewhat enigmatic *obiter dictum* in *Westminster City Council v Croyalgrange Ltd* [1986] 2 All ER 353, 359.

referred to have been decisions on handling stolen goods under section 22(1) of the Theft Act 1968, where the relevant words are 'knowing or believing'. As has been pointed out,[129] the word 'believing' was included in the draft Bill by the Criminal Law Revision Committee precisely in order to render liable persons who are 'wilfully blind'. The word chosen is not very apt for the purpose, however: hence the decisions. It is arguable that in the absence of the alternative 'or believing', as in the Performers' Protection Acts, it is open to the court to apply the earlier line of authority. It is submitted, however, that the recent approach of treating it as a matter of evidence is to be preferred.

2.66   A contrast may be drawn in this respect between the wording of the Performers' Protection Act and that of the Copyright, Designs and Patents Act 1988. Section 198 of the 1988 Act provides that a person is guilty of an offence if he 'knows or has reason to believe' that the recording is illicit. It is submitted that this wording is more apt to catch 'wilful blindness'.[130]

Unreasonable belief

2.67   What if the defendant honestly believed that the performer had consented but had no reasonable grounds for that belief or the belief was positively unreasonable? A simple application of *Gaumont v Henry* would suggest that in those circumstances he is entitled to an acquittal. The matter is not so straightforward as that, however.

2.68   It has been held in a number of cases[131] that 'an honest and reasonable belief' in the existence of circumstances which, if true, would make an act for which a person has been indicted innocent is a good defence. The significance of this is that it suggests that *mens rea* is only absent if the belief is reasonable as well as honest, in other words that the test is objective rather than subjective. This issue was considered by the House of Lords in *Director of Public Prosecutions v Morgan*[132] where the trial judge directed the jury that on a charge of rape a defendant was not entitled to be acquitted on the ground that he believed that the woman was consenting unless that belief was also reasonable. Their Lordships held by a majority of 3–2 that that direction was wrong. The reasoning of the House left considerable room for doubt, however, as to the general applicability of the *Tolson* rule.[133] At present the approach of the courts seems to be that the reasonableness or unreasonableness of the defendant's belief is material only to the question of whether he actually held

129   Smith and Hogan, *Criminal Law*, 6th edn, (Butterworths 1987) p. 632.
130   See Ch. 8, para. 8.19. See also Ch. 5, paras. 5.52–56.
131   See especially *R v Tolson* (1889) 23 QBD 168 and *Bank of New South Wales v Piper* [1897] AC 383.
132   (1975) 61 Cr App R 156.
133   See Archbold, 43rd edn, vol. 2, ch. 17, paras. 17–5,6.

the belief at all.[134] If the belief was in fact held, its unreasonableness is irrelevant.[135]

2.69   It is at least arguable that the *Tolson* rule is in any event inapplicable where the statute defines the mental element of the offence, as do the Performers' Protection Acts. This argument would hold that a man cannot make a record knowing that the perfomers have not consented if he believes that they have. Even if that is wrong, it is submitted that the approach just outlined ought now to be applied.[136]

Recklessness

2.70   Does a defendant who proceeds to make a record or film knowing that there is a risk that a performer may not have consented to it[137] – that is, is reckless – 'knowingly' make it without the performer's consent so as to commit an offence if in fact the performer has not consented? It appears from the *Peter Sellers* case (a civil case) that he does.

2.71   In the *Peter Sellers* case, the defendants argued that although they had not obtained any specific consent from Sellers' estate to the use in *The Trail of the Pink Panther* of out-takes and clips from earlier Pink Panther films, Sellers himself had consented in advance to such use being made of out-takes and clips in the agreements under which his services were provided for the earlier films. This was a question of the construction of the agreements on which both the trial judge and the Court of Appeal held against the defendants.

2.72   As to the defendants' state of mind, Hobhouse J found[138] that they knew that they had not obtained consent unless it was contained in the agreements; that, having obtained two Opinions from counsel, the defendants did not have a positive belief that no consent from the estate was necessary, but merely a belief that they had a fully arguable case under English law that such consent was unnecessary; and that they decided to go ahead on a commercial assessment of the risk that this would be held to be wrong. The judge expressed his conclusion on the issue of the defendants' knowledge as follows:

> On the findings of fact that I have made each of the defendants knew all the material facts at all material times and were not acting under mistake, whether of fact or law. It follows that the requirement of knowledge for the purposes of proof of an offence under the section have been made out. Also because the relevant acts were done deliberately any element of *mens rea* was likewise made out.[139]

---

134   Compare the approach to wilful blindness discussed in para 2.64.
135   See *R v Kimber* (1983) 77 Cr App R 225, *R v Williams* (1984) 78 Cr App R 276 and *Beckford v R* [1987] 3 All ER 425.
136   Again, the position will be different under the Copyright, Designs and Patents Act 1988. See Ch. 8, para. 8.19.
137   To be in this position the defendant would need to know that consent was required, cf. *Gaumont v Henry* [1939] 2 KB 711. See para. 2.61.
138   This aspect of the case is unreported but see [1986] FSR 502, 505.
139   [1986] FSR 502, 508.

This state of mind is best described as recklessness. It is submitted that this is not the same as making the film 'knowingly', and furthermore that it does not constitute an alternative *mens rea* under the Performers' Protection Act. As in his finding that the Acts conferred a civil right of action, Hobhouse J effectively anticipated the 1988 Act.[140]

2.73   If, contrary to the author's view, recklessness does constitute sufficient *mens rea* for an offence to be committed under the Acts, it becomes necessary ask whether the 'objective' or the 'subjective' test should be applied. The distinction, which has arisen following the decisions of the House of Lords in *R v Lawrence*[141] and *R v Caldwell*,[142] is that the latter requires that the defendant have realised that there was a risk that his act would have certain consequences but proceeded anyway, while the former holds that the defendant is reckless even if he gave no thought to the possibility of there being any such risk (that is, is careless). Since the defendants' state of mind in the *Gaumont* case[143] was close to that covered by the objective test,[144] it may be arguable that the subjective test is the correct one. Hobhouse J effectively applied a subjective test in the *Peter Sellers* case.

Corporations

2.74   Unless a contrary intention appears, 'person' includes a body corporate.[145] There is nothing to show a contrary intention, and the insertion of section 4A into the Performers' Protection Act 1963[146] confirmed that corporations may be guilty of offences under the Performers' Protection Acts. It would seem that in such cases the requisite *mens rea* must be possessed by a 'directing mind'[147] of the corporation. It appears to have been taken for granted in the *Gaumont* case[148] that the appellants' general manager did qualify as a directing mind.

Dealings in records or films made in the UK

2.75   It is clear from *Gaumont v Henry* that, where a defendant is charged with dealing in a record or film 'made in contravention of' the Performers' Protection Acts contrary to sections 1(b) or (c) or 2(b) or (c) of the 1958 Act, the prosecution must show knowledge on the part of the defendant that the performers had not consented to the making of the record or film. It is not clear

---

140   See Ch. 5, paras. 5.52–56 and Ch. 8, para. 8.19.
141   [1981] 1 All ER 974.
142   [1981] 1 All ER 961.
143   [1939] 2 KB 711.
144   See paras. 2.61–63.
145   Interpretation Act 1978, section 5 and Schedule 1.
146   See para. 2.59.
147   See *Tesco Supermarkets Ltd v Nattrass* [1972] AC 153.
148   [1939] 2 KB 711.

(since the appellants in that case had been charged under section 1(a)) whether the prosecution must also prove that the *maker* of the record or film knew that the performers had not consented. Although it is perhaps arguable that this is not necessary, it is submitted that the better view is that it is, for it is not a contravention of the Acts to make a record or film without the consent of the performers, but merely to do so knowingly. It is also submitted that this is supported by the interpretation of section 2 of the 1963 Act advanced below,[149] according to which the position is different where a record made in a foreign country having a law requiring consent is dealt in.

Dealings in records made abroad

2.76 Section 2 of the Performers' Protection Act 1963 provides as follows:

> For the purposes of [section 1(b) and (c) of the 1958 Act], a record made in a country outside the United Kingdom directly or indirectly from or by means of a performance to which [the 1958 Act] applies shall, where the civil or criminal law of that country contains a provision for the protection of performers under which the consent of any person to the making of the record was required, be deemed to have been made in contravention of [the 1958 Act] if, whether knowingly or not, it was made without the consent so required and without the consent of the performers.

2.77 At least five different possible constructions of this section have been advanced:

(1) Only performances which take place in a foreign country having a law requiring consent are protected. The reasoning behind this is that, if the performance takes place in a country where the law does not require consent, then – since no consent is required – a record could not be made 'without the consent so required' and so would not be deemed to have been made in contravention of the Act.[150] It is submitted, however, that the section is not concerned with the venue of the *performance* but with that of the *making of the record*.

(2) Only records which are made in foreign countries having a law requiring consent (regardless of where the performance took place) are protected. The reasoning is the same as in (1), that is, that, if the record is made in a country where the law does not require consent, then – since no consent is required – the record could not be made 'without the consent so required' and so would not be deemed to have been made in contravention of the Act. The effect of this construction is to make reciprocity of foreign countries' laws a condition of protection.[151]

---

149 See para. 2.78.
150 See Laddie *et al.*, para. 18.4.
151 The Whitford Committee felt that, if this construction was the correct one, it was unjust and should be amended accordingly: Cmnd 6723 at para. 412(vi).

(3) All records made abroad are protected. The reasoning behind this is that the section only deals with the situation where the laws of a foreign country do contain a provision requiring consent, in which case two consents are necessary, namely under that country's law and under the 1958 Act. Where the law of the foreign country contains no such provision consent is still necessary, but only under the 1958 Act.[152]

(4) Dealing in records made in a foreign country whose law requires consent but not in writing is not an offence under the 1958 Act if oral but not written consent has been given. This depends on reading the first 'consent' in 'without the consent so required and without the consent in writing of the performers' as referring to oral consent.[153]

(5) Dealings in records made abroad may be an offence regardless of whether the maker of the record knew that the performers had not consented in writing: all that matters is whether the dealer in the United Kingdom knew.[154]

2.78   Although, as the variety of interpretations set out above makes clear, the construction of this section is extremely difficult, it is ventured to submit that the true construction is a combination of (3) and (5) above. Where a record is made in a foreign country which does not have a provision requiring consent, the situation is the same as with a record made in the United Kingdom, namely that dealing in the record is only an offence if, to the knowledge of the dealer, the record was made in contravention of the 1958 Act, that is, it was made, to the knowledge of the maker, without the consent in writing of the performers. Where the foreign country has provision requiring the consent of 'any person', whether that person be the performer or not, the record shall be *deemed* to have been 'made in contravention of [the 1958 Act]' if it was made both without the consent of that person and without the consent in writing of the performers *whether the maker knew it or not*. In those circumstances the only question will be whether the dealer has the requisite knowledge.

2.79   The 1963 Act only applies in relation to performances taking place after its commencement,[155] which was on 1 September 1963. Thus section 2 does not apply to records made before that date.

Defences

2.80   The following defences are available under the Performers' Protection Acts:

---

152   *Ibid.*
153   *Ibid.*
154   See Cornish, 1st edn, page 448.
155   Performers' Protection Act 1963, section 5(3).

(i) consent;[156]
(ii) private or domestic use;[157]
(iii) reporting current events;[158]
(iv) inclusion incidental to the principal matters;[159]
(v) made by the IBA.[160]

It should be noted that although the burden of proof of making out defences (ii) to (v) and the section 7 defence in (i)[161] is on the defendant, the burden is not so onerous as that laid on the prosecutor as regards proving the offence: whereas the latter must prove it beyond reasonable doubt, it is sufficient for the defendant to prove these defences as to a preponderance of probability.[162]

1. Consent

By the performer

2.81 Consent in writing by the performer is, of course, a defence to any charge under the Acts. 'Writing' includes other modes of representing or reproducing words in a visible form.[163] It would seem that oral consent is insufficient. Although, as was said by Sir Robert Megarry V-C in *Apple Corps Ltd v Lingasong Ltd*,[164] an attempt at civil proceedings under the Acts,

> Equity has a long tradition, in proper cases, of decorously disregarding a statutory requirement of writing,

it does not appear that this would extend to a criminal charge. This may give rise to difficulties, however. For example, a person who orally agrees to give an interview on television has clearly consented, but not in writing. Although the makers of films and records may be able to arrange to obtain written consent from all performers, this may not be practicable for broadcasters.

By the performer's agent

2.82 Section 7 of the 1958 Act,[165] the rubric for which is 'Consent on behalf of performers', provides as follows:

> Where in any proceedings under this Act it is proved –

---

156 See paras. 2.81–87.
157 See paras. 2.88–89.
158 See para. 2.90.
159 See para. 2.91.
160 See para. 2.93.
161 See para. 2.82.
162 *R v Carr-Briant* [1943] KB 607, *R v Dunbar* [1958] 1 QB 1.
163 Interpretation Act 1978, section 5 and Schedule 1.
164 [1977] FSR 345 at 351.
165 As amended by Performers' Protection Act 1963, section 3(3) and Cable and Broadcasting Act 1984, section 57(1) and Schedule 5, para. 7(2).

(a) that the record, cinematograph film broadcast or cable programme to which the proceedings relate was made or included with the consent in writing of a person who, at the time of giving the consent, represented that he was authorised by the performers to give it on their behalf, and

(b) that the person making or including the record, film broadcast or cable programme had no reasonable grounds for believing that the person giving the consent was not so authorised,

the provisions of this Act shall apply as if it had been proved that the performers had themselves consented in writing to the making or including of the record, film broadcast or cable programme.

It appears that the intention behind this curiously-drafted section is to provide a defence where a person makes a record etc. on the strength of consent obtained from someone who *falsely* holds himself out as the performers' agent.[166] It will be noted, however, that the words of the section are equally apt where the representation is *true*. It therefore seems that consent may be given on behalf of a performer by his agent, in which the performer himself is to be deemed to have consented.[167] Note that consent given by an agent must still be in writing.

By a person holding himself out as the performer's agent

2.83   Section 7 of the 1958 Act gives a defence where there is written consent by a person who represented that he was authorised by the performers to give it on their behalf if the maker of the record, film, broadcast or cable programme had no reasonable grounds for believing that the person giving the consent was not so authorised.[168] Where the offence charged is one of making the record or film in question, the section would appear to be superfluous, since it is difficult to see that such a person would have the requisite *mens rea* in any event.[169] Where the offence charged is one of dealing in the record or film in question, the effect of the section appears to be that it does not matter that the dealer (as opposed to the maker) had reasonable grounds, or even knew, that the person purporting to consent did not have authority to do so if the maker did not.

By a person holding himself out as the performer's assignee

2.84   As is discussed elsewhere,[170] it is open to doubt whether it is possible for a performer validly to assign his rights under the Performers' Protection

---

166   As to which, see para. 2.83.
167   That this is so also appears to be implicit in section 4 of the 1963 Act: see para. 2.57.
168   See para. 2.82.
169   If he had no reasonable grounds for believing that the person giving the consent was not authorised, he could not even be 'wilfully blind'.
170   See Ch. 3, paras. 3.02–08.

Acts. A performer may nevertheless attempt to do so; and someone else may represent that he has obtained an assignment of such rights from a performer when in fact he has not. Although it might be argued that this situation is not covered by words of section 7 of the 1958 Act if strictly construed,[171] it is submitted that a broader construction would cover it. Again, a maker of a record etc. who relied upon such a representation would probably not have the requisite *mens rea* in any event, but a dealer who knew better will if this is right have a defence.[172]

By the performer's estate

2.85 After a performer's death, consent may be given by his personal representatives, who stand in his shoes for this purpose.[173]

By a person holding himself out as the performer's personal representative

2.86 It is arguable that the construction placed upon section 7 of the 1958 Act by the Court of Appeal in the *Peter Sellers* case[174] means that it is *not* a defence to prove that (a) the record, film, broadcast or cable programme was made with the written consent of a person who represented that he was the personal representative of a deceased performer and (b) the maker of the record, film or broadcast had no reasonable grounds for disbelieving him. The argument would be that such a person does not represent that he is 'authorised *by the performers* to give *on their behalf*' (emphasis added), which would require a representation of agency, but that he is authorised *by law* to give it *on his own behalf* standing in the performers' shoes. It is submitted, however, that this is to adopt too legalistic an approach to the section.[175] Again, a maker of a record etc. who relied upon such a representation would probably not have the requisite *mens rea* in any event, but a dealer who knew better will, if this is right, have a defence.[176]

Consent upon terms

2.87 There is no reason why a performer should not give his consent to the exploitation of his performance upon terms, in particular terms limiting the ambit of the permitted exploitation or as to consideration. If the act in question is clearly outside the ambit of the performer's consent, for example if

---

171 Cf. the construction adopted by the Court of Appeal in the *Peter Sellers* case, discussed in para. 2.86.
172 Cf. para. 2.83.
173 *Rickless v United Artists Corp.* [1988] QB 40.
174 [1988] QB 40, 56–7. See para. 2.22.
175 See the discussion in para. 2.58.
176 Cf. para. 2.83.

consent is given to record the performance for broadcast only but copies are sold commercially, then, it is submitted, there is no doubt that an offence is committed. The position is less clear if it is merely a matter of non-compliance with terms, for example as to payment. In the civil context, there is conflicting authority as to whether failure to comply with the terms of a licence results in infringement or merely breach of contract.[177] It may seem rather harsh if non-compliance with terms of consent were to render criminal an act that would not be criminal if the terms were complied with, but it is submitted that it is reasonable to apply the same test as in civil law, namely that applicable under the general law of contract. If the breach of the terms of the consent is insufficiently severe to permit the performer to treat the contract as having been repudiated, then the act in question should be treated as having been done with consent for the purposes of the criminal law. If the breach of the contract is severe enough to permit the performer to treat the contract as having been repudiated, then (unless the performer elects to affirm the contract) the act in question should be treated as having been done without consent for the purposes of the criminal law.[178]

2.   Private or domestic use

2.88   It is a defence to charges under sections 1(a) and 2(a) of the 1958 Act to show that the record or film was made for the defendant's private and domestic use only. This is in contrast to the position under the Copyright Act 1956, where (except with respect to importation) private and domestic use is not a defence to infringement.[179] The defence does not extend to subsequent dealings, however.

2.89   It is not clear whether 'private' is intended to add anything to 'domestic'. The copyright cases decide that a 'public' performance is one for which the audience is not a 'domestic or quasi-domestic' one, and that a 'domestic or quasi-domestic' audience is one that lives under one roof.[180] It is submitted that the same test ought to be applied under sections 1(a) and 2(a), so that the words 'private and' are to be treated as mere surplusage.

3.   Reporting current events

2.90   By section 6(a) of the 1958 Act as amended by section 3(3) of the 1963 Act it is a defence to any charge under the Acts to prove that the record, film, broadcast or transmission was made only for the purpose of reporting current events. If the copyright cases may be taken as indicative, this defence is a

---

177   See Ch. 6, para. 6.42.
178   Cf. *R v Morris (David)* [1984] AC 320, a difficult decision under the Theft Act 1968 in which the House of Lords purported to eschew this approach but achieved a similar result.
179   See *CBS Songs Ltd v Amstrad Consumer Electronics plc* [1988] AC 1013.
180   See para. 2.44.

narrow one.[181] It is not clear, for example, whether the defence would cover a wide-ranging interview with a politician let alone an interview with, for example, a musician.

4. Incidental to the principal matters

2.91   By section 6(b) of the 1958 Act as amended it is a defence to any charge under the Acts to prove that the inclusion of the performance in question in the record, film, broadcast or transmission in issue was only by way of background or was otherwise only incidental to the principal matters comprised or represented in the record, film or broadcast.

5. Independent Broadcasting Authority

2.92   By section 4(7) of the Broadcasting Act 1981 the IBA may make and use visual and sound records of programmes (including advertisements) or any part thereof broadcast by the Authority for the purpose of maintaining supervision and control over such programmes without committing any offence under the Performers' Protection Acts.

Delay

2.93   Informations alleging offences under the Performers' Protection Acts which are only triable summarily must be laid within six months of the commission of the offence if the justices are to have jurisdiction to try the case.[182] Those which are triable either way, however, are not subject to any statutory limitation period,[183] and at common law there is no time limit on criminal prosecutions.[184] Nevertheless, delay in bringing a prosecution may give rise to prejudice and unfairness which by itself amounts to an abuse of process such that the tribunal may decline to entertain the proceedings.[185]

---

181   See *Independent Television Publications Ltd v Time Out Ltd* [1984] FSR 64. Cf. the position under the Copyright, Designs and Patents Act 1988, Schedule 2 paragraph 13. See Ch. 6, paras. 6.21–22.
182   Magistrates Courts Act 1980, section 127(1).
183   See *Kemp v Liebherr-GB Ltd* [1987] 1 All ER 855.
184   *Halsbury's Laws*, 4th ed. (reissue), vol. 11 (1), para. 786.
185   *R v Bow Street Stipendiary Magistrate ex parte Director of Public Prosecutions* The Times, 20 December 1989.

Penalties

Fine and/or imprisonment

2.94   The penalty on summary conviction under section 1 of the 1958 Act[186] is a fine not exceeding 'the prescribed sum'[187] (presently £2,000[188]). The penalty for conviction on indictment is a term of imprisonment not exceeding two years or a fine or both.[189] There is no limit to the fine which may be imposed by the Crown Court, but it should be within the offender's capacity to pay.[190] The penalty on summary conviction of all other offences under the Acts[191] is a fine not exceeding level 5 on the standard scale[192] (presently £2,000[193]).

Destruction of records etc.

2.95   Under section 5 of the 1958 Act, the Court also has power, on conviction of the offender, to order that all records, films, plates[194] or similar contrivances in the offender's possession which appear to the Court to have been made in contravention of the Act, or to be adapted for making records in contravention of the Act, and in respect of which the offender has been convicted, be destroyed or otherwise dealt with as the Court thinks fit.

Private Prosecutions

2.96   This subject is dealt with in relation to the 1988 Act in Chapter 8.[195] The position is the same with regard to prosecutions under the Performers' Protection Acts.

---

186   Dramatic and Musical Performers' Protection Act 1958, section 1 as amended by the Magistrates Courts Act 1980, section 32(2).
187   That is, the prescribed sum within the meaning of the Magistrates Courts Act 1980, section 32: Criminal Justice Act 1982, section 74(1).
188   Magistrates Courts Act 1980, section 32(9) as amended.
189   Dramatic and Musical Performers' Protection Act 1958, section 1 as amended by Performers' Protection Act 1972, section 2.
190   *R v Churchill (No. 2)* [1967] 1 QB 190 (reversed on other grounds *sub nom Churchill v Walton* [1967] 2 AC 224).
191   Dramatic and Musical Performers' Protection Act 1958, sections 2, 3 and 4 and Performers' Protection Act 1963, sections 3(1) and 4(1) as amended by Criminal Justice Act 1982, sections 38 and 46.
192   That is, the standard scale set out in Criminal Justice Act 1982, section 37(2).
193   Criminal Penalties etc (Increase) Order 1984, S.I. 1984 No. 447, Article 3(4) and Schedule 4.
194   See para. 2.56 for the definition of 'plate'.
195   See para. 8.29.

3 Civil Law

Introduction

3.01 On their face, the Performers' Protection Acts merely create criminal offences and do not confer any civil right of action. Nevertheless the Court of Appeal in the *Peter Sellers* case[1] held that the Acts did confer civil rights of action on performers. The Court's reasoning, in short, was that an offence under the Acts was actionable as a breach of statutory duty since the Acts fell into the category of statutes passed for the benefit of a particular class of individuals.[2]

Transmission of Rights

Assignment

3.02 An important question which still remains unanswered after the *Peter Sellers* case is whether a performer's rights under the Performers' Protection Acts may validly be assigned by him. In *MPPA v BIP*,[3] this issue was argued before but not decided by McCardie J.

3.03 In that case the performers after having given the performances in question executed assignments to the plaintiff association. The assignments assigned

> all that the right of consent to the making of records directly or indirectly from or by means of the assignor's performance of a musical work in conjunction with the film production known as *Blackmail*, and all that the right of consent to the sale, hire, or distribution of such records.

---

1 *Rickless v United Artists Corp.* [1988] QB 40.
2 See Appendix 2 for a full discussion of the Court of Appeal's reasoning and of the preceding cases.
3 (1930) 46 TLR 485.

The defendants argued first that the right to consent was not assignable at all whether before or after the commission of an offence, and secondly that even if assignable it was not a 'debt or other legal thing in action' within section 136 of the Law of Property Act 1925 so as to enable the assignee to sue without joining the assignors. The judge decided the case on other grounds, however.[4]

3.04   It is not clear how the defendants' first argument in *MPPA v BIP* was put, but it may have proceeded by analogy with contracts for personal service, which are not assignable.[5] If so, it is submitted that the analogy does not hold: there is a clear difference between assigning a right to give or withhold consent to a person doing an act on the one hand, and assigning a contract for a person to do an act on the other hand. As to the second argument, there does not appear to be any clear authority as to whether an equitable chose in action is a 'debt or other legal thing in action' within section 136 of the Law of Property Act 1925; but there are *dicta* which suggest that it is.[6] Even if not, however, it is submitted that joinder of the assignor is not necessary if the assignment is absolute since the chose in action is equitable (if it were legal joinder would be required unless the assignment was within section 136).[7]

3.05   Even if these two arguments are wrong, however, it does not necessarily mean that the right is assignable. In the absence of any authority, the following analysis is offered. The performer's right to give or withold consent is a statutory right. If the performer did not have a civil cause of action for breach, the argument that the right was purely personal would be strong. Given that the performer does have a civil right of action, the next question is to what species of personal property the right belongs. The three possibilities are that it is (a) a chose in possession, (b) a chose in action or (c) a *sui generis* right.

3.06   If the right to bring civil proceedings for breach of the Performers' Protection Acts is property in possession, it is assignable in the absence of any statutory restriction. If it is a chose in action, the chose must (notwithstanding that the right is statutory) be equitable since it is only actionable as a breach of statutory duty, which requires the assistance of equity. As such, it is assignable in equity provided that (a) the assignment is for consideration (since equity does not assist volunteers) and (b) the assignment is not of a bare cause of action (which would constitute maintenance).[8] Finally, if the right is *sui generis* subject to its own statutory regime, the absence of any provision in the

---

4   See Appendix 2, para. A2.02.
5   See *Halsbury's Laws*, 4th edn, vol. 6, para. 88.
6   *Ibid.*, para. 15 and cases cited in note 2.
7   *Ibid.*, para. 69 and cases cited in note 3.
8   Assignments of causes of action incident to property are valid, however. It is therefore submitted that the assignment in *MPPA v BIP* did not fall foul of this restriction. See *Halsbury's Laws*, 4th edn, vol. 6, paras. 86 and 87. In addition, there was probably sufficient common interest between the assignors and the assignee to permit such an assignment. See *Trendtex Trading Corp. v Credit Suisse* [1981] 3 All ER 520.

Performers' Protection Acts expressly or impliedly permitting or enabling assignment would seem to be fatal.

3.07   Comparison may be made with copyrights and patents, both of which are expressly provided by statute to be personal property or transmissible as such.[9] But to what species of personal property are patents and copyrights to be regarded as belonging? The point does not appear to have been decided, the various *dicta* in the cases being largely explicable by reference to statutes in force at the time.[10] The question was debated in the Law Quarterly Review at the end of last century. Elphinstone[11] argued that patents and copyrights were not choses in action since there was no cause of action unless and until an act of infringement occured, but did not seem inclined to regard them as choses in possession. Brodhurst[12] agreed that they were not choses in action, and argued that they were to be classified as property in constructive possession: a patent or copyright could not be property in possession since it was incorporeal, yet the proprietor had enjoyment of the property so far as was possible and neither could nor needed to sue to reduce the property or its fruits to possession. Pollock[13] agreed that if they had to be classified as either in possession or in action, they were choses in possession. Williams[14] and Sweet,[15] on the other hand, argued that the categories of choses in action had been extended to embrace patents and copyrights, and that they could not sensibly be regarded as being in possession, constructive or otherwise.

3.08   The most sensible conclusion therefore seems to be to regard patents and copyrights (and trade marks) as *sui generis* species of personal property, each right being subject to its own statutory regime. The same conclusion would apply to the right of action under the Performers' Protection Acts. If so, it follows that the right is not assignable.

Transmission on death

3.09   It appears to have been accepted in the *Peter Sellers* case that if the right to give or withhold consent survived Peter Sellers' death, then the right would devolve upon his personal representatives in the same way as any other personal property. As such it would be susceptible of specific bequests. Equally it seems to have been assumed that any consent given by the deceased would bind the estate.

---

9   Copyright Act 1956, section 36(1) and Patents Act 1977, section 30(1).
10   Thus section 30(1) of the Patents Act 1977 expressly provides that a patent is not a chose in action, repealing section 54(5) of the Patents Acts 1949 which implied the opposite. See also *British Nylon Spinners Ltd v Imperial Chemical Industries Ltd* [1953] Ch 19, 26 per Sir Raymond Evershed MR.
11   (1893) 9 LQR 311.
12   (1895) 11 LQR 64.
13   (1895) 11 LQR 75.
14   (1894) 10 LQR 143, (1895) 11 LQR 223.
15   (1894) 10 LQR 303, (1895) 11 LQR 238.

Collecting Societies

3.10   Collecting societies (more correctly termed collective licensing bodies) are organisations which license and monitor the use of copyright works, enforce the conditions under which licensees use copyright works and collect and distribute royalties.[16] The system of collective licensing, under which users normally pay a tariff according to the type of use, is convenient both for users, who are saved the necessity of seeking specific licences from copyright owners, and owners, who are saved the burden of identifying users of their works and enforcing their rights against those users. Among the better known collecting societies in the United Kingdom are Phonographic Performance Limited (PPL), Mechanical Copyright Protection Society Limited (MCPS), Performing Right Society Limited (PRS) and Video Performance Limited (VPL). Of these bodies, it is the practice of some to take assignments of copyright from the owners; others merely act as the owners' agent. The advantage of taking an assignment is that it makes enforcement easier, for the collecting society can thus bring proceedings in its own name.

3.11   Prior to the coming into force of the Copyright, Patents and Designs Act 1988, there was no collecting society for the collection of moneys due to performers.[17] The gap was filled to some extent by Equity and by the Musicians' Union, each of which collected and distributed certain payments on behalf of its members. For example, Equity collected and distributed 'residuals', that is, payments to actors for sales of British television programmes abroad.

3.12   It is to be anticipated that with the coming into force of Part II of the Copyright, Designs and Patents Act 1988, one or more collecting societies may be established to licence performers' rights and recording right. Given that acts done in pursuance of arrangements made before commencement of the 1988 Act will not be infringements of the new rights granted by that Act, but will (following the *Peter Sellers* case) be actionable breaches of statutory duty under the Performers' Protection Acts, such collecting societies may wish to collect royalties under the Performers' Protection Acts as well as under the 1988 Act. Since these rights are probably unassignable,[18] any such society will be forced to act as agent and not as assignee.[19]

---

16   Monopolies and Merger Commission Report on Collective Licensing, Cm 530, glossary and para. 3.4.
17   Although Musical Performers' Protection Association Limited was apparently such a body while it existed.
18   See paras. 3.02–08.
19   As they will with the new rights. See Ch. 4, para. 4.66.

Who May Sue?

Performers

3.13 Any person whose performances are protected under the Performers' Protection Acts 1958–72 may be a plaintiff in civil proceedings. That is, the performances

> of any actors, singers, musicians, dancers or other persons who act, sing, deliver, declaim, play in or otherwise perform literary, dramatic, musical or artistic works.[20]

See Chapter 2, paragraphs 2.03–19 for a full analysis.

Performers' estates

3.14 After the death of a performer title to sue vests in the performer's personal representatives standing in his or her shoes.[21] Thus the first two plaintiffs in the *Peter Sellers* case were his executors. See Chapter 2, paragraphs 2.20–3.

Record and film companies

3.15 It is common for performers of certain types – particularly musicians – to enter into contracts for the exclusive exploitation of their performances. Such contracts may be of considerable value to the record or other company in question, for (in the absence of any assignable performers' right[22]) they provide the only means by which the output of a valuable commodity – fixations of performances – can be controlled. Those with whom performers have such exclusive contracts therefore have a considerable interest in preventing third parties from rendering their contractual rights less valuable by unauthorised exploitation of performances. It is nevertheless clear that such persons do not themselves have any right of action under the Performers' Protection Acts.[23]

Who May Be Sued?

3.16 The persons against whom performers have a cause of action under the

---

20 Dramatic and Musical Performers' Protection Act 1958, section 8(1) as amended by the Performers' Protection Act 1963, section 1(1).
21 *Rickless v United Artists Corp.* [1988] QB 40.
22 As to which see paras. 3.02–08. Comparison may be made with copyright: it is common practice for a record company (or its publishing arm) to take an assignment of future copyright in songs to be written by a musician.
23 *RCA Corp. v Pollard* [1983] Ch 135. This is unaffected by *Rickless v United Artists Corp.*

Acts fall into two categories: (a) those who make records, films or broadcasts in contravention of the Acts, and (b) those who deal in contraband records and films. Joint tortfeasors may also be sued on normal principles.[24]

3.17   In each case all the same matters must be proved as in a criminal prosecution for the relevant offence. The standard of proof, however, is the civil standard, namely on the balance of probabilities. The requirements are discussed in Chapter 2, paragraphs 2.24–56.

Territoriality

3.18   In construing Acts of Parliament there is a well-established presumption that, in the absence of clear and specific words to the contrary, an offence-creating section of an Act is not intended to make conduct taking place outside the jurisdiction triable in England.[25] In the case of the Performers' Protection Acts, there are no such words. Indeed, section 1(2) of the Performers' Protection Act 1963 clearly implies the opposite, for it provides that, although the Acts apply to any performance wheresoever it took place, this does not make anything done outside the United Kingdom an offence. It follows that the civil right of action under the Acts is strictly territorial, like copyright and other intellectual property rights. The consequences of territoriality are discussed in relation to performers' rights under Part II of the 1988 Act in Chapter 5.[26]

Defences

3.19   The following defences are available: consent; private or domestic use; reporting current events; inclusion incidental to the principal matters; and made by the IBA. See Chapter 2, paragraphs 2.80–92. In addition, general defences to torts may be relied upon, in particular acquiescence and expiry of limitation period. The latter is six years, for section 2 of the Limitation Act 1980 applies to a breach of statutory duty as to any other tort.[27]

---

24   *Grower v BBC* (*The Times*, 6 July 1990), where it was held that the BBC was not liable as a joint tortfeasor where it had licensed its sound recording copyright in a recording on terms that the licensee obtain all necessary consents but the licensee failed to do so in the case of one performer. See generally *C. Evans & Sons Ltd v Spritebrand Ltd* [1985] 1 WLR 317, *CBS Songs Ltd v Amstrad Consumer Electronics plc* [1988] AC 1013 and *Unilever plc v Gillette UK Ltd* [1989] RPC 583.
25   *Cox v Army Council* (1962) 46 Cr App R 258, *Air India v Wiggins* (1980) 71 Cr App R 213.
26   See paras. 5.58–62.
27   *Clarkson v Modern Foundries Ltd* [1957] 1 WLR 1210. This was conceded in *Grower v BBC*, Note 24 above.

Oral consent

3.20   Although the Performers' Protection Acts require consent in writing by the performer, it was pointed out by Sir Robert Megarry V-C in *Apple Corps v Lingasong Ltd*[28] that

> Equity has a long tradition, in proper cases, of decorously disregarding a statutory requirement of writing.

Although the Vice-Chancellor came to no decision on the point, the passage suggests that oral consent by the performer might be a defence to a civil action. This would be an application of the equitable maxim that equity looks to the intent rather than the form. The defence might be categorised as a species of promissory estoppel.

Remedies

Injunction

3.21   It is clear from the decision of the Court of Appeal in *Rickless v United Artists Corp.*[29] that an injunction will issue to restrain breach of the Performers' Protection Acts. Curiously, although an injunction was claimed by the writ in that action, no injunction was actually granted. No reason for this appears in the reported judgments. It may be surmised that the plaintiffs waived the claim to an injunction, preferring to maximise their financial compensation; the film had completed its theatrical release by the time the matter came to trial in any event.

Damages

3.22   It is a requirement for any action for breach of statutory duty that the plaintiff establish damage of a kind against which the statute was designed to give protection.[30] The damages recoverable will include damages which are the natural consequence of the breach; in other words, subject to the normal rules on causation and remoteness in tort. In the case of breaches of the Performers' Protection Acts, the measure of damages recoverable will presumably be similar to that recoverable as damages for infringement of copyright under section 17 of the Copyright Act 1956. This may give rise to problems of quantification, for a discussion of which see Chapter 7.[31]

---

28   [1977] FSR 345 at 351.
29   [1988] QB 40.
30   See *Halsbury's Laws*, 4th edn, vol. 45, para. 1279.
31   See para. 7.09.

Account of profits

3.23   It does not appear that an account of profits may be awarded.[32]

Delivery up or destruction

3.24   It does not appear that there is any basis upon which delivery up of records or films made in contravention of the Acts might be ordered. Nor can any order for destruction under section 5 of the 1958 Act can be made in a civil case, for the Court's powers under that section are only available 'on conviction of the offender'.[33]

---

32   The account of profits ordered in *Rickless v United Artists Corp.* was awarded on a different ground.
33   See Ch. 2, para. 2.95.

Part II

The New Law of Performers' Rights and Recording Rights

4 Subsistence and Ownership

Introduction

4.01   Part II of the Copyright, Designs and Patents Act 1988 came into force on 1 August 1989.[1] The Act applies to all performances which took place before commencement.[2] Effectively, this means all performances from 1 January 1939 onwards, since any rights under Part II in earlier performances expired on 31 December 1988.[3]

4.02   In short, Part II of the 1988 Act respectively endorses and reverses the decisions of the Court of Appeal under the Performers' Protection Acts in *Rickless v United Artists Corp.*[4] and *RCA Corp. v Pollard.*[5] Thus for the first time both performers and those with whom they enter into exclusive recording contracts have statutory civil rights of action to prevent the unauthorised exploitation of performances. Although Part II is studiously (and, in places, cumbersomely[6]) drafted so as to avoid use of the word 'copyright',[7] the effect is to confer on performers and recording companies two new copyrights. The new rights are not full copyrights[8] (they are not assignable,[9] and imitation of a performance is not an infringement[10]), but they are bundles of rights subject to very similar provisions as to subsistence, ownership, infringement and remedies for infringement as those applicable under Part I of the 1988 Act.

---

1   Copyright, Designs and Patents Act 1988 (Commencement No. 1) Order 1989, 1989 S.I. No. 816.
2   Copyright, Designs and Patents Act 1988, section 180(3).
3   See para. 4.56.
4   [1988] QB 40.
5   [1983] Ch 135.
6   See, for example, Ch. 5, para. 5.03.
7   Although the draughtsman has had to admit defeat in one or two places. Thus the Copyright Tribunal is given jurisdiction over rights under Part II. See Ch. 6, paras. 6.52–69.
8   They are 'neighbouring rights' in both the narrow and wide senses of the phrase. See Appendix 2, para. A2.13 and Note 44.
9   See paras. 4.57 and 4.61.
10   See Ch. 5, para. 5.08.

Indeed, much of the drafting (for example, the provisions as to exceptions, infringement and remedies) is identical.

4.03   The result is that application of copyright concepts (and copyright case law) is, in the author's view, essential to understanding the new provisions. In this work, therefore, Part II will be treated as having created two new species of copyright which will be referred to as 'performers' rights'[11] and 'recording rights' respectively. These are the terms by which the draughtsman describes the new rights conferred: the terms will merely be used in a slightly different way. It is hoped that this will enable the reader more easily to appreciate the effect of the Act without introducing non-statutory terminology.

Performances

4.04   Part II of the Copyright, Designs and Patents Act 1988 confers rights on performers in relation to their performances. As we shall see, a performer has rights which may be infringed in any 'qualifying performance'. Although, in contrast to Part I of the Act, the word 'subsist' is not used in Part II, the requirements for the existence of performers' rights are similar to those for the existence of copyright. In the case of copyright, there must first be a work in which copyright is capable of subsisting (for example, a literary work) and then copyright will subsist if the work is original and stipulations as to qualification are complied with. In the case of performers' rights, there must first be a performance in which performers' rights are capable of subsisting and then performers' rights will subsist if stipulations as to qualification are complied with. There is no requirement of originality for performances, and so an actor, for example, will have performers' rights in each and every performance he gives in a particular play.

4.05   Section 180(2) of the 1988 Act defines 'performance' for the purposes of Part II[12] as meaning

   (a) a dramatic performance (which includes dance and mime),
   (b) a musical performance,
   (c) a reading or recitation of a literary work, or
   (d) a performance of a variety act or any similar presentation,

   which is, or so far as it is, a live performance given by one or more individuals.

These are therefore the categories of performance in which performers' rights are capable of subsisting.

---

11   Not, of course, to be confused with perform*ing* rights (sometimes referred to in older sources as perform*ance* rights), which are among the bundle of rights comprising copyright.
12   Note that the different definition of 'performance' contained in section 19(2) of the 1988 Act only applies to Part I.

4.06　The definition of 'performance' is something of a hybrid in that the first two categories are not on their face defined in terms of any work or type of work performed, but the second two categories are. Furthermore, it is expressly provided in Part II that the expression 'literary work' is to have the same meaning as in Part I,[13] but there is no equivalent provision relating to 'dramatic' or 'musical'. Although it is tempting to assume that these terms are to be construed in accordance with the meaning that they have in Part I, this suggests that there may be some difference. An important question, which bears upon this, is whether the four categories are mutually exclusive.

4.07　'Performer' is not defined by the 1988 Act.[14] This may be compared not only with the Performers' Protection Acts[15] but also with the Rome Convention, Article 3(a) of which defines 'performers' as

> actors, singers, musicians, dancers, and other persons who act, sing, declaim, play in, or otherwise perform literary or artistic[16] works.

Article 9 expressly states, however, that Contracting States may extend the protection provided for in the Convention to persons who do not perform literary or artistic works. The Convention is therefore of little or no assistance in construing section 180(2) of the 1988 Act.

Dramatic performances

4.08　Just as 'dramatic work' in Part I of the 1988 Act includes a work of dance or mime,[17] so too 'dramatic performance' includes dance and mime. The definitions are not necessarily co-extensive, however, for it would seem that a dramatic performance need not be a performance of a 'work'. It is submitted that this makes it clear that performers' rights may subsist in an improvised dramatic performance (that is, even if a purely improvised dramatic piece is not a work[18]).

4.09　Other than this, 'dramatic performance' is not defined. It is arguable, however, that 'dramatic performance' excludes the other three categories of performance. This argument depends partly upon the structure of the subsection, which is comparable to that of section 3(1) in Part I, and partly upon a consideration of the definitions of the other categories.[19] If it is right, it is submitted that 'dramatic performance' is to be understood as comprising one

---

13　Copyright, Designs and Patents Act 1988, section 211(1).
14　See, however, paras. 4.28–30 and 4.37.
15　See Ch. 2, para. 2.03.
16　'Artistic' in this context has the same meaning as in the Berne Convention. See Ch. 2, para. 2.10.
17　Copyright, Designs and Patents Act 1988, section 3(1).
18　Contrary to the view advanced in Ch. 2, para. 2.07. See also paras. 4.13–15.
19　See in particular paras. 4.10–12.

or both of two aspects:[20] (a) speech, that is to say, the use of the human voice to convey dramatic meaning to an audience but excluding any musical performance (that is, singing); and (b) action, that is to say, the use of bodily or facial movement to convey dramatic meaning to an audience.

Musical performances

4.10   'Musical performance' is undefined in Part II. In Part I of the 1988 Act 'musical work' is defined as

> a work consisting of music, exclusive of any words or action intended to be sung, spoken or performed with the music.[21]

Again, it is submitted that a musical performance need not be a performance of a 'work', so that an improvised musical performance will suffice.[22]

4.11   On the other hand, it is submitted that 'musical performance' should be understood as excluding performances in other categories; in particular, that 'musical performance' should exclude any dramatic performance that accompanies it. Such an interpretation may be supported both by analogy with the definition of musical work ('exclusive of . . . any action . . . performed with the music') and by reference to the structure of section 180(2).

4.12   The point is not an idle one, for the significance of the definition of musical work is that separate copyrights subsist in, say, the music and words of a song. Similarly, separate performers' rights should subsist in, for example, the musical performance and the dramatic performance of an opera. A rough and ready distinction in this example is between what the audience hears (musical performances) and what the audience sees (dramatic performances). The two categories of performances may involve different performers, for example, orchestral musicians who give musical performances but do not appear on stage or dancers who give dramatic performances but neither sing nor play an instrument. The two categories of performances may also involve different recording rights: for example, a record company may have recording rights in the orchestral musicians' musical performances while a film or television company may have recording rights in the dancers' dramatic performances. Then the two categories of performance may be exploitable in different ways: for example, the musical performances alone by the publication of records etc.; the dramatic performances alone by the publication of still photographs; and the musical and dramatic performances together by the publication of films or videos.

---

20   See para. 4.27, however.
21   Copyright, Designs and Patents Act 1988, section 3(1).
22   Cf. para. 4.08.

Readings and recitals

4.13 'Literary work' is defined in section 3(1) of the Act to mean

> any work, other than a dramatic or musical work, which is written, spoken or sung, and accordingly includes:
>
> (a) a table or compilation, and
> (b) a computer program.

A performance which consists of reading or reciting will therefore not be one in which performers' rights subsist unless what is read or recited is a 'work'. This raises the question of fixation: whether an improvised reading or recital is within the definition. This question can be approached in two stages.

4.14 First, suppose that what is read or recited (a poem or legal judgment, for example) existed in the author's mind but had not been reduced to writing or other material form prior to the performance. In this case, it is submitted that it is even clearer under the 1988 Act than under the 1956 Act[23] that a literary work may exist before it is recorded. This follows from the inclusion of the words 'any work . . . which is . . . spoken' in the definition just quoted. This is confirmed by subsections 3(2) and (3) of the 1988 Act, which provide that copyright does not subsist in a literary, dramatic or musical work unless and until it is recorded and that, where it is recorded by someone other than the author, the question whether copyright subsists in the record is distinct from the question whether it subsists in the work.

4.15 Secondly, suppose that the piece is composed and performed entirely extempore. Again, it is submitted that the position is clearer under the 1988 than under the 1956 Act.[24] 'Any work . . . which is spoken' must include works spoken extempore. An example may help. A prominent contemporary instance of the extempore literary work is the diary dictated into a tape recorder. It is submitted that there can be no doubt that this is a 'literary work' so as to qualify for copyright protection. It is an interesting question how far this may be taken: is all speech a literary work?[25] It is tentatively suggested that this is not so, for there must be an identifiable 'work'. The 'work' may be a work in progress or unfinished or improvised, but it must be in some way a distinct and identifiable creation. A mere snippet of speech is not a literary work.[26] An alternative view might be that all speech is a literary work, but that

---

23   As to which see Ch. 2, para. 2.05–2.06.
24   As to which see Ch. 2, para. 2.07.
25   Cf. Molière, *Le Bourgeois Gentilhomme*, Act II, scene iv: M. Jourdain: *Par ma foi! il y a plus de quarante ans que je dis de la prose sans que j'en suisse rien.* (M. Jourdain: Good heavens! For more than 40 years I have been speaking prose without knowing it.) But did M. Jourdain speak literary works without knowing it?
26   Cf. *Exxon Corp. v Exxon Insurance Consultants International Limited* [1982] RPC 69, in which the Court of Appeal held that the invented word 'Exxon' was not a literary work. See also paras. 4.24–25 in which interviews are considered.

copyright protection is reserved for those speeches upon which the author has expended a significant degree of skill or labour and which are recorded.

4.16   It may be objected that, whatever the position is under Part I of the Act, a work that is composed extempore is not read or recited, for these words imply that the work existed prior to the performance. It is submitted that this construction is too narrow. If it were adopted, it would lead to an arbitrary distinction between works composed but not recorded prior to performance and works truly extempore. The Oxford English Dictionary definition suggests that the word 'recite' is capable of bearing the wider construction even if it is not the most natural:

> **recite** . . . 1. a. *trans.* To repeat or utter aloud (something previously composed, heard, or learned by heart); now *spec.* to repeat to an audience (a piece of verse or other composition) from memory and in an appropriate manner. Also, to read out or aloud (now *rare*) . . . 2. a. To relate, rehearse, narrate, tell, declare; to give an account of; to describe in detail. ?*Obs.* . . . 3. To compose; to write *down*. *Obs. rare.* . . . 6. a. *intr.* (or without direct object) To relate, rehearse, etc. *Obs.* (Cf. sense 2).[27]

4.17   Similarly, it is submitted that there is a performance within the meaning of section 180(2) even if only part of a literary work (for example, a novel) is read or recited. Such a performance is a reading or recitation from the work, and in that sense is a reading or recitation of the work even though not of the whole work.

Performances of variety acts – circus performers

4.18   'Variety act' is nowhere defined in the 1988 Act. Furthermore, the term has no previous statutory history, having appeared neither in the Copyright Act 1956 nor in the Performers' Protection Acts 1958–72. On the face of section 180(2), it would appear that subsubsection (d) is intended to cover performances of a nature not within categories (a) to (c). The Oxford English Dictionary, however, gives the following:

> **variety** . . . 9b. Used to designate music-hall or theatrical entertainments of a mixed character (songs, dances, impersonations, etc.). Also applied to things or persons connected with such entertainments.

Everything within this definition falls within one of categories (a) to (c). Thus an impersonation is a dramatic performance. If 'variety act' is given its dictionary definition, subsubsection (d) will be mere surplusage.

4.19   The use of the term 'variety act' appears to stem from the Report of the Whitford Committee which used the term 'variety artistes' compendiously to describe performers such as jugglers and acrobats.[28] This usage may derive

---

27   2nd edn.
28   Cmnd 6732 at para. 407.

from the name of the Variety Artistes' Federation.[29] While some performances given by circus performers could be regarded as dramatic performances (clowning, for example[30]), others do not fit into this category so easily. Interpreting 'variety act' in this way will therefore serve a useful purpose. It remains to be seen, however, whether the courts will feel free to ignore the natural meaning of the words and adopt a meaning that is only apparent from a consideration of the legislative history of the 1988 Act.[31]

4.20   On normal principles, the words 'or any similar presentation' would be construed *ejusdem generis* with 'variety act'. The words may allow some latitude, however, for covering borderline cases. Either way, it would seem clear that an improvised performance will be within subsection (d).

Sporting performances

4.21   In general sporting performances are outside the categories of performance listed in section 180(2). Certain sports are arguably exceptions to this, however. Thus it is submitted that performances of ballroom dancing, ice dancing and figure skating are forms of dance and therefore within category (a); the mere fact of competition should not alter this. In addition, if 'variety act' is interpreted as referring to circus performances, it may be possible to include certain forms of sport, such as gymnastics, within the ambit of the words 'or any similar presentation' in category (d). It would be difficult, after all, to distinguish between gymnastics and circus performances such as high-wire or trapeze acts.

4.22   An interesting theoretical question is whether a general distinction between sportsmen and women and other performers can be justified. Given the possible latitude in interpretation of section 180(2), this question has practical relevance also, for the answer to it may (if only subconsciously) influence courts in how widely they are prepared to extend the ambit of the definition. The author's view is that, if improvised performances are regarded as worthy of the protection given by Part II of the Act, no such general distinction can be drawn, for sportsmen and women are simply performers whose performances are always improvised within the constraints imposed by the rules of the particular sport. This is true even of athletes who are judged merely on the criterion of speed. Although the presence of competition in sport

---

29   The Report of the Gregory Committee refers to a submission made by the Variety Artistes Federation, even though this is not one of the organisations listed in the relevant appendix: Cmnd 8662 at para. 165. The Variety Artistes' Federation is now incorporated within Equity. The Variety & Allied Entertainments' Council, however, is a confederation of unions representing performers who appear in clubs, cabarets and 'variety venues'.
30   See Ch. 2, para. 2.12.
31   In general it is not permissible for the Court to have regard in construing a statute to the report of a Royal Commission or government committee which preceded its enactment. Such a report may be considered to show the mischief aimed at, however. See *Halsbury's Laws*, 4th edn, vol. 44, para. 901.

might be cited as a distinction, it is surely not relevant to whether or not protection should be granted.[32] Certainly it must be accepted that sporting performances are equally susceptible of commercial exploitation by diffusion and/or fixation as other performances. To put it more shortly, sportsmen are entertainers too. Thus the economic considerations are the same. Prior to the enactment of the Copyright Act 1956 the Gregory Committee was urged to extend copyright to sportsmen but rejected the proposal, essentially on the ground that it had never been done before.[33] The question does not seem to have been reconsidered by the Whitford Committee, or in any of the Green Papers leading up to the 1988 Act.

Improvised performances

4.23   Although the point is not explicitly addressed by the Act, it is submitted that the width of the definitions in section 180(2) is sufficient to embrace improvised performances of every description. For further details, see the commentary on each subsubsection.

Interviews

4.24   It is submitted that performers' rights may subsist in an interview as being an improvised performance of two or more individuals within category (c) of section 180(2). At first sight the words 'reading or recitation' may appear to militate against this. If, however, it is accepted that a monologue composed extempore as it is performed is 'read or recited' just as much as one that has been written prior to performance,[34] it is difficult to see why the same principle should not apply to an interview. An interview can be regarded as a collective literary improvisation in the same way that a jazz performance is a collective musical improvisation.

4.25   It may be objected (on the assumption that not all speech is a literary work) that an interview is no different from any conversation and that therefore there is no 'work'. It is submitted that a distinction (albeit a somewhat precarious one) can be drawn between an interview and a conversation so as to make the former and not the latter a 'work'. This is that an interview is distinct, identifiable and takes place for a particular purpose.[35]

---

32   Particularly since it could be said that the arts are becoming increasingly competitive as more and more prizes are instituted.

33   Cmnd 8662 at para. 180.

34   See paras. 4.16–17.

35   Cf. *Donoghue v Allied Newspapers Ltd* [1938] 1 Ch. 106 in which Farwell J held that on the facts an interviewee was neither the author nor the joint author of articles derived from the interview, and so not the owner of any copyright in them. It was not suggested that no copyright subsisted in the articles, and the judgment implies that if the articles had consisted of a transcript of the interview, the interviewee would have been a joint author of the work and therefore a co-owner of the copyright. See also para. 4.15.

The provisions of paragraph 13 of Schedule 2 of the 1988 Act, which in the words of the rubric permit 'use of recordings of spoken works in certain cases', suggest that the draughtsman of the Act envisaged that performers' rights would subsist in an interview.[36]

Aleatoric works

4.26   An aleatoric (or aleatory) work is a work which is 'dependent on uncertain contingencies',[37] for example one in which the author gives the performer (or even the audience) a number of options to choose between or one in which options are selected by some random means. Works of this character have recently become quite common in music and drama.[38] Performances of such works are clearly musical or dramatic performances and within section 180(2).

Artistic works

4.27   In contrast to section 8(1) of the Dramatic and Musical Performers' Protection Act 1958 as amended,[39] section 180(2) does not extend to performances of artistic works. This probably does not reduce the scope of protection, however, since the only works that might be performable are almost certainly within one of categories (a) to (d): for example, performance art is probably more accurately categorised as a species of dramatic performance than as an artistic work. Perhaps the only activity that might be affected is conceptual art.[40] It is suggested in Chapter 2 that section 8(1) of the 1958 Act might protect the performances of persons such as lighting technicians.[41] The basis for this suggestion is that the lighting design for a play or opera is, typically, a part literary and part artistic work which is in a real sense 'performed' by a technician each night.[42] Under the 1988 Act such a performance might be considered to be a dramatic performance on the basis that it helps to convey dramatic meaning to an audience. It does not fit into either of the two subdivisions of dramatic performance advanced in paragraph 4.09 above, however.

---

36   Similarly with section 58 (the rubric to which reads 'use of notes or recordings or spoken words in certain cases') and copyright if the interview is recorded. See Ch. 6, paras. 6.21–22.
37   Oxford English Dictionary, 2nd edn. The word is derived from *aleator*, a dice player, from *alea*, a die.
38   For example, certain plays by the dramatist Alan Ayckbourn.
39   See Ch. 2, para. 2.10.
40   See Ch. 2, para. 2.10 and Note 23.
41   See para. 2.10.
42   Although lighting desks are increasingly computerised. To the extent that the performance is computer-generated it will fall outside the definition in section 180(2): see paras. 4.35–36.

Interpreters and executants

4.28   Section 180(1) of the Copyright, Designs and Patents Act 1988 states that Part II of the Act 'confers rights on a performer, by requiring his consent to the exploitation of his performances'. 'Performer' is not defined in the Act. Commonsense suggests that a performer is one who gives a performance. Not all performances are within Part II of the Act, however. It would appear from the definition of 'performance' in section 180(2) that a 'performer' for the purposes of Part II is an individual who gives a live performance as defined.

4.29   This leaves the question whether interpretative (as opposed to executive) artists such as conductors and directors are performers who can have rights under Part II. At first blush, a theatre director does not 'give a performance' of a play, for he merely directs the rehearsals beforehand. On the other hand, much of a conductor's work is done in rehearsal too. Is a distinction to be drawn between a conductor who rehearses an orchestra but does not appear in the concert hall and one who does appear in the concert hall? It is submitted that 'performer' should be construed broadly so as to avoid such distinctions.[43]

4.30   Support for such a broad construction can be gained from the Rome Convention. Although the English text of the Rome Convention only refers to 'performers', the French text uses the expression '*artistes interprètes or executants*'.[44] This makes it clear that both *artistes interprètes* and *artistes executants* should be protected. The 1988 Act should therefore be construed so as to comply with the Convention.

Performance or adaptation

4.31   Some interpretative artists – particularly theatre directors – alter a work to such an extent that it is arguable that their contribution should be categorised as adaptation rather than 'mere' performance. This would have the consequence that the artist acquired a separate copyright in the adaptation. If this proposition seems strange, it may be instructive to compare the work of a theatre director with that of a film director.[45] Few would question that a film is a separate copyright work from any antecedent work such as a play; that, even if there is a detailed screenplay, there can be no question of 'mere' interpretation such that there would be no copyright in the film separate from that in the screenplay. This might be explained[46] in one of two ways. First, that 'translating' a work from one medium to another, namely, paper to celluloid,

---

43   See also para. 4.37.
44   See Ch. 2, para. 2.13.
45   Ignoring, for this purpose, the fact that under section 9(2) of the Copyright, Designs and Patents Act 1988 a film director may not be the 'author' of a film for the purposes of copyright ownership.
46   As a matter of principle, rather than simply of what the Copyright Act provides.

and so creating a new object for consumption, must give rise to a fresh copyright. Second, that no matter how detailed a screenplay is, it must necessarily give the director considerable latitude in selecting the images that will constitute the film. But if these explanations are tested against the work of a theatre director, their cogency may be doubted. For a theatre director also 'translates' a work from one medium to another, namely, from paper to speech and action, so as to create a new object for consumption. It might be objected that speech and action do not constitute a material form, but since they are capable of fixation there is no reason why copyright should not subsist.[47] Then again, a play gives a director considerable latitude in how he directs his actors. Why then should copyright not subsist in a production of a play?[48]

4.32 It could be argued by extension of this that every performer interprets the work he or she performs and in doing so adapts it to some extent – a musician, for example, may vary tempi or dynamics or phrasing. Thus, it might be said, every performer is protected by copyright in any event. This is almost certainly not the law (though the argument does not seem ever to have been put in this way). It is not easy, however, to explain why not. The difficulty – the fineness of the distinction that needs to be drawn – may perhaps best be seen by comparing the work of a performer with the work of an editor of a musical score. There seems little doubt that the latter but not the former attracts copyright for his labours.[49]

4.33 This raises the question of where to draw the line – or rather, of what test to apply in drawing it. It might be thought that in deciding whether there has been an adaptation rather than merely an interpretation, the ordinary test of originality for copyright purposes should be applied, namely whether sufficient skill and labour has been been expended. Almost all performances, however, require considerable skill and labour. Nor it is possible, it is submitted, to make a clear distinction between the skill and labour expended merely in performing or interpreting from that expended in adapting. Some objective test is required. The Copyright, Designs and Patents Act 1988 gives no guidance on this, however, and it remains to be to seen what attitude the courts might take.

4.34 It is worth pointing out, finally, that this question is not an entirely academic one. There are two main reasons for this, one technical and one more general. The technical reason is that the period of copyright protection is longer than that of performers' rights: 50 years from the end of the year of the author's death as opposed to a simple 50 years from the end of the year of the

---

47 As it may in an improvised dramatic performance: see para. 4.08.
48 Particularly if the director has cut or re-ordered the text.
49 The fineness of the distinction is emphasised by the fact that, with the rise of the Early Music movement, it has become increasingly common for one person – the musicologist-performer – to do both tasks. Where this happens, it is inevitable that 'interpretative' considerations will influence the 'musicological' task of editing, and 'musicological' consider-ations will influence the 'interpretative' task of performing.

performance. This may make a substantial difference. The more general reason is that artists such as film directors and theatre directors are becoming more concerned to protect their work through copyright. One recent result of this is the according of limited *droits morals* to film directors under Chapter IV of Part I of the 1988 Act. It may be expected that pressure to give such artists further protection will increase.

Live

4.35   'Live' is not defined in the Act, and has no previous statutory history.[50] There would appear to be two possible meanings: first, a performance that is not pre-recorded; and secondly, a performance given in the presence of an audience. Curiously, the Oxford English Dictionary definition gives only the first meaning, although the illustrative quotations contain both:

> live . . . 2. *trans.* and *fig.* in various applications . . . d. Of a performance, heard or watched at the time of its occurrence, as distinguished from one recorded on film, tape, etc. Also quasi-*adv.*

> 1934 *B.B.C. Year-Bk.* 248 Listeners have . . . complained of the fact that recorded material was too liberally used . . . but . . . transmitting hours to the Canadian and Australasian zones are inconvenient for broadcasting 'live' material . . . 1944 *Ann. Reg. 1943* 348 It was still felt . . . that attendance at concerts and listening to 'live' performances belonged to a better order of things.[51]

Thus a performance by an orchestra in a broadcasting studio may be broadcast 'live' in the first sense although no audience is present in the studio; conversely, a recording of a performance by an orchestra when an audience is present may be described as a 'live' recording in the second sense even though the recording is broadcast some time after the event.

4.36   It is submitted that the first meaning is to be preferred in the context of section 180(2), for a number of reasons. The simplest is that this seems to be the sense in which the word is used elsewhere in Part II, notably in section 182(1)(b).[52, 53] Then, to apply the second meaning might have the effect of denying performers' rights to many performers. For example, a film actor's only immediate audience (other than the film crew[54]) is the camera. It would be surprising if the legislature intended by introducing the word 'live' to reverse the decision in the *Peter Sellers* case,[55] where the performances in question were film performances. Next, it is submitted that the first, but not

---

50   But see Ch. 2 paras. 2.15–17.
51   2nd edition.
52   See Ch. 5, para. 5.20.
53   See also para. 4.49.
54   Although the presence of the crew perhaps makes it easier to argue that a film director gives a live performance than that a theatre director does, on the assumption that no one is present at theatrical rehearsals save the cast.
55   [1988] QB 40.

the second, interpretation is in accordance with the Rome Convention. If a performance was unprotected simply because it did not take place in front of an audience, the performers could not prevent their performance being fixed without their consent as required by Article 7. On the other hand, the Convention does not provide for protection of fixed performances other than against reproduction for purposes other than those for which the fixation was made.[56] Finally, to interpret 'live' in the first way does not render it surplusage, for it ensures that the duration of performers' rights cannot be indefinitely extended by including an old recording in a new performance.[57] It may also mean that performances, or parts of performances, that are computer-generated are excluded from protection, at least where the computer is effectively being used as a substitute for a recording.[58]

One or more individuals

4.37   'Individual' would appear to mean natural person. Thus corporations are excluded. It might be argued that computer-generated performances are also excluded in this way, but it is submitted that this is not so, for an individual must at least give the computer the instruction to start at a particular time. The real distinction is between using the computer as an instrument and using it as a form of recording, and this distinction is provided by the word 'live'.[59] It has been suggested[60] that, in the context of circus performances,[61] a performance by animals should nevertheless be regarded as a performance given by an individual, namely the trainer, notwithstanding that the animals are not individuals. This is to stretch the concept of interpretation[62] nearly to breaking point, but it may be justifiable on grounds of policy.

4.38   The definition of 'performance' as a performance given by 'one *or more* individuals' (emphasis added) might be thought to suggest that, for example, a concert given by an orchestra is *one* performance given by a number of individuals in respect which there is *one* performers' right shared among the participants. Reading Part II as a whole, however, it seems clear that the

---

56   Compare Article 7 paragraphs (a) and (b) with paragraph (c).
57   The use of recordings during otherwise live performances has recently become common in pop music. It may become more common in theatre: in 1987 Laurence Olivier appeared in the musical *Time* in London by way of a hologram.
58   Computers are increasingly being used in performances of both avant-garde and popular music. The computer may be used simply as an instrument or part of an instrument, for example by generating a variety of pitches and tones that are then played in performance through conventional control means (typically a keyboard, but guitars, wind instruments and percussion have been used). Alternatively, the computer may be used instead of a recording, for example, to produce a pre-programmed rhythm track.
59   See the preceding footnote.
60   Lester and Mitchell, *Joynson-Hicks on UK Copyright Law*, (Sweet & Maxwell 1989), para. 12.12.
61   See paras. 4.18–20.
62   See paras. 4.29–30.

intention is that *each* individual performer has his *own* performers' right in any particular collective performance.[63]

Subsistence of Performers' Rights

4.39   Performers' rights subsist in a performance if it is a 'qualifying performance',[64] that is, if it given by a qualifying individual or takes place in a qualifying country.[65] Although not expressly stated in relation to performances which qualify by virtue of having taken place in a qualifying country, it seems clearly to be intended that performers' rights are only to subsist in a performance by an individual, so that each performer in, say, an orchestra, has his own performers' right. On the other hand, performers' rights are personal. Unlike copyright,[66] there is no provisions for first ownership by the performers' employer. Furthermore, performers' rights are unassignable,[67] which would seem to indicate that there can be no beneficial ownership separate from the legal ownership.

No formalities

4.40   No formalities are required for the subsistence of performers' rights. Thus there is no need for any registration, deposit or marking of recordings: the rights arise automatically if the performance qualifies.

Performers' rights independent of copyright

4.41   Performers' rights are independent of any copyright that may subsist in any work performed or any film or sound recording of or broadcast or cable programme including the performance.[68]

Qualifying individual

4.42   A qualifying individual is an individual who is either (a) a citizen or subject of a qualifying country or (b) resident in a qualifying country.[69]

---

63   For example, this is the rationale for the powers given to the Copyright Tribunal to give consent on behalf of a performer: see Ch. 6, paras. 6.52–69. See also para. 4.39.

64   The Act does not express it in this way, but this is the effect since only rights in qualifying performances may be infringed: Copyright, Designs and Patents Act 1988, sections 182, 183 and 184. See also Ch. 5, para. 5.03.

65   Copyright, Designs and Patents Act 1988, section 181.

66   *Ibid.*, section 11(2).

67   See para. 4.57.

68   Copyright, Designs and Patents Act 1988, section 180(4)(a).

69   *Ibid.*, section 206(1).

Citizen or subject

4.43   In the case of the United Kingdom, a person is a citizen or subject if he is a British citizen.[70] In the case of a colony of a United Kingdom, a person is a citizen or subject if he is a British Dependent Territories' citizen by connection with that colony.[71] Whether a person is a citizen or subject of another country must be decided according to the law of the country concerned.[72] This will be a question of fact to be proven by expert evidence in English proceedings.

Resident

4.44   Whether a person is resident in a particular country must be decided according to the appropriate United Kingdom law – in other words, the *lex fori* rather than the law of the country in question.[73] Unfortunately, 'residence' is a word that has different meanings in different branches of the law, at least so far as the law of England and Wales is concerned.[74] Taxation cases would seem to provide a suitable guide, however. These indicate that a man is resident in a particular country if he is present there other than casually or as a visitor, or if he has a home that is (in substance) constantly available to him for his own use and which he occupies from time to time.[75] Residence implies a degree of permanence and continuity, a genuine and substantial connection. Even prolonged absence does not cause a person to cease to be resident.[76] It is possible to be resident in more than one country at once.[77]

Qualifying country

4.45   The following are qualifying countries:[78]

(a) the United Kingdom;[79]
(b) other Member States of the European Economic Community;[80] and
(c) countries designated by Order in Council as enjoying reciprocal protection.[81]

---

70   *Ibid.*, section 206(2)(a). For the definition of British citizen see Nationality Act 1981.
71   *Ibid.*, section 206(2)(b). For the definition of British Dependent Territories' citizen see Nationality Act 1981.
72   *Stoeck v Public Trustee* [1921] 2 Ch 67, *Re Chamberlain's Settlement* [1921] 2 Ch 553.
73   Dicey and Morris, *The Conflict of Laws*, 11th edn, Rule 8 and *Re Annesley* [1926] Ch 692. Both the Rule and the case are concerned with domicile, but it seems clear that the same rule must apply to residence.
74   Dicey and Morris, p. 163.
75   *Re Young* (1875) 1 TC 59, *Cooper v Cadwallader* (1904) 5 TC 101.
76   *Re Young*, above, *Levene v Inland Revenue Commissioners* [1928] AC 217.
77   *Inland Revenue Commissioners v Lysaght* [1928] AC 234.
78   Copyright, Designs and Patents Act 1988, section 206(1).
79   See Ch. 5, para. 5.57.
80   Presently France, the German Federal Republic, the Netherlands, Italy, Belgium, Luxembourg, the Republic of Ireland, Denmark, Greece, Spain and Portugal.
81   Copyright, Designs and Patents Act 1988, section 206(1).

Countries enjoying reciprocal protection

4.46   A country may be designated by Order in Council as enjoying reciprocal protection if it is either:

(a) a country which is party to a Convention relating to performers' rights to which the United Kingdom is a party;[82] or

(b) a country which the Crown is satisfied has given or will give adequate protection to British performances, that is, performances either given by individuals who are British citizens or resident in the United Kingdom or taking place in the United Kingdom.[83]

Countries which have acceded to or ratified the Rome Convention fall within the first category.[84] The Channel Islands, the Isle of Man and colonies of the United Kingdom may be designated in the second category.[85] If a country provides adequate protection only for certain descriptions of British performances, the Order designating it may be limited to a corresponding extent.[86]

Exclusive Recording Contracts

4.47   In addition to performers, Part II of the Copyright, Designs and Patents Act 1988 confers rights on persons who have the benefit of exclusive recording contracts with performers or their licensees. These rights, referred to as 'recording rights', subsist if the relevant person is qualified.

Exclusive recording contracts

4.48   An 'exclusive recording contract' is defined as

a contract between a performer and another person under which that person is entitled to the exclusion of all other persons (including the performer) to make recordings of one or more of his performances with a view to their commercial exploitation.[87]

The performances to which this applies are those in which performers' rights are capable of subsisting.

---

82   *Ibid.*, section 208(1)(a),(2).

83   *Ibid.*, section 208(1)(b),(3).

84   Presently Austria, Barbados, Brazil, Burkina Faso, Chile, Columbia, People's Republic of Congo, Costa Rica, Czechoslovakia, Denmark, Dominican Republic, Ecuador, El Salvador, Fiji, Finland, France, Federal Republic of Germany, Guatemala, Honduras, Republic of Ireland, Italy, Japan, Lesotho, Luxembourg, Mexico, Monaco, Niger, Norway, Panama, Paraguay, Peru, Philippines, Sweden, Uruguay. All of these countries, except Honduras, Japan, and Lesotho, which only acceded on 26 October 1989, 26 January 1990 and 16 February 1990 respectively, have been designated as enjoying reciprocal protection by the Performances (Reciprocal Protection) (Convention Countries) (No. 2) Order 1989, S.I. 1989 No. 1296.

85   Copyright, Designs and Patents Act 1988, section 208(5).

86   *Ibid.*, section 208(4).

87   *Ibid.*, section 185(1).

Recordings

4.49   'Recording' is defined as meaning

a film or sound recording

(a) made directly from the live performance,
(b) made from a broadcast of or cable programme including the performance, or
(c) made, directly or indirectly, from another recording of the performance.[88]

'Film' and 'sound recording' bear the same meanings as in Part I.[89] Thus a film is a recording on any medium from which a moving image may by any means be produced.[90] This definition is broad enough to encompass conventional films, videotapes and videodiscs or indeed moving pictures stored in any other medium (but not a still photograph). A sound recording is either a recording of sounds, from which the sounds may be reproduced, or a recording of the whole or part of a literary, dramatic or musical work, from which sounds reproducing the work or part of it may be produced, in either case regardless of medium or method of reproduction.[91] It should be noted that the soundtrack of a film falls within the definition of a sound recording, but not within the definition of a film. Assuming that 'live' means 'not pre-recorded',[92] the word 'live' in (a) would appear to be surplusage.

Performance

4.50   The definition of 'performance' is the same for the purpose of recording rights as for the purpose of performers' rights,[93] so that recording rights are capable of subsisting in all performances in which performers' rights may subsist.

With a view to commercial exploitation

4.51   This is defined to mean 'with a view to the recordings being sold or let for hire, or shown or played in public'.[94] This does not advance matters greatly. It is not clear whether a mere test of intention is intended, or whether something more will be required. Equally, if it is merely a test of intention, is it subjective or objective? It is submitted that the definition should be read as imposing an objective test, so that the question to be asked is whether the contract on its true construction gives the other person the exclusive right to make recordings for any commercial purpose. Thus the performer may have

---

88   *Ibid.*, section 180(2).
89   *Ibid.*, section 211(1).
90   *Ibid.*, section 5(1).
91   *Ibid.*
92   See paras. 4.35–36.
93   See paras. 4.04–36.
94   Copyright, Designs and Patents Act 1988, section 185(4).

the right to make recordings of his own performances for his private and domestic use[95] without preventing the contract from being an exclusive recording contract within the meaning of section 185(1).

Subsistence of Recording Rights

4.52   Recording rights may subsist in a performance in either of two ways:

(i) Where the person who has the benefit of an exclusive recording contract to which the performance is subject (either by virtue of that person being a party to the contract or by virtue of an assignment of the benefit of the contract) is a qualifying person;[96] or

(ii) (If the person referred to in (i) is not a qualifying person) where another person who is licensed to make recordings of the performance with a view to their commercial exploitation (either by virtue of an agreement with the person who has the benefit of an exclusive recording contract to which the performance is subject or by virtue of an assignment of the benefit of such an agreement) is a qualifying person.[97]

The difference between the two situations is that in (i) a licence from the person having the benefit of the recording contract permitting another to make recordings of a particular performance will operate as a licence of the first person's recording rights as well as of his contractual rights, whereas in (ii) there will only be a licence of the first person's contractual rights, and the recording rights will belong to the second person, the licensee. Interestingly, the licensee in (ii) need not be exclusive.

No formalities, rights independent of copyright

4.53   As with performers' rights, there are no formalities to be observed, and the rights are independent of any copyright.

Qualifying person

4.54   A qualifying person is either (i) a qualifying individual[98] or (ii) a body corporate or other body having legal personality which (a) is formed under the law of a qualifying country and (b) has in any qualifying country a place of business at which substantial business activity is carried on.[99] There appears to be no requirement that the qualifying country in which business is carried on

---

95   Cf. the definitions of category (i) infringements of performers' rights and recording rights. See Ch. 5, paras. 5.11 and 5.45.
96   Copyright, Designs and Patents Act 1988, section 185(2).
97   *Ibid.*, section 185(3).
98   See para. 4.42.
99   Copyright, Designs and Patents Act 1988, section 206(1).

be the same as that under the law of which the body is formed. In determining whether substantial business is carried on, however, no account is to be taken of dealings in goods which are at all material times outside the country in question.[100] Thus mere brokerage businesses are excluded.

First ownership of recording rights

4.55 Recording rights are first owned either (i) by the person having the benefit of the recording contract to which the performance is subject if that person is qualified or (ii) if not, by that person's licensee if the licensee is qualified.

Duration of Performers' Rights and Recording Rights

4.56 Performers' rights and recording rights which subsist in a performance by virtue of Part II of the Copyright, Designs and Copyright Act 1988 continue to subsist until the expiration of 50 years from the end of the calendar year in which the performance took place.[101] This is comfortably in excess of the 20 year minimum stipulated in Article 14 of the Rome Convention. Assuming that performances are not required to take place before audiences for it to be possible for rights to subsist in them at all,[102] the limitation is unaffected by whether or not the performance is broadcast or recordings of it published at the time when it was first given. In other words' performers' rights and recording rights do not subsist indefinitely if the work remains unpublished.[103]

Transmission of Performers' Rights and Recording Rights

Performers' rights: assignment

4.57 Performers' rights may not be assigned.[104] Apart from the limited provision for transmission on death,[105] therefore, performers' rights are personal to the performer.

---

100 *Ibid.*, section 206(3).
101 *Ibid.*, section 191.
102 As to which see paras. 4.35–36.
103 Following the rule for copyright now that section 2(3) of the Copyright Act 1956 has been repealed.
104 Copyright, Designs and Patents Act 1988, section 192(1).
105 See paras. 4.58–59.

Performers' rights: disposition

4.58   Performers' rights may be passed on death to

> such person as [the performer] may by testamentary disposition specifically direct.[106]

This might be taken to suggest that the rights – that is, all rights in any one performance – can only be transmitted to *one* person.[107] Section 192(3), however, makes it clear that rights may be transmitted to more than one person, in which case the recipients will be able to exercise the performers' rights independently of each other.[108]

4.59   Part II of the Act does not stipulate whether or not a performer's rights in any one performance can be the subject of partial dispositions, that is, the rights divided up between different heirs as to category of infringing act and/or time.[109] It is not clear whether this omission is deliberate or inadvertent. Since there is no prohibition upon partial disposition, it is submitted that Part II should be interpreted as permitting it.

Performers' rights: transmission on death in absence of disposition

4.60   Where there is no express provision in the will, performers' rights are exercisable after death by the deceased's personal representatives.[110] Damages recovered by the personal representatives in respect of an infringement occurring after the deceased's death devolve as part of the deceased's estate as if the right of action had subsisted and been vested in the deceased immediately before death.[111] In either case, any consent which was binding upon the deceased will bind the person or persons to whom the rights pass.[112]

Recording rights

4.61   Recording rights may not themselves be assigned or otherwise transmitted.[113] This would not appear to matter greatly,[114] however, since the contractual rights upon which they depend are assignable and it is expressly provided[115] that the restriction on the transmissibility of recording rights does

---

106   Copyright, Designs and Patents Act 1988, section 192(2)(a).
107   Although in general the single includes the plural unless the contrary intention appears: Interpretation Act 1978, section 6(c).
108   See para. 4.59.
109   Cf. section 90(2) in Part I.
110   Cf. *Rickless v United Artists Corp.* [1988] QB 40.
111   Copyright, Designs and Patents Act 1988, section 192(5).
112   *Ibid.*, section 193(3).
113   *Ibid.*, section 192(1).
114   Save in relation to collecting societies: see para. 4.66.
115   Copyright, Designs and Patents Act 1988, section 192(4).

not affect sections 185(2)(b) or (3)(b), under which assignees of such rights may acquire recording rights. Thus if A has recording rights in a performance by virtue of an exclusive recording contract with the performer to which the performance is subject, he cannot assign those rights to B. He can, however, assign the benefit of the contract to B who will, if he is a qualified person, automatically acquire the recording rights thenceforward. Such an assignment would probably not carry with it any accrued rights of action (unlike an assignment of copyright), but these could be assigned to B together with the benefit of the contract. If B is not a qualified person, he will be able to license someone to make recordings (includings recordings made from a recording) of the performance with a view to commercial exploitation who is a qualified person. Any consent which was binding upon the assignor or licensor of such contractual rights will bind the assignee or licensee.[116]

Co-ownership

Performers' rights

4.62   During the lifetime of a performer, his performers' rights remain both unitary and personal to him. There can therefore be no question of co-ownership. After his death, however, the rights may enter multiple ownership. Where this occurs, section 192(3) provides that the rights are

> exercisable by each of them independently of the other or others.

It is not quite clear what this means. It is submitted that this must mean that each owner may sue for infringement without the presence of the others (although possibly he may have to account to the others for their share of the damages). It is arguable that it also means that (a) each owner may himself do acts within the scope of the performer's rights without committing an infringement even if he does not have the permission of the others; and/or (b) he may grant a licence without the consent of the others. This argument may be supported by the fact that Part II of the Act contains no provision corresponding to section 173(2) of Part I, which expressly states that, where the licence of the copyright owner is required, that means the licence of all the owners. On the other hand, it would be surprising if joint owners of performers' rights were able to act in a way possibly detrimental to each others' interest without the others' consent. It is therefore submitted that section 193(2) should not be construed as permitting this.

Recording rights

4.63   Since recording rights are neither assignable nor otherwise transmissible

---

116   *Ibid.*, section 193(2).

it is not possible for multiple ownership of them to arise in the same way as for performers' rights. What would appear to be possible, however, is for the benefit of the underlying recording contract to be jointly owned by two or more persons and hence for the recording rights arising out of it to be jointly owned. It is submitted that in such circumstances, each owner should be able to take proceedings for infringement without the presence of the other owners, but should not be able to exploit or license the exploitation of the rights without the consent of the others.

Licensing

4.64   It is expressly provided that an owner of performers' rights or recording rights may grant licences in relation to a specific performance, a specific description of performances or performances generally, whether past or future.[117] There is no reason why licences should not also be granted in relation to specific acts concerning specific performances, so that for example the right owner may license one person to record the performance and another to broadcast it.

4.65   Licences will be subject to normal contractual principles, so that, for example, they may be express or implied and may be revocable at will if bare or in accordance with the contract if supported by consideration.[118]

Collecting Societies[119]

4.66   Since neither performers' rights nor recording rights are assignable, any collecting societies which may be established to license users and collect royalties under Part II of the 1988 Act will have to act as agent for the right owner in each case. This will mean that they will not be able to take enforcement proceedings in their own name. They will therefore function in a manner akin to, say, Mechanical-Copyright Protection Society Ltd rather than, say, Phonographic Performance Ltd.

---

117   Copyright, Designs and Patents Act 1988, section 193(1).
118   See Ch. 6, para. 6.42.
119   See also Ch. 3, paras. 3.10–12.

5 Infringement

Introduction

5.01 Although Part II of the Copyright, Designs and Patents Act 1988 came into force on 1 August 1989,[1] so that it was possible for performers' rights and recording rights to be infringed from that day, the Act provides that no act done

in pursuance of arrangements made before [1 August 1989]

is to be regarded as infringing.[2] Since the Performers' Protection Acts 1958–72 were repealed in their entirety on 1 August 1989,[3] acts done after that day, but pursuant to 'arrangements made' before it, are not caught by either the Performers' Protection Acts or by Part II of the new Act. This suggests that 'arrangements' should be narrowly interpreted.[4]

Infringement of Performers' Rights

5.02 Like other forms of copyright, performers' rights and recording rights are bundles of rights. They may thus be infringed in a number of different ways. Performers' rights which subsist[5] in a performance are infringed by the doing of any of the following acts without the consent of the performer:[6]

---

1 Copyright, Designs and Patents Act 1988 (Commencement No. 1) Order 1989, S.I. 1989 No. 816.
2 Copyright, Designs and Patents Act 1988, section 180(3).
3 *Ibid.*, section 303(2) and Schedule 8; Copyright, Designs and Patents Act 1988 (Commencement No. 1) Order 1989, Note 1 above.
4 See Ch. 6, para. 6.51. In *Grower v BBC* (*The Times*, 6 July 1990) it was conceded that the plaintiffs had no cause of action under the 1988 Act in relation to acts done pursuant to a copyright licence granted in July 1988.
5 See para. 5.03.
6 In all three of sections 182, 183 and 184 of the Copyright, Designs and Patents Act 1988, the word 'his' in 'without his consent' has two possible antecedents: 'a performer' and 'a person'. The former is clearly correct. Matters are not helped, however, by the reappearance of the word 'his' in the phrase 'otherwise than for his private and domestic use' in sections 182(1)(a) and 184(1)(a), where it has the same possible antecedents but the latter must be intended.

(i) making (otherwise than for private and domestic use) a recording of the whole or any substantial part of the performance;[7]

(ii) broadcasting live or including live in a cable programme service the whole or any substantial part of the performance;[8]

(iii) showing or playing in public the whole or any substantial part of the performance by means of a recording which, as the exhibiter knows or has reason to believe, was made without the performer's consent;[9]

(iv) broadcasting or including in a cable programme service the whole or any substantial part of the performance by means of a recording which, as the broadcaster knows or has reason to believe, was made without the performer's consent;[10]

(v) importing into the United Kingdom otherwise than for the private and domestic use of the importer a recording of the whole or any substantial part of the performance which, as the importer knows or has reason to believe, was made otherwise than for private purposes and without the performer's consent (an 'illicit recording');[11]

(vi) in the course of a business possessing, selling, letting for hire, offering or exposing for sale or hire or distributing a recording of the whole or any substantial part of the performance which, as the dealer knows or has reason to believe, was made otherwise than for private purposes and without the performer's consent (an 'illicit recording').[12]

Subsistence of rights

5.03   It should be noted that (as a consequence of the avoidance of copyright-style drafting), the infringement-defining provisions in Part II in fact refer to a 'qualifying performance'. There is no explicit limitation to performances in which performers' rights subsist. This must be the intention, however, for otherwise section 191 (duration of rights)[13] would be of no effect. The various sections must be read together. For the sake of clarity, therefore, reference is made in this Chapter to performances in which performers' rights subsist rather than to qualifying performances.

Primary and secondary infringement

5.04   Infringements in categories (i) and (ii) and those in categories (iii) to (vi) will be referred to as primary and secondary infringements respectively, by analogy with the customary usage that grew up under the Copyright Act 1956.

---

7   Copyright, Designs and Patents Act 1988, section 182(1)(a). See paras. 5.10–14.
8   *Ibid.*, section 182(1)(b). See paras. 5.15–20.
9   *Ibid.*, section 183(a). See paras. 5.21–24.
10   *Ibid.*, section 183(b). See para. 5.25.
11   *Ibid.*, section 184(1)(a). See paras. 5.25–32.
12   *Ibid.*, section 184(1)(b). See paras. 5.33–43.
13   See Ch. 4, para. 4.56.

It should be noted, however, that this description is incorrect in one respect. Secondary infringements are so called because they are dealings in an article the making of which was (or is deemed to have been) a primary infringement. Conversely, a primary infringement consists of making an article which may be dealt in in the ways that constitute a secondary infringement. Category (ii) infringement is not true primary infringement in this sense, for the broadcast or cable programme that is made cannot be dealt in in any way that constitutes an infringement of categories (iii) to (vi), unlike a recording made in category (i) infringement. Category (ii) infringement does, however, share with category (i) infringement another characteristic of primary infringement, namely that both are torts of strict liability, since no particular mental state is required to accompany the overt act. The opposite is true of infringements in categories (iii) to (iv), for which knowledge or reason to believe is an ingredient of the tort. For this reason it is useful to classify category (ii) infringement as primary infringement, provided that it is remembered that in this case it cannot lead to any secondary infringement.

Substantial part

5.05 Part II of the 1988 Act contains no guidance as to what might constitute a substantial part of a performance. A question which presents itself is whether or not substantiality is to be measured by reference to any works performed. 'A performance' might be either the performance of a single work or the performance of all works performed on one occasion. Thus a concert in which 20 songs are sung might be one performance or 20. The definition of 'performance' in section 180(2) provides little assistance in answering this question. On the one hand, paragraph (c) could be taken to indicate that the reading of each literary work is a performance; but, on the other hand, paragraphs (a) and (b) could be taken as indicating the opposite.

5.06 It is submitted that the question whether infringement has taken place should not depend on the correct resolution of this question. Instead, the traditional approach of the courts when faced with deciding questions of substantiality in connection with copyright should be adopted. This approach may be expressed in two ways. The first is in the rule of thumb or maxim, 'what is worth copying is *prima facie* worth protecting'.[14] The second is in the series of *dicta* which support the proposition that substantiality is a matter of impression, taking into account the quality of what has been taken as well as the quantity.[15] In short, if what is taken is substantial, the courts will not concern themselves with whether many works or only part of a work is involved.

---

14 Per Petersen J in *University of London Press Ltd v University Tutorial Press Ltd* [1916] 2 Ch 601, 610. This dictum was approved by the House of Lords in *Ladbroke (Football) Ltd v William Hill (Football) Ltd* [1964] 1 Wl.R 273, 279, 288, 294.
15 See in particular *Ladbroke v William Hill*, above, Note 13.

5.07   Nevertheless modern technology may give rise to some difficult questions on substantiality. A particular example is provided by the use of digital electronic sampling, which permits a musician using a computer to 'sample' any pre-existing sound and then manipulate it. If the pre-existing sound is a performance, say by an opera singer, and a very short phrase is taken and then manipulated in various ways, has a substantial part been taken? It is submitted that no clear answers can be given to such hypothetical cases in advance, but that each case will be decided on its facts in accordance with the approach just described.

5.08   This does not mean that it is an infringement of performers' rights to take a substantial part by *imitating* a performance. The reason is that (by contrast with infringement of copyright under Part I[16]) copying or reproduction is not a primary infringement, only making a recording from or broadcasting a performance. Performers' rights will therefore be of little assistance to those seeking legal protection for personality merchandising, that is to say, the exploitation of a persons' name, likeness and performance characteristics. Thus in the United States of America 'sound alikes', persons who can imitate a performer's manner of speaking, have become a popular form of advertising. A performer who sought to restrain such activities in the United Kingdom could not rely on performers' rights for this purpose, but would have to rely on such rights in passing off as he or she might have.[17]

Without consent

5.09   Although absence of consent is an element of the tort, it is convenient to deal with this topic when dealing with defences.[18]

1.   Making a recording

5.10   Section 182(1)(a) of the 1988 Act makes it an infringement without the consent of the performer to make, otherwise than for the maker's[19] private and domestic use, a recording of the whole or any substantial part of a performance in which performers' rights subsist.

---

16   Copyright, Designs and Patents Act 1988, section 17(1).
17   In *Sim v H.J. Heinz Co. Ltd* [1959] 1 WLR 313 an application for an interlocutory injunction was refused, but the judge and the Court of Appeal declined to express an opinion as to whether such an action would lie. In *Midler v Ford Motor Co.* 849 F. 2d 460 (9th Cir., 1988) a US Circuit Court of Appeals held that such imitation was actionable, but it is not certain that this would be followed in the United Kingdom. See Frazer, 'Vox-Pop: US Law Finds a Voice on Sound-Alikes' [1990] ENT. LR 26.
18   See Ch. 6, paras. 6.34–46. See also para. 5.24.
19   See Note 6 above.

Recording

5.11 'Recording' is defined as meaning

a film or sound recording

(a) made directly from the live performance,
(b) made from the broadcast of or cable programme including the performance, or
(c) made, directly or indirectly, from another recording of the performance.[20]

This definition is discussed in Chapter 4.[21]

Directly or indirectly

5.12 The inclusion of paragraph (c) in the definition of 'recording' quoted in the preceding paragraph has the effect that copying, say, a compact disc – and thus making another recording directly from the recording of the performance(s) embodied in the disc, and hence indirectly from the original recording (assuming that there is one) from which the disc was made – is a category (i) infringement of any performers' rights subsisting in the performance(s) unless the copy is made for private and domestic use. Similarly, use of out-takes and clips from previous films to make a new film such as was done by the defendants in the *Peter Sellers*[22] case would be an infringement. As this example shows, consent will be needed to the making of the recording or recordings in question; consent to the making of the original recording will not be enough.

Otherwise than for private and domestic use

5.13 Under the Performers' Protection Acts 1958–72 it was a defence to charges under sections 1(a) and 2(a) of the 1958 Act to show that the record or film was made for the defendant's private and domestic use only.[23] Thus the burden of proof that the use intended was private and domestic was clearly upon the defendant. It is not quite so clear upon whom the burden of proof falls under the new Act. It would appear, however, that by snifting the exception from a separate proviso to the substantive definition of the tort, the draughtsman has made 'otherwise than for his private and domestic use' an element of the tort that the burden is upon the plaintiff to prove. It may well be, on the other hand, that if the legal burden is upon the plaintiff, there will nevertheless be an evidential burden upon the defendant: if no evidence is adduced to show what use was intended, it will be inferred that the use intended was not private and domestic.

5.14 Although it is clear that the essential thrust of the phrase is that the use

---

20 Copyright, Designs and Patents Act 1988, section 180(2).
21 See para. 4.49.
22 [1988] QB 40.
23 See Ch. 2, paras. 2.88–89.

must be non-commercial, it is not clear whether 'private' is intended to add anything to 'domestic'. There are copyright cases which decide that a 'public' performance is one for which the audience is not a 'domestic or quasi-domestic' one, and that a 'domestic or quasi-domestic' audience is one that lives under one roof.[24] It is submitted that a similar test should be applied, so use will be private and domestic if it is by persons living under one roof. Too much stress should not be laid on the word 'his' in this context, for it is unlikely that the draughtsman intended to restrict the exception to the *personal* private use of the maker of the recording: if he had so intended, it would have been easy enough to say so, and in that case the word 'domestic' would surely have been omitted.

2.   Broadcasting live or including live in a cable programme

5.15   Section 182(1)(b) makes it an infringement without the consent of the performer to broadcast live or include live in a cable programme the whole or any substantial part of a performance in which performers' rights subsist.

Broadcast

5.16   'Broadcast' has the same meaning as in Part I.[25] Thus a broadcast is a transmission by wireless telegraphy of visual images, sounds or other information which is either (a) capable of being lawfully received by the public or (b) transmitted for presentation to members of the public.[26] The definition includes satellite television broadcasts. Encrypted transmissions are to be regarded as capable of being lawfully received by members of the public only if decoding equipment has been made available to the public by or with the authority of the person making the transmission or the person providing the contents of the transmission.[27]

Cable programme service

5.17   'Cable programme service' has the same meaning as in Part I.[28] Thus a cable programme service is a service which consists wholly or mainly in sending visual images, sounds or other information by means of a telecommunications system, otherwise than by wireless telegraphy, for reception (a) at two or more places (whether simultaneously or at different times in response to

---

24   *Jennings v Stephens* [1936] 1 Ch 49 explaining *Duck v Bates* (1884) 13 QBD 843. See also para. 5.22.
25   Copyright, Designs and Patents Act 1988, section 211(1).
26   *Ibid.*, section 6(1).
27   *Ibid.*, section 6(2). See *BBC Enterprises Ltd v Hi-Tech Xtravision Ltd* [1990] FSR 217.
28   *Ibid.*, section 211(1).

requests by different users) or (b) for presentation to members of the public.[29] The following are excepted:[30]

(i) interactive services;[31]

(ii) services run for the internal purposes of businesses rather than to render a service or provide amenities for others, the apparatuses of which are under the sole control of the businesses and which are not connected to any other telecommunications system;[32]

(iii) services run by individuals solely for domestic purposes of the individuals, the apparatuses of which are under the control of the individuals and which are not connected to any other telecommunications system;[33]

(iv) services where all the apparatus is situated in or connects premises under single occupation which are not operated as part of the amenities provided for residents or inmates of premises run as a business and which are not connected to any other telecommunications system;[34] and

(v) services run for broadcasters or cable programme transmitters or persons providing programmes.[35]

Person broadcasting a performance

5.18   By virtue of section 6(3) of the Act, which it is expressly provided applies to infringements of performers' rights,[36] the following persons are to be regarded as broadcasting a performance:

(i) the person transmitting the programme in question if he has responsibility to any extent for its contents; and/or

(ii) any person providing the programme who makes the arrangements necessary for its transmission with the person transmitting it.

Thus more than one person may be liable for any infringement. It is not clear, however, in what circumstances the person transmitting the programme will be held to be responsible for its contents. The use of the words 'to any extent' would seem to cast the net very wide.

Person including a performance in a cable programme service

5.19   By virtue of section 7(5) of the Act, which it is expressly provided applies to infringements of performers' rights,[37] the person who includes a

---

29   *Ibid.*, section 7(1).
30   Subject to any amendment by the Secretary of State by order under section 7(3).
31   Copyright, Designs and Patents Act 1988, section 7(2)(a).
32   *Ibid.*, section 7(2)(b).
33   *Ibid.*, section 7(2)(c).
34   *Ibid.*, section 7(2)(d).
35   *Ibid.*, section 7(2)(e).
36   *Ibid.*, section 211(2).
37   *Ibid.*, section 211(2).

performance in a cable programme service is the person providing the service. In contrast with the position in respect of broadcasting, the person providing the programme is not liable.

Live[38]

5.20   'Live' is not defined in the Act. It would seem, however, that the only possible meaning is the obvious one, that is, not by means of a recording: compare section 182(1)(b) with section 183(b).

3.   Showing or playing a recording in public

5.21   Section 183(a) makes it an infringement without the performer's consent to show or play in public the whole or any substantial part of a performance in which performers' rights subsist by means of a recording which was, and which the exhibitor knows or has reason to believe was, made without the performer's consent.

In public

5.22   'In public' is not defined in either Part I or Part II of the 1988 Act. Although it is not expressly provided that the expression should have the same meaning in Part II as in Part I, this must be the intention. The meaning of 'in public' was considered in a number of cases under earlier Copyright Acts.[39] It would appear that these authorities are still good law in relation to Part I,[40] and therefore applicable to Part II.[41] They indicate that the decisive factor is the *nature* of the audience, rather than its size or whether it paid for the pleasure or the nature of the venue. A public performance or exhibition is one for which the audience is not a 'domestic or quasi-domestic one'. It seems that a 'domestic or quasi-domestic' audience is one that lives under one roof.[42] Thus a performance of a play by members of the Women's Institute of one village to an audience of members of the Institute of another village was held to have been 'in public' even though non-members had not been admitted and no charge had been made.[43]

Knowledge or reason to believe

5.23   This topic is dealt with separately.[44]

---

38   See also Ch. 4, paras. 4.35–36.
39   See Laddie *et al.*, para. 7.46 and the cases cited there.
40   Copyright, Designs and Patents Act 1988, section 172(2),(3).
41   See also paras. 5.13–14.
42   *Jennings v Stephens* [1936] 1 Ch 469 explaining *Duck v Bates* (1884) 13 QBD 843.
43   *Ibid.*
44   See paras. 5.52–56.

Without consent[45]

5.24   It should be noted that in all forms of secondary infringement under Part II, it is a requirement that the performer's consent be absent at two stages. First, the performer must not have consented to the making of the recording in question. Secondly, the performer must not have consented to the particular dealing in question. Thus if the performer consented to the making of the recording there can be no secondary infringement. It would appear that this is the case even if the performer gave his consent to the making of the recording only on condition that the recording be used for a specific, limited purpose but the recording is subsequently used for a different purpose.

4.   Broadcasting or including a recording in a cable programme service

5.25   Section 183(b) makes it an infringement without the performer's consent to broadcast or include in a cable programme service the whole or any substantial part of a performance in which performers' rights subsist by means of a recording which was, and which the broadcaster knows or has reason to believe was, made without the performer's consent.

5.   Importing illicit recordings into the United Kingdom

5.26   Section 184(1)(a) makes it an infringement without the performer's consent to import into the United Kingdom otherwise than for the importer's private and domestic use a recording in which performers' rights subsist which is, and which the importer knows or has reason to believe, an illicit recording.

Import

5.27   Under the Performers' Protection Acts 1958–72 importation *per se* was not a prohibited dealing in contraband recordings,[46] although dealing in the United Kingdom in records made abroad might be prohibited.[47] Under Part II of the new Act, the position has been brought into line with the position in respect of copyright under Part I.[48] It seems that 'import' means simply to bring into the country.[49]

Illicit recording

5.28   An 'illicit recording' is a recording of the whole or any substantial part of a performance made otherwise than for private purposes without the

---

45   See also Ch. 6, paras. 6.34–46.
46   See Ch. 2, para. 2.42.
47   See Ch. 2, paras. 2.76–79.
48   Copyright, Designs and Patents Act 1988, section 22.
49   *Infabrics Ltd v Jaytex Ltd* [1982] AC 1. Cf. *R v Smith (Donald)* [1973] QB 924.

performer's consent.[50] The private purposes are presumably those of the person making the recording. It is not clear whether the omission of the words 'and domestic' in the phrase 'for private purposes' (by comparison with section 182(1)(a)[51]) is intended to have any effect, or if so what effect. A possible interpretation is that in this context a recording made without consent is only not illicit if made for the maker's *personal* private use, but is illicit if made for his domestic use that is, that of his household. It is difficult to see why this distinction should be drawn here and not elsewhere in the Act, however. Again, the Act does not appear to distinguish for this purpose between general and limited consent.[52]

5.29   A recording may also become illicit under the provisions of Schedule 2 to the Act,[53] as to which see elsewhere.[54]

Parallel imports[55]

5.30   What if the performer has consented to the marketing of the illicit recording in another country but not in the United Kingdom? If that country is also a Member State of the EEC, European Community law will prevent the performer from exercising his performers' rights so as to prevent so-called 'parallel imports' of the recording into the United Kingdom.

5.31   This is due to the application of the 'free circulation' rule. This states that the proprietor of an industrial or commercial property right protected by the law of a Member State cannot rely on that law to prevent the importation of a product which has lawfully been marketed in another Member State by the proprietor himself or with his consent.[56] The rule has been elaborated by the European Court of Justice in a series of cases concerning the interpretation of Articles 30, 34 and 36 of the Treaty of Rome. Articles 30 and 34 state the basic rule, namely that quantitative restrictions on imports and exports, and all measures having equivalent effect (which includes the enforcement of industrial property rights), are prohibited as between Member States. Article 36 provides a number of exceptions to this, including restrictions justified on grounds of protection of industrial and commercial property. Whether a particular restriction is justified depends on the 'specific subject-matter' of the right. Thus in the case of patents, 'the substance of a patent right lies essentially in according the inventor an exclusive right of first placing the product on the

---

50   Copyright, Designs and Patents Act 1988, section 197(2).
51   See paras. 5.10, 5.13–14.
52   See para. 5.24.
53   Copyright, Designs and Patents Act 1988, section 197(5).
54   Ch. 6, paras. 6.02–32.
55   This is a very brief precis of an important and complicated topic. The reader is advised to consult a work such as Bellamy and Child, *Common Market Law of Competition*, 3rd edn, (Sweet & Maxwell 1987) for a detailed exposition.
56   *Terrapin v Terranova* [1976] ECR 1039 at 1061, para. 6.

market'.[57] In cases where copyright is for practical purposes a monopoly right,[58] the same is true of copyright.[59]

5.32 The rule is sometimes inaccurately referred to as the 'exhaustion of rights' doctrine. Inaccurately, since the rule applies even if there were no right to be exhausted in the Member State of first marketing. Thus Merck could not enforce its Dutch patent against parallel imports of a drug marketed by it in Italy, where it could not obtain a patent (under a law subsequently ruled unconstitutional by the Italian Supreme Court).[60] Nevertheless the phrase 'exhaustion of rights' is a useful reminder that a proprietor of industrial property rights is not to be taken to have consented to that which he cannot lawfully prevent. Thus a performer will not be prohibited from exercising his performers' rights to prevent importation into the United Kingdom of illicit recordings merely by reason of his performers' rights in another Member State having expired[61] (as may well happen, given that the 50 year term of protection under the 1988 Act is considerably in excess of the 20 year minimum stipulated by the Rome Convention[62]). Similarly, recordings marketed under a compulsory licence (such as that granted by the Copyright Tribunal[63]) are not in free circulation.[64] It has been suggested in a copyright case that products made under licence outside the EEC and imported into a Member State where there is no right corresponding to the licensed right should thereafter be treated as in free circulation;[65] but it is submitted that this is wrong.

6. Dealing in illicit recordings

5.33 Section 184(1)(b) makes it an infringement without the consent of the performer in the course of a business to possess, sell or let for hire, offer or expose for sale or hire, or distribute a recording in which performers' rights subsist which is, and which the dealer knows or has reason to believe is, an illicit recording.

---

57 *Merck v Stephar* [1981] ECR 2063 at 2081, para. 9.
58 See Ch. 1, para. 1.04.
59 *Musik Vertrieb Membran v GEMA* [1981] ECR 147. See also Opinion of Darmon AG in *EMI Electrola GmbH v Patricia Im- und Export Verwaltungsgesellschaft GmbH* [1989] 2 CMLR 413.
60 *Merck v Stephar*, Note 57 above.
61 *EMI Electrola GmbH v Patricia Im- und Export Verwaltungsgesellschaft GmbH*, Note 59 above. In that case the ECJ held that EMI was not prevented from exercising its German copyright in sound recordings against parallel imports from Denmark, where the sound recording copyright had already expired.
62 See Ch. 4, para. 4.56.
63 See Ch. 6, paras. 6.52–69.
64 *Hoechst v Pharmon* [1985] 3 CMLR 775 (a patent case).
65 *The Who Group Ltd v Stage One (Records) Ltd* [1980] FSR 268, 276.

In the course of a business

5.34   There are two possible interpretations of subsubsection (b). The first is that it is only an infringement to possess an illicit recording without consent if the possession is in the course of a business, but that it is an infringement to sell etc. an illicit recording without consent even if this is not done in the course of a business. The second is that all the acts listed must be done in the course of a business in order to amount to infringement.

5.34   There are two possible interpretations of subsubsection (b). The first is that it is only an infringement to possess an illicit recording without consent if the possession is in the course of a business, but that it is an infringement to sell etc. an illicit recording without consent even if this is not done in the course of a business. The second is that all the acts listed must be done in the course of a business in order to amount to infringement.

5.35   Comparison with section 23 in Part I of the Act suggests that the latter construction is the correct one, for in that case the wording is unambiguous:

> The copyright in a work is infringed by a person who, without the licence of the copyright owner −
>
> (a) possesses in the course of a business
> (b) sells or lets for hire, or offers or exposes for sale or hire,
> (c) in the course of a business exhibits in public or distributes, or
> (d) distributes otherwise than in the course of a business to such an extent as to affect prejudicially the owner of the copyright, an article which is, and which he knows or has reason to believe is, an infringing copy of the work.

5.36   Comparison with the definition of the corresponding offence[66] is inconclusive. The offence is defined so as to make it absolutely clear that the acts of selling etc., must be committed in the course of a business. One may conclude from this that the same must be true of the tort; or one may conclude that the legislature has deliberately drawn the offence more narrowly.

5.37   The phrase 'in the course of a business' in itself gives rise to two questions of construction. The first is what is meant by 'business'. This 'includes a trade or profession',[67] but is otherwise undefined. The word is not a term of art, and its meaning depends on its context.[68] Thus decisions on its meaning in other contexts are unhelpful. It would seem that two main elements must be present, namely that transactions are carried out for money or money's worth (though not necessarily for profit) and with a degree of regularity. Thus it is submitted that a person who engages in home taping, even if regularly, will not be held to be conducting a business in this activity, while a person who makes a one-off sale for profit will not either.

---

66   Copyright, Designs and Patents Act 1988, section 198(1)(d). See Ch. 8, para. 8.09.
67   *Ibid.*, section 178.
68   Per Lord Diplock in *Town Investments Ltd v Department of the Environment* [1978] AC 359, 383.

5.38 The second is what is meant by 'in the course of'. In the leading case on this point under section 1 of the Trade Descriptions Act 1968, *Davies v Sumner*,[69] the House of Lords held that a sale by a self-employed courier of his car was not in the course of a trade or business. Although the courier was in business, he was not in the business of selling cars. In order for there to be transactions which had some degree of regularity so that they formed part of the normal practice of the business.[70] It is submitted that Part II will be construed in the same way.

Possession

5.39 Making mere possession of recordings tortious is new to both Part I and Part II of the Copyright, Designs and Patents Act 1988.[71] On the face of the Act, persons who have recordings made otherwise than for private purposes without consent in their possession and who have the requisite knowledge or reason for belief prior to commencement will, after midnight on the day of commencement, suddenly become secondary infringers. This is because the Act is partially retrospective, yet has only the crudest transitional provision.[72] It is difficult to imagine, however, that the courts will interpret the Act strictly in this respect. Presumably some positive act of reducing a recording to possession after commencement will be required.[73] Note that 'possession' may be wider than actual physical possession: control over goods in the custody of a bailee may be enough.[74]

Sale or return

5.40 It was suggested by Neville J in *E.W. Savory Ltd v The World of Golf Ltd* [75] that a person who supplied goods to another on sale or return and subsequently received notice that the goods infringed a third party's copyright would be liable for secondary infringement if he failed to demand the return of the goods. This was later doubted by Clauson J,[76] who relied on *Moss v Sweet*[77] as authority for the proposition that the buyer of goods on sale or return had an option to return the goods within the time specified or within a reasonable time, but that the seller could not demand their return, his only remedy for failure to return being an action for the price. That being the case the seller had no control over the buyer's acts and should not be liable.

---

69   [1984] 1 WLR 1301.
70   Although Lord Keith was careful to say that this did not mean that a one-off sale could not be a trade!
71   Cf. Ch. 2, para. 2.38 in the case of performers' rights.
72   See Ch. 4, para. 4.01.
73   Cf. the corresponding offence: see Ch. 8, paras. 8.07–08.
74   See *Towers & Co. Ltd v Gray* [1961] 2 QB 351.
75   [1914] 2 Ch 566.
76   In *Schofield & Sims Ltd v Robert Gibson & Sons Ltd* [1928–35] MCC 64.
77   (1851) 16 QB 493.

5.41   Both Courts seem to have overlooked the fact that the common law had been substantially codified by the Sale of Goods Act 1893.[78] What is now the fourth rule set out in section 18 of the Sale of Goods Act 1979 provides that, unless a different intention appears,

> when goods are delivered to the buyer on approval or on sale or return or other similar terms the property in the goods passes to the buyer: (a) when he signifies his approval or acceptance to the seller or does any other act adopting the transaction; (b) if he does not signify his approval or acceptance to the seller but retains the goods without giving notice of rejection, then, if a time has been fixed for return of the goods, on the expiration of that time, and, if no time has been fixed, on the expiration of a reasonable time.

Thus the buyer may prevent the passing of property by giving notice of rejection without returning the goods as was required under *Moss v Sweet*. Nevertheless it is submitted that the Act makes it clear that Clauson J's view is the correct one.

Exposure for sale

5.42   Showing a sample to a potential customer and asking for orders is apparently not an exposure for sale and so cannot be an infringement of copyright.[79]

Distribution for the purposes of trade

5.43   It is possible for a trader to handle goods without distributing them. For example, a bookbinder who bound infringing copies of trade lists did not distribute them because his only intention was to return them to the printer after binding.[80] It is not clear, however, whether a carrier or warehouseman who does no more than carry or store goods for a consignor or consignee could be said to be distributing the goods so as to be liable if given the requisite knowledge. It is submitted that a person who merely holds goods to someone else's order in this way should not be regarded as a distributor[81] (though he may possess them in the course of a business).

Dealing outside the United Kingdom

5.44   This is dealt with elsewhere.[82]

---

78   See *Benjamin's Sale of Goods*, 3rd edn, (Sweet & Maxwell 1988) para. 302.
79   *Britain v Kennedy* (1903) 19 TLR 122.
80   *J. Whitaker & Sons Ltd v Publishers Circular Ltd* [1946–49] MCC 10.
81   Cf. *Smith Kline & French Laboratories Ltd v R.D. Harbottle (Mercantile) Ltd* [1979] FSR 555.
82   See paras. 5.57–63.

Infringement of Recording Rights

5.45   Recording rights which subsist[83] in a performance are infringed by the doing of any of the following acts without the consent of the owner of the recording rights or (in category (i), in any event, and in categories (ii) to (v), if performer's rights subsist in the performance) the performer:

(i) Making a recording of the whole or any substantial part of the performance otherwise than for the maker's private and domestic use;[84]

(ii) Showing or playing in public the whole or any substantial part of the performance by means of a recording which, as the exhibiter knows or has reason to believe, was made without the consent of either the performer or the owner of the recording rights at the time that the recording was made;[85]

(iii) broadcasting or including in a cable programme service the whole or any substantial part of the performance by means of a recording which, as the broadcaster knows or has reason to believe, was made without the consent of either the performer or the owner of the recording rights at the time that the recording was made;[86]

(iv) importing into the United Kingdom otherwise than for the importer's private and domestic use a recording of the performance which, as the importer knows or has reason to believe, is a recording of the whole or any substantial part of a performance made otherwise than for the maker's private purposes without the consent either of the performer or of the owner of the recording rights (an 'illicit recording');[87]

(v) in the course of business possessing, selling, letting for hire, offering or exposing for sale or hire, or distributing a recording of the performance which, as the dealer knows or has reason to believe, is a recording of the whole or any substantial part of a performance made otherwise than for the maker's private purposes without the consent either of the performer or of the owner of the recording rights (an 'illicit recording').[88]

5.46   As can be seen, these are parallel to category (i) and (iii) to (vi) infringements of performers' rights. Again, they divide into primary infringements (category (i)) and secondary infringements (category (ii) to (v)). The comments made in relation to infringements of performers' rights are equally applicable here.[89]

---

83   Again, the draughtsman avoids use of the word 'subsist', referring instead to 'the rights of a person having recording rights in relation to a performance'. For the sake of clarity, reference is made to performances in which recording rights subsist in this chapter. Cf. para. 5.03.

84   Copyright, Designs and Patents Act 1988, section 186(1). Cf. paras. 5.10–14.

85   *Ibid.*, section 187(1)(a). Cf. paras. 5.21–24.

86   *Ibid.*, section 187(1)(b). Cf. para. 5.25.

87   *Ibid.*, section 188(1)(a). Cf. paras. 5.26–32.

88   *Ibid.*, section 188(1)(b). Cf. paras. 5.33–44.

89   See the paras. noted below each category.

Without his consent or that of the performer

5.47   Section 186(1) reads in full as follows:

> A person infringes the rights of a person having recording rights in relation to a
> performance who, without his consent or that of the performer, makes a recording
> of the whole or any substantial part of the performance, otherwise than for his
> private and domestic use.

This presents two problems of construction. The first is the usual problem of
multiple antecedents.[90] The second is less straightforward. This is that there
are two possible interpretations of 'without his consent or that of the
performer'. First, that the consent of *both* the performer and the owner of the
recording rights is required if infringement is to be avoided ('without his
consent or without that of the performer'). Secondly, that the consent of *either*
will suffice ('without either his consent or that of the performer'). Either
reading is possible, and both lead to odd results. The former reading would
have the odd result that the maker of the recording would have to obtain
consent from the performer in addition to any consent from the owner of the
recording rights even if performers' rights did *not* subsist in the performance.
The latter reading would have the odd result of making the performer an
alternative source of consent to the owner of the recording rights – even if the
owner has specifically refused consent.[91]

5.48   Support for both readings can be found in the definition of the other
categories of infringement. Section 187(1) reads as follows:

> A person infringes the rights of a person having recording rights in relation to a
> performance who, without his consent or, in the case of a qualifying performance,
> that of the performer, [(a) or (b)] by means of a recording which was, and which
> that person knows or has reason to believe was, made without the appropriate
> consent.

The 'appropriate consent' is:

the consent of

(a) the performer, or
(b) the person who at the time the consent was given had recording rights in

---

90   The word 'his' in the phrase 'without his consent' has two possible antecedents, 'a
person' and 'a person having recording rights'; while in the phrase 'his private and domestic
use' it has three: 'a person', 'a person having recording rights' and 'the performer'. It is
reasonably clear that in the former case the owner of the recording rights is meant and in the
latter case the infringer. Cf. Note 6 to para. 5.02.
91   It is true that the owner of the recording rights will in all probability have recourse
against the performer under the contract between them if the performer improperly gives
consent; but this may be of small comfort to the owner of the recording rights if the
performer has improperly consented to a valuable transaction yet is himself a man of straw.
The owner may have a cause of action against the 'infringer' for inducing breach of contract,
but only it can be shown that the 'infringer' had notice of the relevant term of the contract.

relation to the performance (or, if there was more than one such person, of all of them).[92]

(It would seem that 'at the time the consent was given' means 'at the time the consent was required'). It is reasonably clear that the recording 'by means of' which this category of secondary infringement is committed must be one the making of which constituted a primary infringement contrary to section 186(1). Thus paragraph (a) of the definition of 'appropriate consent' is not restricted to where the performance is a qualifying performance. Now the use of the singular 'consent' rather than the plural 'consents' in 'appropriate consent' suggests that the consent of one of the two alternatives rather than both is what is required. If this construction of section 187(1) is correct, the same should apply to section 186(1).

5.49   On the other hand, both section 187(1) and section 188(1) substitute 'without his consent or, in the case of a qualifying performance, that of the performer' for 'without his consent or that of the performer' in section 186(1). It would seem to make more sense only to *require* consent of the performer to secondary acts in addition to consent of the owner of the recording rights if the performance is one in which performers' rights subsist than only to *permit* the performer to be an alternative source of consent in those circumstances. To put it another way, if the performance is non-qualifying, it would seem to make more sense nevertheless to require the performer's consent to avoid primary infringement of recording rights but not to require it to avoid secondary infringement than to permit the performer to consent to primary acts in the alternative to the owner of the recording rights but to permit him to consent to secondary acts. Interpretation is not assisted by the fact that it is hard to see what object the draughtsman had in mind when drafting these sections. Why was it thought that the performer should be either required or permitted to give consent to interference with another's rights?

5.50   A final possible source of assistance in dealing with the problem is the definition of 'sufficient consent' in the offence-creating provision, section 198.[93] Although this is not the simplest of definitions either, it seems reasonably clear that a person obtains 'sufficient consent' to avoid committing an offence if he obtains consent *either* from the performer *or* from the owner of the recording rights. Of course, this is not conclusive, for it would not be unreasonable that the legislature should require only one consent to prevent the commission of a criminal offence, yet provide for a civil tort to be committed if less than two were obtained. Nevertheless, the general parallels that can be drawn between the offences created by section 198 and the infringements defined by sections 182–4 and 186–8 suggests that one consent is sufficient.

---

92   Copyright, Designs and Patents Act 1988, section 187(2).
93   See Ch. 8, para. 8.03.

5.51   On balance, therefore, it is submitted that the better view is to construe 'or' in section 186(1) as disjunctive rather than conjunctive. It must be recognised, however, that it is not a foregone conclusion that the courts will adopt this construction.

Knowledge or Reason for Belief

5.52   It is a requirement for all forms of secondary infringement of performers' rights and recording rights that the infringer knows or has reason to believe that the recording he is using or dealing in was made without consent. The same words are used in sections 22, 23, 24 and 26 of Part I of the 1988 Act to define forms of secondary infringement of copyright. This represents a change from both the Performers' Protection Acts 1958–72 and the Copyright Act 1956, in each of which there was a requirement of knowledge. The Courts approached those statutory provisions somewhat differently, however.

5.53   In the only case on the mental element of the offence under the Performers' Protection Acts, *Gaumont British Distributors Ltd v Henry*,[94] it was held that the word 'knowingly' imported a requirement that the defendant had actual knowledge of all the relevant matters.[95] The cases under the Copyright Acts 1911 and 1956 proceeded somewhat differently, however. In *Van Dusen v Kritz*[96] the facts were as follows. On 16 October the plaintiff wrote a letter before action complaining about posters and show-cards being displayed by the defendant. The defendant consulted his solicitors forthwith and took down the show-cards. On 18 October the defendant's solicitors received copies of the copyright works relied upon. On 23 October the defendant's solicitors wrote to the plaintiff's solicitors denying the allegation of infringement but offering to withdraw the posters and show-cards and to undertake not to issue any more. A writ was issued on the same day. The action was dismissed on the ground that there was no cause of action at the date of writ since the defendant did not have the requisite knowledge.

5.54   That decision (which was approved by the House of Lords in *Infabrics Ltd v Jaytex Ltd*[97]) was subsequently interpreted[98] as establishing the following propositions:

(i) 'Knowledge' for the purposes of secondary copyright infringement might be actual or imputed;

---

94   [1939] 2 KB 711.
95   See Ch. 2, paras. 2.61–63. Note, however, that the decision in the *Peter Sellers* case (discussed in para. 5.56) is not easy to reconcile with this authority: see Ch. 2, paras. 2.70–72.
96   [1936] 2 KB 176
97   [1982] AC 1, 20.
98   See *Hoover plc v George Hulme (Stockport) Ltd* [1982] FSR 565.

(ii) If a dealer in articles did not have actual knowledge that the articles were infringing copies, he could be fixed with knowledge by giving him notice;

(iii) Knowledge would not be imputed to the dealer unless –

(a) the notice contained sufficient particulars of the claim to copyright to enable it to be investigated; and

(b) the dealer was given a reasonable period in which to investigate the claim to copyright.

Thus if notice was duly given, and the dealer continued the acts complained of after the expiry of a reasonable period, he would be taken to have the requisite knowledge. It should be noted, however, in those circumstances he would not have actual knowledge of the facts which meant that the articles were infringing copies still less that they were infringing copies (which could not be known for certain until the court gave judgment).

5.55 Has the position been altered by the 1988 Act? Section 172(2) of Part I provides that

> A provision of this Part which corresponds to a provision of the previous law shall not be construed as departing from the previous law merely because of a change of expression.

The change from knowledge to knowledge or reason to believe would appear to be more than a mere change of expression, but nevertheless it is submitted that the law has not been changed. The natural interpretation of 'knows or has reason to believe' is the same as the way 'knows' was actually interpreted by the courts: it imports an objective test which means that the defendant cannot say that though he had all the relevant information, he did not *know*. To put it another way, 'wilful blindness' is not a defence.[99] In effect, Parliament has endorsed the decisions of the courts under the Copyright Acts, and extended them to performers' rights.

5.56 Once again Parliament appears to have been anticipated in this by the decisions of the courts in the *Peter Sellers* case.[100] What Hobson J found in that case[101] was not that the defendants had actual knowledge that Peter Sellers had not consented, but in effect that they had reason to believe that he had not. The defendants' case was that Sellers had given his consent in the contracts under which the earlier films were made. Having taken legal advice, they believed that this case was fully arguable and decided to take the risk of proceeding; but it followed that they had reason to believe that Sellers had not consented.

---

99 See the discussion of 'wilful blindness' in Ch. 2 at paras. 2.64–66.
100 *Rickless v United Artists Corp.* [1988] QB 40.
101 See Ch. 2, para. 2.72 for the relevant findings of fact.

Territoriality[102]

5.57   Part II of the Copyright, Designs and Patents Act 1988 'extends to' England and Wales, Scotland and Northern Ireland[103] (but not to the Channel Islands, the Isle of Man or any colony[104]). Things done in the following places are to be treated as done in the United Kingdom:

(a) the territorial waters of the United Kingdom;[105]

(b) on a structure or vessel which is present in the United Kingdom sector of the continental shelf[106] for purposes directly connected with the exploration of the sea bed or subsoil or the exploitation of their natural resources;[107]

(c) on a British ship,[108] aircraft or hovercraft.[109, 110]

5.58   A consequence of the avoidance by the draughtsman of copyright-style definitions is that most of the rights conferred by Part II, unlike those conferred by Part I, are not specifically expressed to be territorially limited. Thus whereas section 16(1) of the Act states that the owner of the copyright in a work has the exclusive right to do certain acts *in the United Kingdom*, section 182(1) of the Act merely states that a performer's rights are infringed by the doing of certain acts without his consent. The question therefore arises whether acts committed abroad[111] are actionable under Part II in the United Kingdom.

5.59   The first stage is to consider whether, on the true construction of Part II of the 1988 Act, the rights granted are territorially limited. The main argument against territoriality is the omission from most of the infringement-defining sections of the words 'in the United Kingdom'. It is arguable that this omission must be given effect, particularly when comparison is made with the corresponding sections in Part I of the Act. Against this are the following points:

(1) It is difficult to see what the effect of section 207, which provides that Part II 'extends to' the United Kingdom, is if not to make the operation of Part II territorial.

---

102   See generally Arnold, 'Can One Sue in England for Infringement of Foreign Intellectual Property Rights?' [1990] 7 EIPR 254.
103   Copyright, Designs and Patents Act 1988, section 207.
104   *Ibid.*, section 208(5).
105   *Ibid.*, section 209(1).
106   That is, the areas designated by order under section 1(7) of the Continental Shelf Act 1964: Copyright, Designs and Patents Act 1988, section 209(3).
107   Copyright, Designs and Patents Act 1988, section 209(2).
108   That is, a ship which is British for the purposes of the Merchant Shipping Acts (see section 2 of the Merchant Shipping Act 1988) otherwise than by virtue of registration in a country outside the United Kingdom: Copyright, Designs and Patents Act 1988, section 210(2).
109   That is, an aircraft or hovercraft registered in the United Kingdom: Copyright, Designs and Patents Act 1988, section 210(2).
110   Copyright, Designs and Patents Act 1988, section 210(1).
111   That is, other than in the places listed in para. 5.57.

(2) Section 194 of the Act provides that infringement of performers' rights and recording rights is actionable as breach of statutory duty. Although there does not appear to be any direct authority on the point,[112] it is submitted that a statutory duty does not extend outside the United Kingdom unless the statute in question expressly so provides.[113] Thus, it can be said, section 194 explains the omission from most of the infringement-defining sections of the words 'in the United Kingdom'.

(3) It is significant that importation of illicit recordings into the United Kingdom is made an infringement.[114] This would seem clearly to imply a territorial scheme: if making recordings abroad was an infringement, it would not be necessary to make importation an infringement.

(4) Similarly, if making recordings abroad were in itself an infringement, it would be unnecessary to stipulate in defining 'illicit recording' for the purposes of Part II that it is immaterial where the record was made.[115]

(5) Interpreting Part II as territorial in operation is consistent with the provisions for reciprocal protection of nationals of other countries which by their law provide adequate protection for British performances.[116]

It is therefore submitted that the better view is that Part II rights are territorial in the same way as Part I rights.

5.60   The next stage is to consider whether the English courts have jurisdiction to entertain an action for an alleged infringement of performers' rights committed outside the United Kingdom; or whether such an action is barred by the *Moçambique* rule[117] as modified by section 30(1) of the Civil Jurisdiction and Judgments Acts 1982, namely that the English courts do not have jurisdiction over actions principally concerned with title to or right to

---

112   Perhaps the nearest is *Coupland v Arabian Gulf Oil Co.* [1983] 1 WLR 1136, a case concerning an accident to a British citizen in the course of employment in Libya, in which Robert Goff LJ said:

> The pleaded case of the plaintiff, as one would expect, puts forward the claim on three grounds: first on the basis of negligence; second on the basis of breach of contract; and third on the basis of breach of statutory duty, which I understand to mean breach of Libyan statutory duty.

It is not clear from the report, however, precisely what statutory duty was being alleged; nor was the question addressed how breach of Libyan statutory duty could be actionable in England.

113   This is an application of the well-established presumption in construing offence-creating statutes that, in the absence of clear and specific words to the contrary, such statutes are not intended to make conduct taking place outside the jurisdiction an offence triable in England: *Cox v Army Council* (1962) 46 Cr App R 258, *Air India v Wiggins* (1980) 71 Cr App R 213.

114   Copyright, Designs and Patents Act 1988, sections 184(1)(a) and 188(1)(a).

115   *Ibid.*, section 197(6).

116   *Ibid.*, sections 181, 206 and 208. See Ch. 4, paras. 4.39–46.

117   *British South Africa Co. v Companhia de Moçambique* [1893] AC 602, *Hesperides Hotels Ltd v Muftizade* [1979] AC 508. See Dicey and Morris, *The Conflict of Laws*, 11th edn (Stevens 1987), Rule 117.

possession of foreign immovables.[118] If the action is framed in terms of local rights, this will depend on whether performers' rights are regarded as immovable property by the law of the country in question. If no evidence of that law is before the Court, however, the Court will apply the English rule. Thus in *Tyburn Productions Ltd v Conan Doyle*,[119] Vinelott J held that intellectual property rights in general and copyrights in particular are immovables,[120] and so an action concerning US copyrights was struck out. If it is right that rights under Part II of the 1988 Act are territorial in the same way as rights under Part I, this decision also applies to performers' rights. It might be said that *Tyburn* is distinguishable on the ground that performers' rights are not property rights. While this is arguably true of recording rights, however, it is not true of performers' rights, which are transmissable on death.[121]

5.61   The third stage is to consider what the effect of the double actionability rule is upon such an action. This stage will be of particular importance if the *Moçambique* rule as modified by section 30(1) of the 1982 Act is inapplicable because neither title nor validity is seriously in issue; or if the action is framed in terms of a purported breach of *United Kingdom* performers' rights committed abroad, so as to circumvent the *Moçambique* rule. The double actionability rule is a rule for choice of law in tort actions which permits the application of English law (the *lex fori*) to foreign torts subject to the condition that the tort in question is actionable according to the local law (the *lex loci delicti commissi*) as well as according to English law.[122] It is stated in Rule 205(1) of Dicey and Morris' *The Conflict of Laws*[123] as follows:

> As a general rule an act done in a foreign country is a tort and actionable as such in England, only if it is both
> (a) actionable as a tort according to English law, or in other words is an act which, if done in England, would be a tort; and
> (b) actionable according to the law of the foreign country where it was done.

In *Def Lepp Music v Stuart-Brown*[124] the plaintiffs, who claimed to be the owners of United Kingdom copyrights, attempted to sue two defendants in England for acts committed in Luxembourg and Holland. The action was struck out on the basis that the plaintiffs could not bring themselves within what is now Rule 205(1) since the acts complained of, being committed

---

118   In addition, where the country in question is a Member State of the European Community and a Contracting State of the Brussels Convention 1968, Article 16(1) of the Convention grants exclusive jurisdiction over such actions to the courts of the country in question.
119   [1990] 1 All ER 909.
120   Following a decision of the High Court of Australia, *Potter v The Broken Hill Pty Co. Ltd* (1906) 3 CLR 479.
121   See Ch. 4, paras. 4.58–60.
122   *Boys v Chaplin* [1971] AC 356, 389 (per Lord Wilberforce), *Coupland v Arabian Gulf Oil Co.*, Note 112 above.
123   11th edn (Stevens 1987).
124   [1986] RPC 273.

outside the UK, were not an infringement of any UK copyright and so were not actionable in accordance with requirement (a). Sir Nicolas Browne-Wilkinson V-C observed that it could not be right to determine actionability (as suggested by the concluding words of Rule 205(1)(a)) by asking what the position would be if the acts had been done in England when the statute only made acts *in fact* done in England actionable.[125]

5.62   The absence from the relevant provisions of Part II of the 1988 Act of the words 'in the United Kingdom' makes it possible to argue that *Deff Lepp Music v Stuart-Brown* can be distinguished, and that acts committed abroad are (if actionable in the country in question) actionable in this country by virtue of Rule 205(1). If, however, it is correct that rights under Part II are territorial in the same way as rights under Part I, as contended in para. 5.59, the decision is indistinguishable.

5.63   A final point to be borne in mind is the question of *forum conveniens*. Even if it is possible to bring proceedings in the United Kingdom under Part II in respect of acts committed abroad, the UK courts may well not be the most appropriate forum for such proceedings. If there is a more appropriate forum, such an action will be stayed unless there are special circumstances which militate a trial in the UK.[126]

125   *Ibid.*, p. 276. See also *James Burroughs Distillers plc v Speymalt Whisky Distributors Ltd* [1989] SLT 561, a Scottish trade mark case in which the Court of Session came to a similar conclusion.
126   *Spiliada Maritime Corp. v Cansulex Ltd* [1987] AC 460.

6 Exceptions and Defences

Introduction

6.01 Copyright and rights in the nature of copyright such as performers' rights can if rigidly enforced prove oppressive in that they inhibit activities of others that do not cause damage to the right owner or they inhibit them to a degree that is disproportionate to the potential damage to the right owner. For this reason, it is necessary to provide statutory defences to potential infringers in a number of situations. Since these are in truth limitations upon the right itself, they are referred to in the 1988 Act as 'permitted acts' and in this book as 'exceptions'. These are discussed in this chapter together with four more fundamental defences, consent, 'innocence' (that is, lack of knowledge), private and domestic use and arrangements made before commencement, and the Copyright Tribunal, which also acts as a limitation upon copyright and performers' rights.

Exceptions

6.02 The Performers' Protection Acts 1958–72 provided for a number of what were essentially fair dealing defences or exceptions.[1] These have been considerably supplemented in the Copyright, Designs and Patents Act and are now contained in Schedule 2 to the Act. The exceptions run closely parallel to those in Chapter 3 of Part I of the Act. Furthermore, most of the expressions used are expressly stated to have the same meaning as in the corresponding provisions in Part I.[2] Decisions under Part I will therefore be applicable to Schedule 2.

6.03 It should be noted, however, that not all the exceptions contained in

---

1 See Ch. 2, paras. 2.88–93.
2 Copyright, Designs and Patents Act 1988, Schedule 2, paras. 2(2), 3(4), 4(4), 5(3), 6(3), 7(2), 8(2), 9(2), 10(2), 11(4), 12(6), 13(3), 14(4), 15(3), 16(4), 17(4), 18(5), 19(3), 20(2) and 21(2).

Part I are reproduced in Schedule 2. Some, of course, are not reproduced since they are only applicable to copyright. Others, however, are potentially applicable but nevertheless have still not been reproduced. Two in particular should be noticed. First, there is no equivalent in Schedule 2 to the Part I exception for fair dealing for research or private study.[3] It may be that this is because showing or playing a recording is only an infringement if done 'in public': if a student views or listens to a recording privately,[4] there will probably be no infringement. Second, there is no equivalent in Schedule 2 to the Part I exception for time-shifting.[5] It may be that this is for a similar reason: because a recording made for the purposes of time-shifting will almost invariably be made for private and domestic purposes, and so not an infringement.

1. Criticism, reviews and news reporting

6.04   Fair dealing with a performance or recording for the purpose of either (a) criticism or review (whether of that or of another performance or recording or of a work) or (b) reporting current events does not infringe performers' rights or recording rights.[6] It should be noted that (by contrast to section 30), there is no requirement for any acknowledgement.

Criticism, review, reporting current events

6.05   In the context of the corresponding provisions under the Copyright Act 1956,[7] these phrases were narrowly interpreted.[8] It is to be expected that the courts will frown upon attempts to invoke these provisions to protect any use of performances that savours of commercial gain. Nevertheless, so literally have the provisions been interpreted that a wide-ranging interview would probably not qualify as 'reporting current events'.[9]

Fair dealing

6.06   What constitutes fair dealing is a matter of fact and degree in all the circumstances of the particular case.[10] Among the factors that may be relevant, however, are the following:

(a) The amount and importance of what has been taken.[11] In certain

---

3 *Ibid.*, section 29.
4 For example, in a video library which provides individual booths for viewing films.
5 Copyright, Designs and Patents Act 1988, section 70.
6 *Ibid.*, Schedule 2, para. 2(1) (corresponding to section 30(2),(3) of Part I). See also para. 6.21.
7 Sections 6(2),(3).
8 See in particular *Independent Television Publications Ltd v Time Out Ltd* [1984] FSR 64.
9 But see paras. 6.21–22.
10 *Hubbard v Vosper* [1972] 2 QB 84.
11 *Ibid.*, 94, 98.

circumstances it may be proper to take the whole of a performance, especially if it is short. In general, however, the greater and the more important the part that is taken, the more difficult it will be to establish that the dealing is fair.

(b) The nature of the accompanying material and the relation it bears to what has been taken. This may for example show that the taking is not for the purpose of criticism or review but for exposition.[12]

(c) Whether it was necessary to use the performance or whether the use was gratuitous. It is not incumbent on the defendant to show that the use was necessary, but if it was gratuitous, it will be harder to justify as fair dealing.[13]

(d) Whether the performance or recording was published or not. If it was not, it will be more difficult to establish fair dealing.[14]

(e) Whether what is sought to be justified as a fair dealing in fact competes with the performance.[15] The courts will be reluctant to allow performers to be damaged by supposed fair dealing.

(f) The motive for the dealing.[16] Thus if the motive is to gain a commercial advantage, the courts will be slow to recognise the dealing as fair. On the other hand, a hostile motive may not preclude fair dealing, for legitimate criticism may be hostile.

2.   Incidental inclusion

6.07   The incidental inclusion of a performance or recording in a sound recording, film, broadcast or cable programme does not infringe performers' rights or recording rights.[17] It is expressly provided that music and any accompanying words (whether spoken or sung) that are deliberately included are not incidentally included.[18] It is not clear whether this means that any other class of performance must be included non-deliberately in order to be incidental. The exception extends to subsequent dealings in anything the making of which was not an infringement by virtue of paragraph 3(1) and in copies of any such thing.[19]

3.   Instruction or examination

6.08   Copying of a recording of a performance in the course either of instruction or of preparation for instruction in the making of films or film

---

12   *Sillitoe v McGraw-Hill Book Co.* [1983] FSR 545.
13   *Associated Newspaper Group plc v News Group Newspapers Ltd* [1986] RPC 515.
14   *British Oxygen Co. Ltd v Liquid Air Ltd* [1925] Ch 383.
15   *Hubbard v Vosper*, Note 10 above, 93–94.
16   *Johnstone v Bernard Jones Publications Ltd* [1938] Ch 599, 607, *Associated Newspaper Group plc v News Group Newspapers Ltd*, Note 13 above.
17   Copyright, Designs and Patents Act 1988, Schedule 2, para. 3(1) (corresponding to section 31(1) of Part I).
18   *Ibid.*, Schedule 2, para. 3(3).
19   *Ibid.*, Schedule 2, para. 3(2).

sound-tracks does not infringe performers' rights or recording rights provided it is done by a person either giving or receiving instruction.[20] Similarly, copying of a recording of a performance for the purposes of setting or answering questions in an examination does not infringe performers' rights or recording rights, nor does anything done by way of communicating the questions to the candidates.[21] The exception does not extend to any subsequent dealing, however.[22] The apparent oddity of limiting the exception for instruction to film-making but not the exception for examinations is accounted for by the fact that instruction in other subjects is sufficiently allowed for by the following exception.

4. Playing or showing at educational establishments

6.09 A sound recording, film, broadcast or cable programme played or shown at an educational establishment for the purposes of instruction before an audience consisting of teachers, pupils and persons directly connected with the activities of the establishment is not played or shown 'in public' so as to infringe performers' rights or recording rights.[23]

Educational establishment

6.10 'Educational establishment' means any school[24] or any other description of educational establishment specified by order of the Secretary of State under section 174(1)(b) of the Act.[25] These are:[26]

(a) any university empowered by Royal Charter or Act of Parliament to award degrees and any college, or institution in the nature of a college, in such a university;
(b) any institution providing further education within the meaning of section 1(5)(b) of the Education (Scotland) Act 1980 and any educational establishment (other than a school) within the meaning of section 135(1) of that Act;
(c) any institution providing further education within the meaning of Article 5(c) of the Education and Libraries (Northern Ireland) Order 1986 and any college of education within the meaning of that Order;
(d) any institution the sole or main purpose of which is to provide further education within the meaning of section 41 of the Education Act 1944 or

---

20 *Ibid.*, Schedule 2, para. 4(1) (corresponding to section 32(2) of Part I).
21 *Ibid.*, Schedule 2, para. 4(2).
22 *Ibid.*, Schedule 2, para. 4(3).
23 *Ibid.*, Schedule 2, para. 5(1) (corresponding to section 34(2) of Part I).
24 As defined in the Education Act 1944, the Education (Scotland) Act 1962 (but including an approved school as defined in the Social Work (Scotland) Act 1968) and the Education and Libraries (Northern Ireland) Order 1986.
25 Copyright, Designs and Patents Act 1988, Schedule 2, para. 5(3); section 34; section 174(1).
26 Copyright (Educational Establishments) (No. 2) Order 1989, S.I. 1989 No. 1068.

higher education within the meaning of section 120 of the Education Reform Act 1988; and

(e) any theological college.

Persons directly connected with the activities of the establishment

6.11   A person is not directly connected with the activities of an establishment merely because he or she is the parent of a pupil.[27] Otherwise, it is somewhat unclear who is covered by this phrase. Presumably it means ancillary staff, governors and the like; but what about a parents' representative on a Parent-Teacher Association?

5. Recording by educational establishments

6.12   A recording of a broadcast or cable programme, a copy of such a recording, may be made by or on behalf of an educational establishment for educational purposes without thereby infringing performers' rights or recording rights in any performance or recording included in it.[28] The exception does not extend to subsequent dealings.[29] The exception also applies in relation to teachers who are employed by local education authorities to give instruction elsewhere to pupils who are unable to attend an educational establishment.[30] Curiously, this does not appear to be the case for the preceding exception.[31]

6.13   Unlike the corresponding provision in Part I,[32] this exception is not excluded if or to the extent that a licensing scheme is certified under section 143 of the Act. It would therefore appear that the licensing schemes[33] which have been certified for the purposes of Part I rights do not apply to Part II rights.

6. Copies of works made as a condition of export

6.14   It is not an infringement of performers' rights or recording rights to make a copy of a work of an article of cultural or historical importance for deposit in an appropriate library or archive where this is a condition of

---

27   Copyright, Designs and Patents Act 1988, Schedule 2, para. 5(2).
28   *Ibid.*, Schedule 2, para. 6(1) (corresponding to section 35(1) of Part I).
29   *Ibid.*, Schedule 2, para. 6(2).
30   *Ibid.*, Schedule 2, para. 6(3); section 35; section 174(2); Copyright (Application of Provisions Relating to Educational Establishments to Teachers) (No. 2) Order 1989, S.I. 1989 No. 1067.
31   The statutory instrument does not apply to section 34 and hence does not apply to Schedule 2, para. 5(3).
32   Copyright, Designs and Patents Act 1988, section 35(2).
33   Namely those operated by Educational Recording Agency Ltd and Guild Sound and Vision Ltd: Copyright (Certification of Licensing Scheme for Education and Recording of Broadcasts and Cable Programmes) (Educational Recording Agency Limited) Order 1990, S.I. 1990 No. 879 and Copyright (Certification of Licensing Scheme for Educational Recording of Broadcast and Cable Programmes) (Guild Sound and Vision Ltd) Order 1990. S.I. 1990 No. 878.

export.[34] 'Appropriate' is not defined; it seems likely that it will be broadly construed.

7. Parliamentary and judicial proceedings, Royal Commissions and inquiries

6.15   Performers' rights and recording rights are not infringed by anything done for the purposes of parliamentary or judicial proceedings or for the purpose of reporting such proceedings.[35] The same applies to the proceedings of Royal Commissions and statutory inquiries.[36] It is not clear exactly how widely this exception extends: for example, whether it extends to things done by way of preparation for such proceedings as well as things done during the proceedings. Similarly, it is not clear whether proceedings before courts other than United Kingdom courts are covered. It is submitted that the exception should be broadly construed.

8. Public records

6.16   Material in public records[37] which are open to public inspection may be copied, and a copy supplied to any person, by or with the authority of any officer appointed under the Public Records Act without infringing performers' rights or recording rights.[38]

9. Statutory authority

6.17   To do any act which is specifically authorised by an Act of Parliament is not an infringement of performers' rights or recording rights unless the Act so provides.[39] This applies no matter when the Act was passed.

10. Works in electronic form

6.18   Where a recording of a performance in electronic form has been purchased on terms which allow the purchaser to make further recordings from it, a person to whom the recording is transferred may do anything which the purchaser was allowed to do without infringement of performers' rights or recording rights.[40] This is provided that there are no express terms which

---

34   Copyright, Designs and Patents Act 1988, Schedule 2, para. 7(1) (corresponding to section 44 of Part I).
35   *Ibid.*, Schedule 2, para. 8(1) (corresponding to section 45(1),(2) of Part I).
36   *Ibid.*, Schedule 2, para. 9(1) (corresponding to section 46(1),(2) of Part I). A statutory inquiry is an inquiry held or investigation conducted in pursuance of a duty imposed or power conferred by or under any statute: *ibid.*, Schedule 2, para. 9(2); section 46(4).
37   As defined in the Public Records Act 1958, the Public Records (Scotland) Act 1937 or the Public Records (Northern Ireland) Act 1923.
38   Copyright, Designs and Patents Act 1988, Schedule 2, para. 10(1) (corresponding to section 49 of Part I).
39   *Ibid.*, Schedule 2, para. 11(1) (corresponding to section 50(1) of Part I).
40   *Ibid.*, Schedule 2, para. 12(2) (corresponding to section 56(2) of Part I).

either (a) prohibit transfer of the recording by the purchaser, impose obligations which continue after a transfer, prohibit the assignment of any consent or terminate any consent on transfer or (b) stipulate the terms on which a transferee may do the things that the purchaser was permitted to do. The exception applies whether what is transferred is the original purchased recording or (if this is no longer usable) a copy of it.[41] Otherwise, a recording made by the purchaser which is not transferred together with the original recording will be treated as an illicit recording.

6.19   It therefore appears that the purpose of the exception is to permit transferees from purchasers who are allowed to make back-up copies[42] also to make back-up copies, but to ensure that any back-up copies are transferred together with the original. Thus a purchaser cannot buy a work, make a back-up copy and sell on so as to get free use of the back-up copy.

In electronic form

6.20   'In electronic form' is defined in section 178 of Part I as follows:

> 'electronic' means actuated by electric, magnetic, electro-magnetic, electro-chemical or electro-mechanical energy and 'in electronic form' means in a form usable only by electronic means.

The definition would appear to be broad enough to cover most software media. The following in particular would seem to be within the definition: floppy disks and diskettes, cassettes, videotapes and compact discs (these are only usable when read by a laser, that is, by electro-mechanical energy). LPs, however, would not seem to be within the definition as these are read mechanically (although the mechanical movement of the needle is then translated into an electrical signal). Needless to say, this is an odd result, for there does not seem to be any reason to distinguish between LPs and other media — save, perhaps, that LPs are not subject to corruption in the same way as electronic forms of information storage and so it is not so necessary to make back-up copies.

11.   Spoken works

6.21   It is not an infringement of performers' rights or recording rights to use a recording (or to copy it and use the copy) of the reading or recitation of a literary work for the purposes of either (a) reporting current events or (b) broadcasting or including in a cable programme service the whole or part of the reading or recitation if the recording was made for that purpose.[43] The following conditions must be met, however:[44]

---

41   *Ibid.*, Schedule 2, para. 12(3).
42   A back-up copy is a copy made in case the original becomes corrupt.
43   Copyright, Designs and Patents Act 1988, Schedule 2, para. 13(1) (corresponding to section 58(1) of Part I).
44   *Ibid.*, Schedule 2, para. 13(2).

(a) the recording must be a direct recording of the reading or recital and not taken from a previous recording or from a broadcast or cable programme;

(b) the making of the recording must not have been prohibited by or on behalf of the person giving the reading or recitation;

(c) the use made of the recording must not be of kind prohibited by or on behalf of the person giving the reading or recitation before the recording was made; and

(d) the use is by or with the authority of a person who is lawfully in possession of the recording.

6.22   Although it is nowhere made explicit, it appears that this exception is directed to the use of interviews.[45] Comparison may be made with the corresponding Part I provision, section 58, which is directed to the use of records of spoken words. Subparagraph (b) of the exception appears to have been included to ensure that the broadcasting of an interview for its own sake[46] is permitted, and not just if the interview is included in a news programme.

12.   Recordings of folksongs

6.23   A recording may be made of a performance of a song for the purpose of including it in an archive maintained by a designated body without infringing performer's rights or recording rights.[47] A designated body is one designated by order of the Secretary of State under section 61 of the Act;[48] he must be satisfied that it is not established or conducted for profit.[49] The following conditions must be met, however:[50]

(a) the words must be unpublished and of unknown authorship at the time the recording is made;

(b) the making of the recording must not infringe any copyright; and

(c) the making of the recording must not have been prohibited by any performer.

---

45   See Ch. 4, paras. 4.24–25.
46   For example, as in the television programme *Face to Face*.
47   Copyright, Designs and Patents Act 1988, Schedule 2, para 14(1) (corresponding to section 61(1) of Part I).
48   *Ibid.*, Schedule 2, para. 14(4). The following are designated bodies: The Archive of Traditional Welsh Music, University College of North Wales; The Centre for English Cultural Tradition and Language; The Charles Parker Archive Trust (1982); The European Centre for Traditional and Religious Cultures; the Folklore Society; the Institute of Folklore Studies in Britain and Canada; the National Museum of Wales, Welsh Folk Museum; the National Sound Archive, the British Library; the North West Sound Archive; the Sound Archives, British Broadcasting Corporation; Ulster Folk and Transport Museum; the Vaughan Williams Memorial Library, English Folk Dance and Song Society: Copyright (Recordings of Folksongs for Archives)(Designated Bodies) Order 1989, S.I. 1989 No. 1012.
49   *Ibid.*, section 61(5)(a).
50   *Ibid.*, Schedule 2, para. 14(2).

6.24· Copies of a recording so made may be made and supplied by the archivist if conditions prescribed by the Secretary of State are met.[51] The prescribed conditions are:[52]

(a) that the person requiring a copy satisfies the archivist that he requires it for the purposes of research or private study and will not use it for any other purpose; and

(b) that no person is furnished with more than one copy of the same recording.

13.   Playing sound recordings for clubs etc.

6.25   It is not an infringement of performers' rights or recording rights to play a sound recording[53] as part of the activities of, or for the benefit of, a club, society or other organisation.[54] The following conditions must be met, however:[55]

(a) the organisation (i) must not be established or conducted for profit and (ii) its main objects must be charitable[56] or otherwise concerned with the advancement of religion, education or social welfare; and

(b) the proceeds of any charge for admission to the place where the recording is to be heard must be applied solely for the purposes of the organisation.

6.26   It would seem that 'organisation' is to be construed *ejusdem generis* with 'club' and 'society'. The essence of a club (proprietary and investment clubs apart) is that it is an association of persons for purposes other than those of trade: for social reasons, for the promotion of politics, sport, art, science and so on.[57] Trading activities which are incidental to the club's purposes will not prevent it from being a club. A club may be incorporated or unincorporated.

14.   Incidental recordings for broadcasts or cable programmes

6.27   A person who is able to broadcast or include in a cable programme service a recording of a performance without infringing performers' rights or recording rights is deemed to have consent to the making of a further recording

---

51   *Ibid.*, Schedule 2, para. 14(3), (4) and section 61(5)(a).
52   Copyright (Recordings of Folksongs for Archives) (Designated Bodies) Order 1989, Note 48 above, Article 3.
53   See Ch. 5, para. 5.11 for the definition of 'sound recording'.
54   Copyright, Designs and Patents Act 1988, Schedule 2, para. 15(1) (corresponding to section 67(1) in Part I).
55   *Ibid.*, Schedule 2, para. 15(2).
56   See *Halsbury's Laws*, 4th edn, vol. 5, paras. 502–513 for the definition of 'charitable' objects.
57   See *Halsbury's Laws*, 4th edn, vol. 6., para. 201.

for the purposes of the broadcast or cable programme.[58] The following conditions must be met, however:[59]

(a) the further recording must not be used for any other purpose; and
(b) the further recording must be destroyed within 28 days of being first used for broadcasting the performance or including it in a cable programme service.

If either condition is breached the further recording becomes an illicit recording.[60]

15. Recordings for supervision of broadcasts and cable programmes

6.28   The BBC, the IBA and the Cable Authority may make or use recordings for the purposes of maintaining supervision and control over programmes within their respective regulatory remits without infringing performers' rights or recording rights.[61]

16. Free public shows

6.29   Performer's rights and recording rights are not infringed by the showing or playing in public of a broadcast or cable programme to an audience which has not paid for admission.[62] The audience is be treated as having paid for admission if either:[63]

(a) they have paid for admission to a place of which the place where the broadcast or programme is to be seen or heard forms part; or
(b) goods or services are supplied at prices which either (i) are substantially attributable to the facilities for seeing or hearing the broadcast or programme or (ii) exceed those usually charged at the place in question and are partly attributable to those facilities.

On the other hand, the following are to be treated as not having paid for admission:[64]

(a) residents or inmates of the place in question; and
(b) members of a club or society where the payment is only for membership of the club or society and the provision of facilities for seeing or hearing broadcasts or programmes is only incidental to the main purposes of the club or society.

---

58   Copyright, Designs and Patents Act 1988, Schedule 2, para. 16(1) (corresponding to section 68(2) of Part I).
59   *Ibid.*, Schedule 2, para 16(2).
60   *Ibid.*, Schedule 2, para. 16(3).
61   *Ibid.*, Schedule 2, para. 17(1),(2),(3) (corresponding to section 69(1),(2),(3) of Part I).
62   *Ibid.*, Schedule 2, para. 18(1) (corresponding to section 72(1) of Part I).
63   *Ibid.*, Schedule 2, para. 18(2).
64   *Ibid.*, Schedule 2, para. 18(3).

17.   Reception and retransmission of broadcasts in cable programme services

6.30   A broadcast made from a place in the UK may be included in a cable programme service by reception and immediate retransmission without infringing performers' rights or recording rights if the broadcast is made for reception in the area in which the cable programme service is provided or the inclusion of the broadcast in the cable programme service was required by the Cable Authority.[65]

18.   Subtitled copies of broadcasts and cable programmes

6.31   Recordings of television broadcasts or cable programmes may be made by a designated body for the purpose of providing people who are deaf or hard of hearing or physically or mentally handicapped with copies which are subtitled or otherwise modified for their special needs without infringing performers' rights or recording rights.[66] A designated body is one designated by order of the Secretary of State under section 74 of the Act;[67] he must be satisfied that it is not established or conducted for profit.[68]

19.   Recordings of broadcasts or cable programmes for archival purposes

6.32   A recording or copy of a recording of a broadcast or cable programme of a designated class may be made for placing in an archive maintained by a designated body without infringing performers' rights or recording rights.[69] A designated body is one designated by order of the Secretary of State under section 75 of the Act;[70] he must be satisfied that it is not established or conducted for profit.[71]

Defences

6.33   Other than the exceptions contained in Schedule 2 (which are dealt with above) the following defences are available under Part II: consent, 'innocence'

65   *Ibid.*, Schedule 2, para. 19(2) (corresponding to section 73(2),(3) of Part I).
66   *Ibid.*, Schedule 2, para. 20(1) (corresponding to section 74(1) of Part I).
67   *Ibid.*, Schedule 2, para. 20(2). The National Subtitling Library for Deaf People is a designated body: Copyright (Subtitling of Broadcasts and Cable Programmes) (Designated Body) Order 1989, S.I. 1989 No. 1013.
68   *Ibid.*, section 74(2).
69   *Ibid.*, Schedule 2, para. 21(1) (corresponding to section 75(1) of Part I).
70   *Ibid.*, Schedule 2, para. 21(2). The British Film Institute, the British Library, the Music Performance Research Centre and the Scottish Film Council are all designated in respect of all broadcasts other than encrypted tranmissions and all cable programmes: Copyright (Recording for Archives of Designated Class of Broadcasts and Cable Programmes)(Designated Bodies) (No. 2) Order 1989, S.I. 1989 No. 2510.
71   *Ibid.*, section 75(2).

(that is, lack of knowledge) and private and domestic use and arrangements made before commencement. In addition, general defences to torts may be relied upon, in particular acquiescence and expiry of limitation period. The latter is six years, for section 2 of the Limitation Act 1980 applies to a breach of statutory duty as to any other tort.[72]

1.   Consent

6.34   Consent may be given in relation to a specific performance, to a specified description of performances or to performances generally; the performances may be past or future.[73] Consent may be oral: in contrast to the Performers' Protection Acts,[74] there is no requirement of writing.[75]

a.   Performers' rights

By the performer

6.35   Consent by the performer is a defence to any allegation of infringement of performers' rights. In relation to secondary infringement, consent may be a defence in either of two ways: consent to the making of the recording or consent to the dealing in question.[76]

By the performer's agent

6.36   Part II of the Copyright, Designs and Patents Act 1988 does not contain any provision corresponding to section 7 of the Dramatic and Musical Performers' Protection Act 1958.[77] It is not entirely clear what the effect of this omission is. It continues to be an offence falsely to represent that one is authorised to give consent by a performer.[78] This would seem to imply that the representation may be true, that a performer can authorise another to give consent. Otherwise, the offence would one of purporting to give consent on behalf of a performer rather than of falsely representing.

By a person holding himself out as the performer's agent

6.37   The omission of any provision corresponding to section 7 of the 1958 Act also raises the question whether a person who commits what would

---

72   *Clarkson v Modern Foundries Ltd* [1957] 1 WLR 1210.
73   Copyright, Designs and Patents Act 1988, section 193(1).
74   As to which, see Ch. 2, para. 2.81.
75   Thus bringing performers' rights and recording rights into line with other copyrights, in relation to which an oral licence has long been sufficient.
76   See Ch. 5, para. 5.24.
77   As to which, see Ch. 2, para. 2.82.
78   Copyright, Designs and Patents Act 1988, section 201(1).

otherwise be a primary infringement[79] on the strength of consent purportedly given by another who falsely holds himself out as the performer's agent. It appears that such a person merely has a defence to an award of damages,[80] rather than a complete defence.

By a person holding himself out as the performer's assignee

6.38   Performers' rights under Part II of the Copyright, Designs and Patents Act 1988 are not assignable.[81] A performer may nevertheless attempt to assign his performers' rights; and someone else may represent that he has obtained an assignment of such rights from a performer when in fact he has not. Again, in the case of primary infringement, it appears that a person to whom such a representation is made has at best a defence to damages,[82] rather than a complete defence.

By the performer's estate

6.39   After a performer's death, consent may be given by his legatee or (if there is no legatee) his personal representatives.[83]

By a person holding himself out as the performer's personal representative

6.40   The position is the same as where the representation is that the performer has assigned his rights.

By the Copyright Tribunal

6.41   The Copyright Tribunal can give consent in place of the performer to what would otherwise be an infringement of performers' rights in either of two situations:

(a) where the identity or whereabouts of the performer cannot be ascertained by reasonable inquiry; or
(b) the performer unreasonably witholds his consent.

See paragraphs 6.52–69 for a full discussion.

---

79   In the case of secondary infringement, such a person would doubtless have a defence on the basis that he lacked the requisite knowledge or reason for belief, having instead reason to believe that the recording was made *with* the performer's consent.
80   See Ch. 7, para. 7.16.
81   See Ch. 4, para. 4.57.
82   See Ch. 7, para. 7.16.
83   Copyright, Designs and Patents Act 1988, section 192(2).

Consent upon terms

6.42 Consent may be given upon terms, for example as to payment. This raises the question of what the result is if the terms are not complied with: is it infringement or merely breach of contract? There were conflicting authorities under the Copyright Act 1956 as to the problem of 'conditional licences'. In *Macaulay v Screenkarn Ltd*,[84] it was held[85] that the licence was bound up with the observance of its conditions so that if the conditions were not complied with there was no licence. In *Hunter v Fitzroy Robinson & Partners*,[86] on the other hand, it was held that that non-compliance with the conditions was merely a breach of contract. It is submitted that the answer to this question should depend upon the application of normal contractual principles. Thus if the breach is either of a condition or is of an innominate term and is sufficiently serious to constitute repudiation, the performer may treat the agreement to give consent as at an end so that any acts committed thereafter are infringements. If, on the other hand, the breach either is of a warranty or is of an innominate term but is not serious, the performer is restricted to his right to damages for breach of contract.

b. Recording rights

By the performer

6.43 It is not clear from sections 186–8 of the Act whether consent by the performer without consent by the owner of the recording rights is a defence to an allegation of infringement. For the reasons discussed elsewhere,[87] however, it is submitted that it is.

By the owner of the recording rights

6.44 By the same token, it is not clear whether consent by the owner of the recording rights without consent by the performer is a defence to an allegation of infringement. Again, it is submitted that it is.

By the owner's agent

6.45 Since it is equally an offence under the 1988 Act falsely to represent that one is authorised to give consent on behalf of an owner of recording rights as it is in relation to a performer, it would seem that owners of recording rights may also authorise agents to consent.[88]

---

84 [1987] FSR 257 but not reported on this point.
85 Following Kennedy J in *The Incandescent Gas Light Co. Ltd v Brogden* (1899) 16 RPC 179, 183 (a patent case).
86 [1978] FSR 167.
87 See Ch. 5, paras. 5.47–51.
88 Cf. para. 6.34.

By the Copyright Tribunal

6.46　The Copyright Tribunal is *not* empowered to consent to what would otherwise be an infringement of recording rights.[89]

2.　'Innocence'

6.47　Part II of the 1988 Act contains no explicit defence of innocence.[90] It will, however, be a defence to allegations of secondary infringement (not of primary infringement) that the alleged infringer did not have the required knowledge or reason for belief.[91]

3.　Private and domestic use

a.　Of the maker of the recording

Primary infringement

6.48　It is a defence to allegations of category (i)[92] primary infringement that the recording was made for private and domestic use only. The defence is inapplicable to category (ii) primary infringement, since the infringing act is committed without use of a recording.

Secondary infringement

6.49　Curiously, that the recording was made for private and domestic use only is *not* a defence to category (iii) and category (iv) secondary infringement, but *is* a defence to category (v) and category (vi) secondary infringement. That a recording made without consent was not a primary infringement since it was originally made for private and domestic use is no defence to an allegation of secondary infringement if the recording is subsequently shown in public or broadcast or included in a cable programme without consent.[93] A recording made without consent for private purposes is not an 'illicit recording',[94] however, and so importation of and dealing in the recording cannot amount to secondary infringement.[95] It is difficult to see the rationale for this distinction.

89　See para. 6.65.
90　Although certain innocence-type defences to damages are provided. See Ch. 7, paras. 7.15–19.
91　See Ch. 5, paras. 5.52–56.
92　See Ch. 5, paras. 5.02 and 5.45 for summaries of the categories of infringing acts.
93　See Ch. 5, paras. 5.21–26.
94　See Ch. 5, paras. 5.28–29.
95　See Ch. 5, paras. 5.26–28. By contrast, recordings made for certain excepted purposes (as to which see Ch. 6, paras. 6.08, 6.12–13, 6.18–20, 6.27) are 'illicit' if subsequently dealt in: Copyright, Designs and Patents Act 1988, section 197(5).

b.　Of the importer

6.50　It is a defence to an allegation of category (v) secondary infringement (importation) that the recording was imported for the private and domestic use only of the importer.[96] This is so whether or not the recording was made for private purposes.

4.　Arrangements made before commencement

6.51　Section 180(3) of the 1988 Act provides that no act done 'in pursuance of arrangements made' before 1 August 1989 is to be regarded as an infringement. It is uncertain precisely what is meant by this. It seems clear that it is meant to protect a person who, for example, enters into a contract to sell 10,000 records, sells 5,000 before 1 August and sells 5,000 after 1 August. The rationale for this is unclear, however, for if the records sold after 1 August would otherwise be infringements, it is likely that the sales before 1 August would be actionable under the Performers' Protection Act as interpreted in the *Peter Sellers* case.[97] The explanation may lie in the absence of a requirement of knowledge with respect to certain categories of infringement under the 1988 Act.[98] Whatever the explanation, the lacuna that is created by section 180(3) suggests that 'arrangements' should be construed narrowly. The word is wide enough, however, to cover situations other than direct contractual relationships. Thus a person who makes records pursuant to a sub-contract made after 1 August 1989 but under a main contract made before 1 August is arguably protected.

Copyright Tribunal

6.52　The Performing Right Tribunal established under the Copyright Act 1956 to supervise the collective licensing of performing rights in copyright works has been renamed and given an extended jurisdiction under the Copyright, Designs and Patents Act 1988. Part of the new Copyright Tribunal's juridiction relates to performers' rights and recording rights.

Jurisdiction

6.53　The Copyright Tribunal has jurisdiction on an application by a person who wishes to make a recording from a previous recording of a performance to give consent in place of a performer in either of two cases:[99]

96　See Ch. 5, paras. 5.26.
97　[1988] QB 40.
98　An alternative explanation is that Parliament considers the decision in the *Peter Sellers* case to be wrong and liable to be overruled by the House of Lords.
99　Copyright, Designs and Patents Act 1988, section 190(1).

(a) where the identity or whereabouts of the performer cannot be ascertained by reasonable inquiry; or

(b) where the performer unreasonably withholds his consent.

It therefore appears that the Tribunal has no jurisdiction where the application is made either by a person who wishes directly to record a performance or by a person who wishes to broadcast the recording or include it in a cable programme service.

6.54   The rationale for the former omission is obscure. It is, of course, true that where a person directly records a performance there can be no question of the identity or whereabouts of the performer being unascertainable. It is curious, however, that the Copyright Tribunal should be empowered to give consent to the copying of existing recordings if performers unreasonably withhold consent, but not to give consent to the making of new recordings if performers unreasonably withhold consent. The rationale in each case would appear to be the same, namely to prevent any one performer from exercising a stranglehold on the exploitation of a performance by many performers.

6.55   It is equally difficult to see the rationale for the latter omission. If the Copyright Tribunal can give consent to the making of copies of recordings, and hence to dealings in such copies, why should it not give consent to the broadcasting of recordings?

The performer

6.56   Although section 190 only expressly refers to 'the performer', it would appear that this should be construed as meaning the owner or owners for the time being of the relevant performers' rights.[100] Thus (for example) the Copyright Tribunal will have jurisdiction to give consent in place of a deceased performer's personal representatives where the identity or whereabouts of those personal representatives cannot be ascertained by reasonable inquiry.

Identity or whereabouts of performer cannot be ascertained

6.57   'Reasonable inquiry' will doubtless include taking such steps as writing to Equity or the Musicians' Union and writing to the appropriate collecting society (if any). The Tribunal may not give consent in this case until after 28 days after the service on such persons as it considers are likely to have relevant information and/or the publication in such publications as it considers appropriate of a notice setting out brief particulars of the application and requesting information as to the identity or whereabouts of the performer.[101]

---

100   *Ibid.*, section 192(2).
101   *Ibid.*, section 190(3); Copyright Tribunal Rules 1989, Rule 35.

Consent unreasonably withheld

6.58 It is expressly provided that the Tribunal shall not give consent unless satisfied that the performer's reasons for withholding consent do not include the protection of any legitimate interest of his.[102] It remains to be seen what the Tribunal will regard as a 'legitimate' interest. On the face of it, a performer has two main interests which he may wish to protect by withholding consent, namely his financial interest and his artistic interest.

6.59 As to the former, a performer might withhold consent if he thought that the remuneration offered by the person wishing to make the recording was insufficient. Presumably that person would seek to meet this with evidence as to the going rate for that class of performer and that class of use. Although it may be objected that many performers are unqiue and cannot be assimilated to a class of performers, this sort of approach has a precedent in the fees levied by the collecting societies such as PRS and MCPS.[103]

6.60 A more difficult problem which may arise, however, is that the performer may wish to withhold consent in order to protect his remuneration from other recordings. For example, a pop musician may want to withhold consent to the exploitation of a live recording in order to protect his sales of studio recordings. It is submitted that considerations of this sort are a legitimate interest of the performer.

6.61 Then there is the question of artistic interests. This is likely to prove a delicate area for the Tribunal. It is submitted that it is clearly within the legitimate interests of a performer to withhold consent to any exploitation which if he were an author would amount to an infringement of his moral rights,[104] for example derogatory treatment[105] of his performance, even though performers have not been granted moral rights under the 1988 Act.[106] What if the performer's reasoning is more subtle than this, however? What if a performer who has retired from giving live performances wishes to suppress all recordings of his live performances in favour of studio recordings?[107] What if a performer wishes to prevent any exploitation of recordings of his perform-ances until after his death? It is submitted that the jurisdiction of the Tribunal under section 190(1)(b) must not be regarded as giving the Tribunal carte

---

102 *Ibid.*, section 190(4).
103 For discussion of the desirability or otherwise of standard fees, see the Monopolies & Mergers Commission's *Report on Collective Licensing*, Cm 530, paras. 7.41–43.
104 Under Chapter IV of Part I of the Act.
105 That is, any addition to, deletion from, alteration or adaptation of the performance which amounts to distortion or mutilation or is otherwise prejudicial to the honour or reputation of the performer: Copyright, Designs and Patents Act 1988, section 80(2).
106 Performers are left to such remedies as they may have under the general law, for example for defamation.
107 This was almost the attitude of the concert pianist Glenn Gould. Gould retired from giving concerts at the height of his career essentially on the ground that no concert performance could match the quality of his studio recordings.

blanche to ride roughshod over genuine artistic concerns, no matter how eccentric they may appear to be.

6.62   It should be noted that the Act places the onus on the performer to show what his reasons are for withholding consent. In default of evidence as to his reasons the Tribunal is permitted to draw such inferences as it thinks fit.[108]

Other factors to take into account

6.63   Two other factors are laid down by the Act for the Tribunal to take into account in all cases:[109]

> (a) whether the original recording was made with the performer's consent and is lawfully in the possession of the person proposing to make the further recording; and
> (b) whether the making of the further recording is consistent with the purposes for which the original recording was made.

The implication is that if either is not complied with then the Tribunal will not give consent or at least will only do so on terms as to remuneration of the performer. Certainly, that is how this provision should be interpreted so as to comply with Article 7 of the Rome Convention.

6.64   It may be helpful to compare this provision with the facts of the *Peter Sellers* case.[110] In that case Sellers had made five Pink Panther films. The original footage of those films had been shot with Sellers' consent and United Artists were lawfully in possession of it. Sellers having died, UA wished to make a film containing clips and out-takes from the earlier films. The Sellers estate having refused consent to this, the question was whether Sellers himself had given his consent in the contracts under which the earlier films were made. Had the 1988 Act been in force, it would have been open to UA to apply to the Tribunal for consent to the new film, and to argue that if they did not already have consent the giving of consent would be consistent with the purposes for which the original footage was shot. Although this argument might perhaps not have fared any better than UA's arguments ultimately did fare in Court, UA would at least have had the benefit of knowing in advance what the position was.

Ambit of consent given by the Tribunal

6.65   The Copyright Tribunal can only give consent for the purposes of the provisions of Part II relating to performers' rights, and not for the purposes of

---

108   Copyright, Designs and Patents Act 1988, section 190(4).
109   *Ibid.*, section 190(5).
110   *Rickless v United Artists Corp.* [1988] QB 40.

those relating to recording rights.[111] It is not clear why the latter should have been excluded from the Tribunal's jurisdiction.

6.66 Consent having been given by the Tribunal to the making of a recording, no subsequent dealing in it will be an infringement of performers' rights.

Terms

6.67 The Tribunal may give consent subject to any conditions it thinks fit[112] including, in default of agreement between the applicant and the performer, as to the payment to be made to the performer.[113]

Applications

6.68 An application to the Tribunal for consent is made by service by the applicant on the Secretary to the Tribunal of a notice in Form 14 to the Copyright Tribunal Rules 1989[114] stating:[115]

(a) (where the identity or whereabouts of the performer cannot be ascertained) the inquiries made by the applicant and the result of those inquiries;
(b) (where the identity and whereabouts of the performer are known) the grounds on which the applicant considers that the performer has unreasonably withheld consent.

In the latter case a copy of the notice must be served on the performer.

Procedure in unreasonable withholding of consent cases

6.69 The performer has 21 days from service of the applicant's statement of case in which to serve his statement in answer.[116] A copy of this must be served on the applicant. After the expiry of this period the Chairman must appoint a date for the parties to attend for directions as to the further conduct of the proceedings.[117] On the hearing for directions the Chairman has extensive powers to control the conduct of the proceedings, including for example the power to give directions as to preparation of Scott schedules, discovery and giving of affidavit evidence.[118] The parties may also apply during the course of

---

111 Copyright, Designs and Patents Act 1988, section 190(2); cf. section 198(3)(b).
112 *Ibid.*, section 190(2).
113 *Ibid.*, section 190(6).
114 S.I. 1989 No. 1129. See Appendix 6.
115 Copyright Tribunal Rules 1989, Rule 34.
116 *Ibid.*, Rule 36(1).
117 *Ibid.*, Rules 11(1), 36(2).
118 *Ibid.*, Rules 11(2), 36(2). A standard form of directions is annexed to the Practice Direction.

the proceedings for further directions.[119] Although the rules state that evidence is given orally unless directed to be given by affidavit, in which case the Tribunal may require the deponent to attend for cross-examination,[120] the Practice Direction envisages sequential service of witness statements. Proceedings may be conducted by agents appointed to act on behalf of parties; there does not appear to be any restriction on who can act as an agent.[121] At hearings barristers and solicitors have rights of audience together with any other person whom the Tribunal or Chairman permits to appear.[122] Submissions may be made in writing. Skeleton arguments are expected in any event.[123] A person who claims a substantial interest in the proceedings may apply to intervene by serving on the Secretary a notice in Form 5 to the Rules.[124] It appears that costs orders will follow High Court practice rather than, for example, the practice in the Patent Office.[125] In particular, any offer made without prejudice save as to costs will be taken into consideration.[126]

---

119   *Ibid.*, Rules 12, 36(2).
120   *Ibid.*, Rules 14(3), 36(2).
121   *Ibid.*, Rules 15(1), 36(2).
122   *Ibid.*, Rules 15(5), 36(2).
123   Practice Direction, paras. 7–8.
124   Copyright Tribunal Rules 1989, Rules 23(1), 37.
125   *Ibid.*, Rule 48.
126   Practice Direction, para. 15.

7 Proceedings

Introduction

7.01 After many years of uncertainty as to the position under the Performers' Protection Acts,[1] performers and recording companies now have statutory rights which may be enforced by civil proceedings. The Copyright, Designs and Patents Act 1988 provides for two different means of proceeding, namely a full-blown action for infringement on the one hand and stand-alone applications for delivery-up and forfeiture on the other. In addition, a self-help remedy consisting of a right of seizure is provided.

Who May Sue?

7.02 Any owner of performers' rights or recording rights for the time being may commence proceedings. Since there does not appear to be any scope for separate beneficial ownership of performers' rights or recording rights,[2] this means the legal owner. It appears that one joint owner of performers' rights or recording rights may commence proceedings without joining the other owners whether as plaintiffs or as defendants.[3] Unlike copyright,[4] there is no right of action for an exclusive licensee (though a beneficiary of an exclusive recording contract has his own separate recording rights).

Who May Be Sued?

7.03 Any infringer may be sued, that is to say any person who commits one of the acts restricted by performers' rights or recording rights without the

---

1 See Appendix 2.
2 See Ch. 4, para. 4.57.
3 See Ch. 4, para. 4.62.
4 Copyright, Designs and Patents Act 1988, section 101.

appropriate consent. Persons who procure the commission of such acts or participate in a common design to commit such acts may be sued as joint tortfeasors on normal principles.[5] There is no specific tort of authorisation, as with copyright,[6] however.

Venue

7.04   It is not entirely clear whether actions for infringement of performers' rights and recording rights may be brought in the county court, or whether they must be brought in the High Court. Such an action would appear to be within the general jurisdiction of the county court to hear actions in tort, and not to be excluded by the bar on actions concerning title to a franchise.[7] It is expressly provided, however, that applications for the 'stand-alone' remedies of delivery up and forfeiture may be made in the county court,[8] which suggests that the county court would not otherwise have jurisdiction. It is submitted that the explanation for this is that section 15 of the County Courts Act 1984 only gives the county court jurisdiction to hear 'any action', and that such applications would not fall within this. If this is right, county courts should have jurisdiction to entertain actions under Part II (subject, of course, to the county court limit).

Remedies

7.05   Sections 194 to 197 inclusive of Part II of the 1988 Act are headed by the rubric 'Remedies for infringement'. It is curious, however, that the only remedies expressly provided are delivery up, seizure and forfeiture of illicit recordings.[9] Furthermore, it appears that these three remedies are available independently of an action for infringement (although the Act is not as explicit as it might be about this). Otherwise, it is merely stated that infringement is actionable as breach of statutory duty.[10] Presumably it is to be inferred that the normal remedies for breach of statutory duty are available. The remedies available therefore appear to be as follows: injunction, damages, delivery up, seizure and forfeiture.

---

5 See *BBC v Grower* (*The Times*, 6 July 1990), *C. Evans & Sons Ltd v Spritebrand Ltd* [1985] 1 WLR 317, *CBS Songs Ltd v Amstrad Consumer Electronics plc* [1988] AC 1013 and *Unilever plc v Gillette UK Ltd* [1989] RPC 583.
6 Copyright, Designs and Patents Act 1988, section 16(2).
7 County Courts Act 1984, section 15.
8 Copyright, Designs and Patents Act 1988, section 205(1). See also section 115(1).
9 *Ibid.*, sections 195 and 196. See paras. 7.21–49.
10 *Ibid.*, section 194. Cf. section 96(2) in Part I and section 229(2) of Part III.

1. Injunction

7.06 An injunction will issue to restrain further infringements on normal principles. It should be remembered that injunctions are an equitable remedy, and so may be refused on equitable grounds such as laches or unclean hands.

Innocence

7.07 In addition, the 1988 Act provides two 'innocence' defences which prevent the award of an injunction against an infringer. In both cases the burden of proof is upon the defendant.

a. Secondary infringements of performers' rights

7.08 In actions for category (v) and (vi)[11] infringements of performers' rights, the only remedy available against a defendant who shows that the illicit recording was innocently acquired by him or by a predecessor in title of his is damages not exceeding a reasonable payment in respect of the act complained of.[12] 'Innocently acquired' means that the person acquiring the recording did not know and had no reason to believe that it was an illicit recording.[13] Curiously, this defence is not available in respect of category (iii) and (iv) infringements. What is a 'reasonable payment' will naturally depend on the circumstances of each case, but a possible method of assessment would be to award a reasonable royalty, that is, whatever is the going rate for acts of the kind in question.

b. Secondary infringements of recording rights

7.09 In actions for category (iv) and (v)[14] infringements of recording rights, the only remedy available against a defendant who shows that the illicit recording was innocently acquired by him or by a predecessor in title of his is damages not exceeding a reasonable payment in respect of the act complained of.[15] 'Innocently acquired' means that the person acquiring the recording did not know and had no reason to believe that it was an illicit recording.[16] Again, this defence is not available in respect of category (ii) and (iii) infringements.

2. Damages

7.10 It is a requirement for any action for breach of statutory duty that the plaintiff establish damage of a kind against which the statute was designed to

---

11 See Ch. 5, para. 5.02 for the categories of infringement.
12 Copyright, Designs and Patents Act 1988, section 184(2).
13 *Ibid.*, section 184(3).
14 See Ch. 5, para. 5.45 for the categories of infringement.
15 Copyright, Designs and Patents Act 1988, section 184(2).
16 *Ibid.*, section 184(3).

give protection.[17] In the case of performers' rights and recording rights, it is clear that the statute is designed to give protection against the damage caused by unauthorised exploitation of performances, which will primarily be economic loss. It will be rare for a plaintiff to have difficulty in establishing that he has suffered or will suffer damage of this kind. More problematic will be the question of quantification.

Measure of damages

7.11   In the case of copyright, the measure of damages is assessed on the basis that the defendant has invaded the plaintiff's property: it is expressly stated in Part I of the 1988 A~ that copyright is a property right.[18] Accordingly, the measure of damages for infringement of copyright depends on whether the copyright owner exploits his property and if so how. If the copyright owner exploits his property by making and selling reproductions of the copyright work, then the invasion of his property will cause damage to this business and he will be compensated for the loss subject to the normal principles of causation and remoteness. If the copyright owner exploits his property by licensing it, then *prima facie* the copyright owner has merely lost an opportunity to grant a licence and the damages will be assessed at his normal royalty rate. If the copyright owner does not exploit his property, a reasonable royalty for the use made of the property by the infringer will be awarded.[19]

7.12   Performer's rights and recording rights, however, are *not* stated to be property rights in Part II. Furthermore, the draughtsman has deliberately avoided use of copyright terminology as far as is possible when creating a scheme of protection that is in fact very similar to copyright. This poses a difficulty: should the measure of damages for infringement of performers' rights and recording rights be assessed on the basis that they are property rights or not? It is submitted that the just and convenient course is to proceed on this basis. It is just because it will ensure that performers are properly compensated for infringements of their rights. It is convenient because it will mean that the courts have ready to hand a set of principles established by copyright case law for the assessment of damages (that is, those outlined in the preceding paragraph). Any other approach would be fraught with uncertainty.

Matters to be taken into account

7.13   The Act does, however, contain two provisions as to the quantification of damages in particular circumstances. Although it is not an infringement to

---

17   *Halsbury's Laws*, 4th edn, vol. 45, para. 1279.
18   Copyright, Designs and Patents Act 1988, section 96(2).
19   See *Meikle v Maufe* [1941] 3 All ER 144, *Stovin-Bradford v Volpoint Properties Ltd* [1971] Ch 1007 and *General Tire & Rubber Co v Firestone Tyre & Rubber Co.* [1976] RPC 197.

show or play in public a broadcast or cable programme to an audience who have not paid for admission to the place where the broadcast or programme is played or shown,[20] if the making of the broadcast or the inclusion of the programme in the service was an infringement, then the fact that it was seen or heard in public by reception of the broadcast or programme is to be taken into account in assessing the damages for that infringement.[21] Similarly, although it is not an infringement to re-transmit a broadcast as part of a cable programme service in certain circumstances,[22] where the making of the broadcast was infringement, then the fact that it was re-transmitted is also to be taken into account.[23]

Aggravated and exemplary damages

7.14   There is no provision in Part II corresponding to section 97(2) of Part I, and so there is no basis for an award of additional damages. It appears, however, that additional damages for copyright infringement are merely a statutory form of aggravated damages.[24] Aggravated damages are damages awarded where the defendant has invaded a property right in such a way as to injure the plaintiff's feelings and dignity.[25] If the courts are prepared to assess damages for infringements of performers' rights and recording rights on the basis that they are to be treated as property rights, it will be open to the courts to award aggravated damages if the circumstances warrant it. In addition, if the defendant's conduct was calculated by him to make a profit for himself which might exceed the compensation payable to the plaintiff (he has acted with a 'cynical disregard for the plaintiff's rights'), an award of exemplary damages may be available.[26]

Innocence

7.15   The 1988 Act provides a number of 'innocence' defences which either prevent or limit awards of damages. In all cases the burden of proof is upon the defendant.

a.   Primary infringements of performers' rights

7.16   In actions for category (i) and (ii)[27] infringements of performers' rights,

---

20   See Ch. 6, para. 6.29.
21   Copyright, Designs and Patents Act 1988, Schedule 2, para. 18(4).
22   See Ch. 6, para. 6.30.
23   Copyright, Designs and Patents Act 1988, Schedule 2, para. 19(2).
24   *Rookes v Barnard* [1964] AC 1129, 1225, *Broome v Cassell & Co. Ltd* [1972] AC 1027, 1134, *Beloff v Pressdram Ltd* [1973] 1 All ER 241, 265–6.
25   See *McGregor on Damages*, 15th edn, (Sweet & Maxwell 1988), para. 409.
26   This is the second category of case described by Lord Devlin in *Rookes v Barnard* [1964] AC 1129, 1226.
27   See Ch. 5, para. 5.02 for the categories of infringement.

damages may not be awarded against a defendant who shows that at the time of the infringement he believed on reasonable grounds that consent had been given.[28] It appears that the principal beneficiaries of this provision will be persons who are the victims of false representations of authority to give consent.

b.   Secondary infringements of performers' rights

7.17   In actions for category (v) and (vi) infringements of performers' rights, the only remedy available against a defendant who shows that the illicit recording was innocently acquired by him or by a predecessor in title of his is damages not exceeding a reasonable payment in respect of the act complained of.[29] 'Innocently acquired' means that the person acquiring the recording did not know and had no reason to believe that it was an illicit recording.[30] Curiously, this defence is not available in respect of category (iii) and (iv) infringements.

c.   Primary infringements of recording rights

7.18   In actions for category (i)[31] infringements of recording rights, damages may not be awarded against a defendant who shows that at the time of the infringement he believed on reasonable grounds that consent had been given.[32]

d.   Secondary infringements of recording rights

7.19   In actions for category (iv) and (v) infringements of recording rights, the only remedy available against a defendant who shows that the illicit recording was innocently acquired by him or by a predecessor in title of his is damages not exceeding a reasonable payment in respect of the act complained of.[33] 'Innocently acquired' means that the person acquiring the recording did not know and had no reason to believe that it was an illicit recording.[34] Again, this defence is not available in respect of category (ii) and (iii) infringements.

Account of profits

7.20   In contrast to infringement of copyright,[35] it does not appear that an account of profits may be awarded.

---

28   Copyright, Designs and Patents Act 1988, section 182(2).
29   *Ibid.*, section 184(2).
30   *Ibid.*, section 184(3).
31   See Ch. 5, para. 5.45 for the categories of infringement.
32   Copyright, Designs and Patents Act 1988, section 186(2).
33   *Ibid.*, section 184(2).
34   *Ibid.*, section 184(3).
35   *Ibid.*, section 96(2).

3. Delivery up

7.21 Section 195 of Part II[36] of the 1988 Act enables the owner of performers' rights or recording rights in a performance to apply to the court for an order for delivery up of illicit recordings of that performance. The remedy is subject to certain restrictions and conditions, however. These may be tabulated as follows:

(i) The remedy only applies to 'illicit' recordings.
(ii) Only illicit recordings that are in the possession, custody or control of the respondent (to the application for an order) in the course of a business may be ordered to be delivered up.[37]
(iii) Applications may not be made after the expiry of the limitation period imposed by section 203 of the Act.[38]
(iv) No order for delivery up may be made unless the court also makes, or it appears to the court that there are grounds for making, an order under section 204 of the Act for forfeiture or destruction of the illicit recording.[39]
(v) The person to whom a recording is delivered up must, if an order under section 204 has not been made, retain it pending a decision of the court whether or not to make such an order.[40]

Illicit recording

7.22 'Illicit recording' is defined in section 197 of the Act.[41] By contrast with the corresponding provision in Part I,[42] the remedy provided by section 195 does not extend to articles specifically adapted or designed for making illicit recordings (such as a master).

Possession in the course of a business

7.23 This restriction reflects the corresponding definition of secondary infringement in section 188(1)(b) of the Act, and is subject to the same difficulties of construction.[43]

Limitation period

7.24 No application for an order for delivery up may be made after the end of six years from date on which the illicit recording was made,[44] unless

---

36 Corresponding to section 99 of Part I.
37 Copyright, Designs and Patents Act, section 195(1).
38 *Ibid.*, section 195(2).
39 *Ibid.*
40 *Ibid.*, section 195(3).
41 See Ch. 5, para. 5.28.
42 Copyright, Designs and Patents Act 1988, section 99.
43 See Ch. 5, paras. 5.33–39, particularly para. 5.38.
44 Copyright, Designs and Patents Act 1988, section 203(1).

(a) the applicant is under a disability within the meaning of the Limitation Act 1980, or

(b) is prevented by fraud or concealment from discovering the facts entitling him to apply,

in which case an application may be made up to six years from when the applicant ceases to be under a disability or could with reasonable diligence have discovered the facts.[45]

No order unless grounds for order under section 204

7.25   No order may be made for delivery up unless one is also made for forfeiture or destruction under section 204 or there are grounds for making such an order.[46] For this reason it would seem sensible to combine applications under sections 195 and 204 where this is feasible.[47]

Mode of application

7.26   Applications for delivery up may be made in England, Wales and Northern Ireland in the county court where the value of the illicit recordings in question does not exceed the county court limit for actions in tort.[48] In Scotland such applications may be made in the sheriff court.[49] The jurisdiction of the High Court and Court of Session is stated to be unaffected,[50] and so presumably applications may also be made in these courts. It is not entirely clear what procedure should be followed if the application is made outside an action for infringement. In the High Court the most appropriate procedure would seem to be by way of an originating motion under Order 8 of the Rules of the Supreme Court; applications under section 204, however, are to be made by originating summons under Order 7,[51] and so it may be advisable to adopt this procedure for applications under section 195 as well. If the application is made in a pending action, the appropriate procedure would be on summons or motion; but if relief is only sought at trial there does not appear to be any reason why it should not simply be claimed in the writ and prayer in the normal way.[52]

7.27   Whether application is made in the county court or in the High Court,

---

45   *Ibid.*, section 203(2).
46   See paras. 7.40–49.
47   See paras. 7.47–48 for further discussion.
48   Copyright, Designs and Patents Act 1988, section 205(1).
49   *Ibid.*, section 205(2). Application is by motion or incidental application where proceedings have been commenced and by summary application where no proceedings have been commenced: Act of Sederunt (Copyright, Designs and Patents) 1990, S.I. 1990 No. 380 (S.37), para. 2(2).
50   *Ibid.*, section 205(3).
51   See para. 7.43.
52   But see para. 7.49.

an important question the answer to which is unclear from the Act is whether or not an application may be made *ex parte*. The requirement for service of notice of applications under section 204[53] suggests that applications under section 204 must be made *inter partes*; conversely, the absence of such a requirement under section 195 may indicate that an application under this section can be made *ex parte*.

Interlocutory or final?

7.28 It should be noted that a combined order under sections 195 and 204 is final, regardless of what stage the action (if any) has reached; whereas an order under section 195 alone is in a sense 'interlocutory', in that it is subject to the making or refusal of an order under section 204, although not to judgment in the action (if any). Either way, however, it would seem that there is no requirement for the applicant to give a cross-undertaking in damages pending an order under section 204 or judgment in any action, as is normally the case where interlocutory relief is sought.

4. Seizure of illicit recordings

7.29 Section 196 of Part II[54] provides for what has been described as a 'do-it-yourself Anton Piller order', namely a right for owners of performers' rights and recording rights and persons authorised by them to seize illicit recordings without first obtaining a court order. A more accurate, if less catchy description would be 'do-it-yourself *ex parte* delivery up order', since the section only applies to premises to which the public have access; there is nothing to require a person to permit access to private premises so that they may be searched, as in a true Anton Piller order. Furthermore, the right is only available in limited circumstances and subject to stringent conditions. These may be tabulated as follows:

(i) The right only applies to 'illicit' recordings.
(ii) The right only applies to an illicit recording in respect of which the person by or on whose behalf the right of seizure is exercised would be entitled to apply for an order for delivery up under section 195.[55]
(iii) Only illicit recordings which are found exposed or otherwise immediately available for sale or hire may be seized.[56]
(iv) Before anything is seized notice of the time and place of the proposed seizure must be given to a local police station.[57]
(v) Premises to which the public have access may be entered for the purpose of exercising the right, but nothing in the possession, custody or

---

53 See para. 7.44.
54 Corresponding to section 100 of Part I.
55 Copyright, Designs and Patents Act 1988, section 196(1).
56 *Ibid.*
57 *Ibid.*, section 196(2).

control of a person at a permanent or regular place of business of that person may be seized.[58]

(vi) The person exercising the right of seizure may not use any force.[59]

(vii) At the time when anything is seized notice must be left at the place where it is seized in prescribed form containing prescribed particulars as to the person by whom or on whose authority the seizure is made and the grounds upon which it is made.[60]

(viii)The right is subject to any decision of the court under section 204.[61]

Entitled to apply for an order under section 195

7.30   This appears to be an indirect way of importing into section 196 the limitations:

(a) that an illicit recording can only be seized from a person who has it in his possession, custody or control in the course of a business;[62] and

(b) that an illicit recording cannot be seized after the expiry of the limitation period imposed by section 203.[63]

7.31   It is not, however, a requirement that the right owner would succeed in obtaining an order under section 195. Therefore it would seem that this does *not* import the limitation that the court be satisfied that there are grounds for making an order under section 204.[64] This is important, because otherwise a person exercising the right of seizure would be subject to the notional comparison with other remedies in an action for infringement.[65]

7.32   It is not quite clear what the position is if an illicit recording is seized by or on behalf of a person who is not entitled to apply for such an order. Presumably, though, he would be liable to an action for wrongful interference for goods.

Exposed or otherwise immediately available for sale

7.33   This formulation appears to be apt to cover goods that are either (a) on display or (b) for sale from stock, both of which situations are as a matter of contract law regarded as merely invitations to treat.

---

58   *Ibid.*, section 196(3).
59   *Ibid.*, section 196(3).
60   *Ibid.*, section 196(4).
61   *Ibid.*, section 196(1).
62   See para. 7.23.
63   See para. 7.24.
64   See para. 7.25.
65   See paras. 7.41–43.

Notice of the time and place of the proposed seizure

7.34　It would appear that the requirement of notice to a police station is intended to ensure that exercise of the right of seizure does not cause a breach of the peace.[66] There is no duty upon the police to take any action upon receipt of the notice, however. It will therefore be a matter for the discretion of the duty sergeant whether any action is taken. Many may take the view that their resources are already overstretched without intervening in what is essentially a civil dispute. Curiously, no minimum period of advance notice is required: one minute's notice would appear to comply. Furthermore, the requirement is merely to notify *a* local police station, not *the* local police station, raising the question of how local is 'local' for the purposes of the section. Finally, no set form of notice is prescribed. A notice modelled on that prescribed under section 196(4)[67] would appear to be satisfactory, however. It would seem, on the other hand, that a general notice to the police that any illicit recordings found (for example, any Michael Jackson bootlegs at a Michael Jackson concert) will be seized is insufficient: notice must be given of *the* proposed seizure.

Premises

7.35　'Premises' are defined as including land, buildings, fixed or moveable structures, vehicles, aircraft and hovercraft.[68]

Permanent or regular place of business

7.36　'Regular place of business' covers any place where business is conducted with any regularity. 'Place' is not confined to 'premises' (though 'premises' is itself widely defined for the purposes of section 196[69]). This provision would appear to place considerable limits on the applicability of the remedy, for even a market trader has a regular stall. It would seem that the only persons who are not protected by this provision are unlicensed street traders, in particular those who sell goods from temporary stalls in places like Oxford Street. The remedy may still prove useful against those selling infringing merchandise at pop concerts and the like, however.

May not use any force

7.37　The prohibition on the use of force goes to the heart of the difficulty with this remedy. The stipulation is necessary, for otherwise the existence of the remedy would be tantamount to an invitation to use violence. Two

---

66　See also para. 7.37.
67　See para. 7.38.
68　Copyright, Designs and Patents Act 1988, section 196(5).
69　See para. 7.35.

problems arise, however. The first is that even if the person seeking to exercise the right does not use force, the person from whom the illicit recording is sought to be seized may respond with violence. Second, it is unclear what sanction if any exists if the person from whom the illicit recording is sought to be seized declines to permit it to be seized. In the case of a true Anton Piller order, the sanction is proceedings for contempt of court. No corresponding sanction is provided by section 196. It is perhaps arguable that a person who declined to deliver up an illicit recording could be sued for breach of statutory duty, but this removes the whole point of the provision, which is to avoid cumbersome and lengthy legal proceedings.

Prescribed form and particulars

7.38   The prescribed form and particulars are set out in the Schedule to the Copyright and Rights In Performances (Notice of Seizure Order) 1989.[70]

Subject to decision under section 204

7.39   The provision that the right to seize illicit recordings is subject to any decision of the court under section 204 means that a person from whom recordings are seized may apply for a decision that no order shall be made under that section, in which case the recordings must be returned to him – although it appears that such a person would not be entitled to damages for the period of detention if the recordings were validly seized. In a sense, therefore, seizure under section 196 is an 'interlocutory' form of relief, like an order under section 195. Both forms of relief become final when an order under section 204 is made. Section 196 differs from section 195 in that under section 195 the onus is on the right owner to apply for an order under section 204, while under section 196 the onus is on the person from whom the recordings are seized. In neither case is there is any requirement for the person claiming performers' or recording rights to give a cross-undertaking in damages pending any order under section 204 (still less pending judgment in any action).

5.   Forfeiture or destruction

7.40   Section 204 of Part II[71] provides that an application may be made to the court for an order that an illicit recording shall either be forfeited to the owner of the performers' or recording rights or destroyed or otherwise dealt with, or for a decision that no such order shall be made. Once again, the remedy is subject to certain restrictions and conditions:

(i) It only applies to 'illicit' recordings.
(ii) It only applies to illicit recordings delivered up pursuant to an order

---

70   S.I. 1989 No. 1006. See Appendix 6.
71   Corresponding to section 114 of Part I.

under section 195[72] or section 199[73] or seized pursuant to section 196[74] of the Act.[75]

(iii) In deciding whether to grant such an order the court must consider what other remedies available in an action for infringement would be adequate to compensate the right owner and to protect his interests.[76]

(iv) Notice may be required to be served on persons having an interest in the recording.[77]

(v) Persons having an interest in the recording may appear (whether or not served with notice) and may appeal against any order (whether or not they appeared).[78]

(vi) Where more than one person is interested in a recording, the court may direct that the recording be sold and the proceeds divided.[79]

Whether other remedies adequate

7.41 In considering what order if any to make on an application under section 204, the court must consider what other remedies available in an action for infringement of performers' rights or recording rights would be adequate to compensate the right owner and to protect his interests.[80]

7.42 This is a strange provision, the purpose of which is not entirely clear. It might perhaps be argued that it implies that an order under section 204 can only be made in the context of an action for infringement, but it is submitted that this is not right. Like applications under section 195,[81] it is provided that the county court may entertain applications under section 204. This, together with the fact that the subject-matter of an application under section 204 may be recordings seized pursuant to section 196, suggests that applications under section 204 do not have to be made in the context of an action for infringement.

7.43 If this is right, section 204(2) is asking the court notionally to compare the right owner's actual position on a stand-alone application for forfeiture and his hypothetical position if he were to bring an action for infringement. In effect, this amounts to asking whether an injunction and damages which the right owner has chosen not to ask for would be sufficient protection of his interests. Presumably the purpose of this is to discourage right owners from making applications for forfeiture when damages would be an adequate

---

72 See paras. 7.21–27.
73 The counterpart to section 195 in criminal proceedings: see Ch. 8, para. 8.26–28.
74 See paras. 7.29–39.
75 Copyright, Designs and Patents Act 1988, section 204(1).
76 *Ibid.*, section 204(2).
77 *Ibid.*, section 204(3).
78 *Ibid.*
79 *Ibid.*, secton 204(4).
80 *Ibid.*, section 204(2).
81 And under sections 99 and 114 of Part I.

remedy, but it is not easy to see how the courts will apply this in practice. (There appears to be no reason why an application under section 204 should not if so desired be made in the context of an action for infringement, in which case the test will be easier to apply.)

Service of notice

7.44   Where an application is made under section 204, the applicant must serve notice of the application on all persons so far as reasonably ascertainable having an interest[82] in the recording which is the subject of the application.[83]

Persons having an interest in the recording

7.45   Any person having an interest in the recording is entitled to appear in proceedings for an order for forfeiture or destruction, whether or not he has been served with notice of them, and to appeal against any order made, whether or not he has appeared.[84] Persons having an interest in the recording include:[85]

(a) persons in whose favour an order for forfeiture could be made (that is, other owners of performers' or recording rights in the performance in question);
(b) persons in whose favour an order for forfeiture of infringing copies under section 114 of the 1988 Act could be made (that is, copyright owners, where the illicit recording is also an infringing copy);
(c) persons in whose favour an order for forfeiture of infringing articles[86] under section 231 of the 1988 Act could be made (that is, design right owners, where the illicit recording is also an infringing article);
(d) persons in whose favour an order for forfeiture of goods under section 58C of the Trade Marks Act 1938 could be made (that is, trade mark owners, where the illicit recording bears infringing trade marks).

More than one person interested in the recording

7.46   Where more than one person is interested in a recording, the court has a wide discretion to make whatever order it thinks just. In particular, it has power to order that the recording be sold or otherwise dealt with and the proceeds divided.[87]

---

82   See para. 7.45.
83   Order 93 Rule 24 of the Rules of the Supreme Court, added by R.S.C. (Amendment No. 3) Order 1989, S.I. 1989 No. 1307, made under section 204(3) of the Act. This is applied to county courts by Order 49 Rule 4A of the County Court Rules.
84   Copyright, Designs and Patents Act 1988, section 204(3).
85   *Ibid.*, section 204(6).
86   That is, articles made in infringements of design right.
87   Copyright, Designs and Patents Act 1988, section 204(4).

Timing of application

7.47   The wording of section 204(1) suggests that applications for orders for forfeiture can only be made *after* delivery up or seizure. Section 195(2), however, expressly contemplates that an order for forfeiture may be made *at the same time* as an order for delivery up or subsequently. It seems clear that the latter must prevail, and that therefore an application for an order for forfeiture can be made at the same time as an application for an order for delivery up.

7.48   If no order for forfeiture is made at the time of the application for delivery up (and *a fortiori* if no application is made), the court must nevertheless consider whether there are grounds for making a forfeiture order. Furthermore, delivery up under section 195 merely gives the deliveree custody of the illicit recordings pending a decision under section 204. In addition, it would appear that the respondent to an application for delivery up could counter with a cross-application for a decision that no order for forfeiture should be made (or, perhaps, a declaration that there were no grounds for making such an order): if no order is made, the person in whose possession the illicit recording was before being delivered up or seized is entitled to its return.[88] It would therefore seem sensible to combine applications under sections 196 and 204 rather than to make them separately. Whether this is feasible may depend on whether others are interested in the illicit recording in question.

Mode of application

7.49   Applications for forfeiture or destruction may be made in England, Wales and Northern Ireland in the county court where the value of the illicit recordings in question does not exceed the county court limit for actions in tort.[89] In Scotland, such applications may be made in the sheriff court.[90] In the High Court, applications must be made by originating summons[91] if there is no pending action for infringement or by summons or motion in that action if there is.[92] Whatever procedure is adopted, it seems clear that interlocutory applications can only be made *inter partes*. If relief under section 204 is sought only at trial, there does not appear to be any reason why it should not be claimed in the writ and prayer in the normal way, but this will not obviate the

---

88   *Ibid.*, section 204(5).
89   *Ibid.*, section 205(1). Applications in pending actions should be made under Order 13 of the Country Court Rules and originating applications under Order 3 Rule 4.
90   *Ibid.*, section 205(2). Application is by motion or by incidental application where proceedings have been commenced and by summary application where no proceedings have been commenced: Act of Sederunt (Copyright, Designs and Patents Act) 1990, S.I. 1990 No. 380 (S.37) para. 2(2).
91   Order 7 of the Rules of the Supreme Court.
92   Order 93 Rule 24(2) of the Rules of the Supreme Court, added by R.S.C. (Amendment No. 3) Order 1989, S.I. 1989 No. 1307, made under section 204(3) of the Act.

necessity to serve a summons or notice of motion returnable at the trial on all persons having an interest in the recording.

Interlocutory Proceedings

7.50   There appears to be no reason why all the usual forms of interlocutory relief (including injunctions, delivery up, discovery and inspection) should not be available in actions for infringement under Part II. Two forms of relief are worthy of brief notice here, namely interlocutory injunctions and Anton Piller orders. An appropriate text on civil procedure should be consulted for a full treatment of these and other forms of interlocutory relief.

Interlocutory injunction

7.51   An interlocutory injunction is a temporary order to restrain the infringement complained of pending the trial of the action. Given that it may take one or two years to bring an action to trial, the remedy is a valuable one for plaintiffs. The essence of the jurisdiction, however, is that the court does not know and should not attempt to predict which party will succeed at trial. The task of the court hearing an application for interlocutory injunction is therefore to decide which course will cause the least risk of ultimate injustice, to grant or to refuse an injunction.[93]

7.52   The principles to be applied by the court on an application for an interlocutory injunction were laid down by the House of Lords in *American Cyanamid Co v Ethicon Ltd*.[94] They may be summarised as follows:

(i) Has the plaintiff established that there is a serious question to be tried, that he has a real prospect of succeeding at trial? If not, no injunction will be granted.

(ii) Assuming that the plaintiff will succeed at trial, would an award of damages at trial adequately compensate the plaintiff for the damage that he would suffer by reason of the defendant continuing to infringe until then? If it would, no injunction will be granted.

(iii) Assuming that the defendant will succeed at trial, would an award of damages under the plaintiff's cross-undertaking adequately compensate the defendant for the damage that he would suffer through being injuncted until then? If the plaintiff would suffer uncompensatable or irreparable harm and the defendant would not on these respective assumptions, an injunction will be granted.

(iv) If both parties would suffer uncompensatable or irreparable harm, which party will suffer most if the court decides against it?

93   *Cayne v Global Natural Resources* [1984] 1 All ER 225.
94   [1975] AC 396.

(v) If the balance of irreparable harm is roughly even, are there other factors which make it more just to grant or to refuse an injunction (what is the 'balance of convenience')? For example, has the plaintiff acted promptly or has he delayed unduly in making his application?

(vi) If the balance of convenience is fairly even, the court may consider it prudent to preserve the status quo. In a very close case on balance, the court may be justified in taking into account the respective strengths of the parties' cases.

Anton Piller orders

7.53   In certain cases the plaintiff may have evidence that, if the defendant is given notice of any proceedings, he will destroy or conceal documents or other evidence, perhaps including any illicit recordings. The Anton Piller order[95] is designed to meet this difficulty. The order requires the defendant to permit the plaintiff to enter and search the defendant's premises and to seize categories of documents and other material. The order is made *ex parte* so as to enable the plaintiff to take the defendant by surprise: the first that the defendant will know of the proceedings is when the plaintiff's solicitors arrive at his premises to serve and execute the order. The principles applied by the courts in considering whether to grant such orders may be summarised as follows:

(i) The plaintiff must establish that he has a strong *prima facie* case.

(ii) The plaintiff must adduce evidence tending to show that there is a likelihood that the defendant if given notice of the proceedings would destroy or conceal documents or other materials.

(iii) As with all *ex parte* applications, the plaintiff must disclose to the court all relevant facts within his knowledge.

(iv) The order must contain appropriate safeguards for the defendant, including undertakings by the plaintiff's solicitors to serve the defendant with copies of the evidence in support, to explain the order in everyday language and to keep a record of all material seized.[96]

---

95   *Anton Piller KG v Manufacturing Processes Ltd* [1976] Ch 55.
96   See *Columbia Picture Industries Inc v Robinson* [1987] Ch. 38 for a discussion of the need for safeguards.

8 Criminal Law

Introduction

8.01 The Performers' Protection Acts on their face provided performers with exclusively criminal remedies. By contrast, the Copyright Acts of 1911 and 1956 were primarily concerned with civil remedies, although criminal penalties for copyright infringement had existed since at least the Copyright Act 1842. Since 1956, however, the legislature has enlarged the criminal aspect of copyright law, firstly by increasing the penalties for the offences under the 1956 Act[1] and now by creating a wider scheme of offences with further increased penalties.[2] The criminal side of performers' rights has been brought into line with this. In both cases the criminal offences created are virtually co-extensive with civil infringements.

Principal Offences

8.02 Section 198 of the Copyright, Designs and Patents Act 1988 makes it an offence for a person to do any of the following acts (subject[3] to the exceptions contained in Schedule 2[4]):

(i) make for sale or hire without sufficient consent a recording which is, and which that person knows or has reason to believe is, an 'illicit recording';[5]

(ii) import into the United Kingdom otherwise than for his private or domestic use without sufficient consent a recording which is, and which that person knows or has reason to believe is, an 'illicit recording';[6]

---

1 Copyright (Amendment) Act 1983.
2 Copyright, Designs and Patents Act 1988, sections 107–110.
3 *Ibid.*, section 198(4).
4 As to which, see Ch. 6, paras. 6.02–32.
5 Copyright, Designs and Patents Act 1988, section 198(1)(a). See para. 8.05.
6 *Ibid.*, section 198(1)(b). See para. 8.06.

(iii) in the course of a business possess with a view to committing an infringement of performers' rights or recording rights without sufficient consent a recording which is, and which that person knows or has reason to believe is, an 'illicit recording';[7]

(iv) in the course of a business sell, let for hire, offer or expose for sale or hire or distribute without sufficient consent a recording which is, and which that person knows or has reason to believe is, an 'illicit recording';[8]

(v) cause a recording of a performance made without sufficient consent to be shown or played in public so that, and so that person knows or has reason to believe that, performers' rights or recording rights are infringed;[9]

(vi) cause a recording of a performance made without sufficient consent to be shown or played in public so that, and so that person knows or has reason to believe that, performers' rights or recording rights are infringed;[9]

Sufficient consent

8.03 'Sufficient consent' for the purposes of section 198(1) and (2) is defined as follows:[11]

(a) where performers' rights subsist,[12] the consent of the performer;
(b) where performers' rights do not subsist but recording rights do subsist:[13]

(i) for category (i) above, the consent of the performer or the owner of the recording rights;
(ii) for categories (ii) to (vi) above, the consent of the owner(s) of the recording rights.

Thus if performers' rights subsist, consent of the performer is always sufficient to prevent the commission of an offence. If recording rights also subsist, it is not necessary also to obtain the consent of the owner of those.

Illicit recording

8.04 'Illicit recording' has the same definition as for civil infringement.[14]

---

7 *Ibid.*, section 198(1)(c). See paras. 8.07–08.
8 *Ibid.*, section 198(1)(d). See paras. 8.09–10.
9 *Ibid.*, section 198(2)(a). See para. 8.11.
10 *Ibid.*, section 198(2)(b). See para. 8.12.
11 *Ibid.*, section 198(3).
12 See Ch. 5, para. 5.03.
13 The words used are 'in the case of a non-qualifying performance subject to an exclusive recording contract', but it is clear from the context that it must be a performance in which recording rights subsist rather simply *any* performance subject to an exclusive recording contract.
14 See Ch. 5, paras. 5.28–29.

1.   Making for sale or hire

8.05   This offence corresponds approximately to category (i) infringement of performers' rights and to category (i) infringement of recording rights. The correspondence is not exact, however. Whereas it is an infringement to make a recording without consent for any purpose save private and domestic use, it is only an offence to make it for sale or hire. Thus it is not an offence to make a recording without consent for the purpose of broadcasting it (although it may be an offence then to broadcast it).

2.   Importation

8.06   This offence corresponds to category (v) infringement of performers' rights and to category (iv) infringement of recording rights. It does not appear that there is any difference between the scope of the offence and the scope of the tort.

3.   Possession in the course of a business

8.07   This offence (together with the succeeding offence) corresponds approximately to category (vi) infringement of performers' rights and category (v) infringement of recording rights. The correspondence is not exact, however. Whereas it is an infringement to possess in the course of a business an 'illicit recording' for any purpose, it is only an offence to possess it 'with a view to committing any act infringing' performers' rights or recording rights. Presumably mere possession is not a sufficient 'act' for this purpose.

With a view to committing any act

8.08   It is not clear whether the words 'with a view to committing any act' import a test purely of intention or whether they import something more than that. On the one hand, if what was meant was 'with intent to commit any act', it would have been easy enough for the draughtsman to say so. On the other hand, if what was meant was 'while taking steps to commit any act', the words chosen do not seem very apt for the purpose. Since it is undesirable to criminalise mere states of mind, it is submitted that the words should be construed as importing more than a simple test of intention. For the offence to be committed, the defendant should have taken steps towards committing an act of infringement.

4.   Sale etc. in the course of a business

8.09   This offence (together with the preceding offence) corresponds to category (vi) infringement of performers' rights and category (v) infringement of recording rights. It does not appear that there is any difference between the scope of the offence and the scope of the torts. It is worth noting, however, that the offence is defined in such a manner as to make it absolutely clear that the acts must be committed in the course of a business, whereas this is not so for the torts.[15]

Distribution

8.10   A distinction must be drawn between sale, letting for hire and offering or exposing for sale or hire on the one hand, and distributing on the other hand. The reason for this is that the penalties for the latter act are heavier than those for the former acts.[16] This would seem to imply that, say, offer for sale does not, without more, constitute distribution.

5.   Causing to be shown or played in public

8.11   This offence, though similar to category (iii) infringement of performers' rights and to category (ii) infringement of recording rights, differs in two respects. First, it is sufficient for the offence to be committed if the putative offender causes a recording to be shown or played; he does not have to do the act himself.[17] Second, and more important, the offence is not committed unless the tort is committed; but an additional element has to be present for the offence to be committed. The additional element is the satisfaction of a second, and different, knowledge requirement. For an offence to be committed, the putative offender must know or have reason to believe:

(i) that the recording was made without the appropriate consent; and
(ii) that the playing or showing of the recording is an infringement of performers' rights or recording rights.

It is possible, however, that the courts will take the view that (ii) adds nothing to (i).

6.   Causing to be broadcast or included in a cable programme service

8.12   This offence bears the same relationship to category (iv) infringement of performers' rights and category (iii) infringement of recording rights as the preceding offence does to categories (iii) and (ii) respectively. The same comments therefore apply.

---

15   See Ch. 5, paras. 5.34–38.
16   See paras. 8.23–25.
17   A person who causes a recording to be shown or played may be a joint tortfeasor; but this depends upon the operation of normal common law principles rather than upon any statutory definition.

Additional Offences

1. False representation of authority to consent

8.13   By section 201(1) of the 1988 Act, it is an offence for a person falsely to represent that he is authorised by another to give consent for the purposes of Part II in relation to a performance unless he believes on reasonable grounds that he is so authorised. The anomaly of section 4 of the Performers' Protection Act 1963, that the representor was only guilty of an offence if the representation afforded the representee a defence under section 7 of the Dramatic and Musical Performers' Protection Act 1958,[18] has therefore been removed.

Authorised

8.14   It is arguable (by analogy with the Court of Appeal's construction of section 7 of the 1958 Act in the *Peter Sellers* case[19]) that a person who represents, contrary to the fact, that he is a deceased person's personal representative and as such purports to give consent does not commit an offence under this provision. The argument would be that such a person does not represent that he is 'authorised *by any person*' to give consent (emphasis added), which would require a representation of agency, but that he is authorised *by law* to give it on his own behalf standing in the deceased's shoes. It is submitted, however, that this is to adopt too legalistic an approach. Assuming that both representor and representee are ignorant of the niceties of the law as to executors, it is likely that the representor will represent – and, more importantly, be understood by the representee to represent – that he is authorised to consent on the performer's behalf, notwithstanding that it is as a matter of law impossible for the representation to be true. It is consistent with the purposes of the subsection for the representor in those circumstances to be guilty of an offence.

Reasonable grounds

8.15   It is unclear what the effect of the proviso to the subsection is. One possibility is that the prosecution has to prove, as an element of the *actus reus*, that the defendant did not have reasonable grounds. A second possibility is that the proviso provides a defence but does not otherwise affect the scope of the offence. A third possibility is that the existence of the proviso, in addition to providing a defence, indicates that the offence is to be a treated as one of strict liability. Of these possibilities, the third appears to be the most likely.

8.16   If this is correct, a defendant will be guilty of the offence once it is established that he made the false representation unless he proves (i) that he

---

18   See Ch. 2, para. 2.57.
19   [1988] QB 40. See Ch. 2, paras. 2.22 and 2.58.

believed that the representation was true and (ii) that he had reasonable grounds for doing so. In effect, the proviso is an enactment of the *Tolson* rule.[20]

2.   Connivance of director etc. of body corporate

8.17   Section 202(1) of the 1988 Act provides that where an offence under Part II committed by a body corporate is proved to have been committed with the consent or connivance of a director, manager, secretary or other similar officer of the body, or a person purporting to act in any such capacity, that person too is guilty of the offence. Directors and others are no longer guilty if the commission of the offence by the body corporate is merely attributable to neglect on their part, however, as under section 4A of the Performers' Protection Act 1963.[21] 'Connivance' would seem to imply knowledge of, and acquiesence in, the commission of the offence but not necessarily any active participation.

Director

8.18   In the case of a body corporate whose affairs are managed by its members, 'director' means a member of the body corporate.[22] Presumably if only some members take part in the management, it means a managing member.

Mens rea[23]

8.19   Under the Performers' Protection Acts 1958–72, it was necessary for the prosecution to prove knowledge on the part of the defendant of all elements of the offence charged.[24] It is submitted that on general principles the same ought to apply under Part II of the 1988 Act. It is possible, however, that the way in which section 198 is drafted will lead the courts to hold that it is merely necessary for the prosecution to prove the defendant did in fact do the acts charged and that he knew or had reason to believe[25] that the recording was an 'illicit recording'. If so, the effect will be that the test of *mens rea* in criminal cases is the same as the test of knowledge in civil proceedings under the Act, only the standard of proof will be higher.

---

20   See Ch. 2, para. 2.68.
21   See Ch. 2, para. 2.59.
22   Copyright, Designs and Patents Act 1988, section 202(2).
23   See also Ch. 2, paras. 2.60–74.
24   *Gaumont British Distributors Ltd v Henry* [1939] 2 KB 711. See Ch. 2, paras. 2.60–63.
25   See Ch. 5, paras. 5.52–56.

Corporations

8.20   Clearly a corporation may be guilty of an offence under Part II. It would seem that in such a case the requisite *mens rea* must be possessed by a 'directing mind'[26] of the corporation.

Defences

8.21   The following defences to a prosecution under Part II of the 1988 Act are available: the act was one covered by the exceptions in Schedule 2;[27] sufficient consent; 'innocence' (that is, lack of knowledge); private and domestic use; and arrangements made before commencement. See Chapter 6, paras. 6.02–51 for discussion of these. So far as the last is concerned, although section 180(3), unlike Schedule 2, is not expressly provided to apply to offences under section 198, it is arguably implicit that it does.

Delay

8.22   Informations alleging offences under Part II of the 1988 Act which are only triable summarily[28] must be laid within six months of the commission of the offence if the justices are to have jurisdiction to try the case.[29] Offences which are triable either way,[30] however, are not subject to any statutory limitation period[31] and at common law there is no time limit on criminal prosecutions.[32] Nevertheless, delay in bringing a prosecution may give rise to prejudice and unfairness which by itself amounts to an abuse of process such that the tribunal may decline to entertain the proceedings.[33]

Penalties

Imprisonment and/or fine

8.23   The penalty on summary conviction under sub-subsections (a),(b) and (d)(iii) of section 198 (making, importing and distributing illicit recordings) is imprisonment for up to six months or a fine not exceeding 'the statutory

---

26   See *Tesco Supermarkets Ltd v Nattrass* [1972] AC 153.
27   Copyright, Designs and Patents Act 1988, section 198(4).
28   That is, those under section 198(1)(c), (d)(i) and (ii) and (2).
29   Magistrates Court Act 1980, section 127(1).
30   That is, those under section 198(1)(a), (b) and (d)(iii).
31   See *Kemp v Liebherr-GB Ltd* [1987] 1 All ER 885.
32   *Halsbury's Laws*, 4th ed. (reissue), vol. 11(1), para. 786.
33   *R v Bow Street Stipendiary Magistrate ex parte Director of Public Prosecutions* The Times, 20 December 1989.

maximum'[34] (presently £2,000[35]) or both.[36] The penalty on conviction on indictment is imprisonment for up to two years or a fine or both.[37] There is no limit to the fine which may be imposed by a Crown Court, but it should be within the offender's means.[38]

8.24 The penalty on summary conviction under sub-subsections (c) and (d)(i) and (ii) of section 198 (possession, sale or hire and offer for sale or hire) and under section 201(1) (false representation of authority) is imprisonment for up to six months or a fine not exceeding level 5 on the standard scale[39] (presently £2,000[40]) or both.[41] These offences are only triable summarily.

8.25 It may be noted that the penalties for distributing illicit recordings are heavier than those for selling, letting for hire, offering or exposing for sale or hire. It is not quite clear why this should be. A possible explanation is that it is thought that distribution is more likely to involve organised crime.

Delivery up

8.26 Section 199 of the 1988 Act gives a court seized of proceedings for an offence under section 198[42] power, if satisfied that the defendant at the time of his arrest or charge[43] had in his possession, custody or control in the course of a business[44] an illicit recording[45] of a performance, to order that it be delivered up to an owner of performers' rights or recording rights in the performance or to any other person that the court directs. Unlike the power to order destruction of records and films under section 5 of the 1958 Act,[46] this power may be exercised whether or not the defendant is convicted.[47] The power may also be exercised of the court's own motion.[48]

---

34 Defined by the Criminal Justice Act, section 74 as 'the prescribed sum' within the meaning of the Magistrates' Courts Act 1980, section 32.
35 Criminal Penalties etc (Increase) Order 1984, S.I. 1984 No. 447, Article 2(4) and Schedule 1.
36 Copyright, Designs and Patents Act 1988, section 198(5)(a).
37 *Ibid.*, section 198(5)(b).
38 *R v Churchill (No. 2)* [1967] 1 QB 190 (reversed on other grounds *sub nom Churchill v Walton* [1967] 2 AC 224).
39 Defined by the Criminal Justice Act 1982, section 75 as the scale set out in the Criminal Justice Act 1982, section 37(2).
40 Criminal Penalties etc (Increase) Order 1984, Note 35 above, Article 3(4) and Schedule 4.
41 Copyright Tribunal Rules 1989, section 198(6) and section 201(2).
42 See paras. 8.02–19.
43 That is, when he is orally charged or is served with a summons or indictment or (in Scotland) when he is cautioned, charged or served with a complaint or indictment: Copyright, Designs and Patents Act 1988, section 199(2).
44 See Ch. 5, paras. 5.34–38.
45 See Ch. 5, paras. 5.28–29.
46 See Ch. 2, para. 2.95.
47 Copyright, Designs and Patents Act 1988, section 199(3).
48 *Ibid.*

8.27   No order may be made after the expiry of six years from the date on which the recording in question was made.[49] Nor may any order for delivery up be made if it appears to the court unlikely that any order for forfeiture[50] will be made.[51] A person to whom a recording is delivered up must retain it pending a decision on whether to make an order for forfeiture.[52]

8.28   Where an order for delivery up is made by a Magistrate's Court, an appeal lies against the order to the Crown Court.[53] Since an order may be made in the absence of a conviction, such an appeal may be made even if there is no appeal against conviction.

Search Warrants

8.29   Section 200 of the 1988 Act gives a justice of the peace power to issue a warrant to enter and search premises if certain conditions are satisfied. These are that the justice must be satisfied by information given on oath by a constable that there are reasonable grounds for believing:[54]

(a) that an offence under section 198(1)(a),(b) or (d)(iii) (making, importing or distributing illicit recordings) has been or is about to be committed in any premises; and
(b) that evidence that such an offence has been or is about to be committed is in those premises.

8.30   The 'premises' that may be searched include land, buildings, fixed or moveable structures, vehicles, vessels, aircraft and hovercraft.[55] The warrant may authorise persons to accompany any constable executing the warrant,[56] for example a representative of the record company concerned and/or their solicitor.

Private Prosecutions

8.31   In the early 1980s the Federation Against Copyright Theft Ltd (FACT) was set up by record and film copyright owners in order to investigate copyright infringement, gather evidence and instigate or take proceedings. The

49   *Ibid.*, section 203(4). Cf. the period during which orders for delivery up may be made in civil proceedings: see Ch. 7, para. 7.24.
50   Under section 204: see Ch. 7, paras. 7.39–48.
51   Copyright, Designs and Patents Act 1988, section 199(3)(b).
52   *Ibid.*, section 199(5).
53   *Ibid.*, section 199(4). In Northern Ireland the appeal is to the county court, and in Scotland the appeal is in the same manner as against sentence: *ibid.*
54   *Ibid.*, section 200(1).
55   *Ibid.*, section 200(4).
56   *Ibid.*, section 200(3)(a).

Federation Against Software Theft (FAST) performs similar functions in relation to computer software copyright. One way in which organisations such as this may operate is to bring private prosecutions. A possible pitfall of this procedure was demonstrated in *R v Ealing Justices ex p. Dixon*.[57] In that case the defendant had been charged by police at a police station with an offence of copyright infringement following the execution by the police accompanied by two FACT officers of search warrants obtained under section 21A(1) of the Copyright Act 1956. A subsequent prosecution brought by FACT was dismissed by the magistrates. The Divisional Court dismissed an application by FACT for judicial review of this decision, holding that under section 3(2) of the Prosecutions of Offences Act 1985, all prosecutions of offences charged by the police had to be conducted by the Director of Public Prosecutions or the Crown Prosecution Service. The police had no power to permit FACT to bring the prosecution. The correct course was for FACT to lay an information. The disadvantage of this for a body such as FACT is that it cannot obtain a search warrant itself, and the deterrent value of the defendant being charged by the police is lost. On the other hand, there may be a reluctance to leave prosecution to the overburdened and unspecialised CPS.

---

57 [1989] 2 All ER 1050.

Appendix 1

The Legislative History of the Dramatic and Musical Performers' Protection Act 1925

A1.01   The Dramatic and Musical Performers' Protection Bill was introduced into the House of Commons by Sir Martin Conway MP[1] on 13 February 1925. It was a Private Member's Bill, but received the support of the Baldwin Government. Conway's primary sponsor appears to have been The Gramophone Company Limited (that is, HMV).[2] The Bill received its second reading on 1 May and was reported from standing committee with amendments on 25 June.

A1.02   Moving that the Bill be read for the third time, Conway stated that he had introduced it 'in order to make it possible to improve broadcast programmes'. He explained that at that moment it was inadvisable for artists to perform for broadcasts since records could be made illicitly from the broadcast and sold. The performer had no protection against this, and it had the effect of breaking contracts between the artists and the gramophone companies.[3]

A1.03   The only objection the Bill met with in the Commons came from Sir Henry Slesser, who had been Solicitor-General in the 1924 Labour administration.[4] He argued that the mischief at which the Bill was directed should be remedied by an amendment to the Copyright Act 1911, and protested at the

---

1   Later Lord Conway of Allington. Conway represented the Combined English Universities as a Conservative member of the Coalition Government, having previously been a Liberal. He was a distinguished art historian, critic and collector who had been Slade Professor of Fine Art at Cambridge and the first Director-General of the Imperial War Museum. He was also a noted mountaineer and explorer.
2   Conway's diary entry for 13 February includes the note 'H. of C. & put in the Grammo-[sic]/phone Co's Bill.', while the entry for 25 May includes the note 'Got my Grammo-[sic]/phone Bill thro' Com^{cc} C.': *Conway Papers*, Cambridge University Library, Add. 7676/Y 58. According to Conway's biographer, he was rewarded by the presentation to him of a 'magnificent' gramophone: Joan Evans, *The Conways: A History of Three Generations* (1966), p. 245.
3   *HC Deb.*, 5th Series, vol. 185 (1925), cols. 1970–71.
4   Later Slesser LJ. Slesser had the unusual distinction of being appointed directly to the Court of Appeal at the age of 46 without having first sat as a judge of first instance. He resigned in 1940 at the age of 57 owing to ill-health, but lived on until 1970.

creation of new crimes when the civil law was quite adequate to deal with the situation.[5] Later in the debate, he added that the appropriate remedies were an injunction and damages.[6] The House appears to have regarded this as a technical point of little merit, however, and the Bill was carried to a third reading on 26 June.[7]

A1.04 The Bill received its first reading in the House of Lords shortly thereafter, on 29 June. Moving that the Bill be read a second time on 13 July, the Earl of Shaftesbury stated that it had the support of the Broadcasting Company (that is, the BBC) and of the gramophone companies as well as of artists.[8] When the question was raised whether it was not more appropriate to make it a matter of civil rather than criminal liability, Viscount Haldane, who had piloted the 1911 Act through the Lords, said that that was 'a gigantic Act' as it was without amending it, and it was simpler to proceed by way of the criminal law[9] (thereby, as Shaftesbury put it, overruling his colleague Slesser[10]).

A1.05 The Bill was reported without amendments from the House in committee on 16 July, was given its third reading on 20 July and received the Royal Assent on 31 July.

---

5   *Ibid.*, cols. 1971–72.
6   *Ibid.*, col. 1975.
7   *Ibid.*, col. 1979.
8   *HL Deb.*, 5th Series, vol. 62 (1925), cols. 18–21.
9   *Ibid.*, col. 21.
10   *Ibid.*, cols. 22–23. Haldane had been a member of the Liberal Government in 1911, but was Lord Chancellor to Slesser's Solicitor-General in 1924.

Appendix 2
Is There a Civil Right of Action Under the Performers' Protection Acts 1958–72?

A2.01   On their face, the Performers' Protection Acts merely created criminal offences and did not confer any civil right of action. Nevertheless there were a number of attempts by performers, performers' associations and those interested in exploiting performances, such as record companies, to enforce the Acts by civil proceedings. The principal reason for this, of course, was the availability of an injunction through the civil process, a remedy not available from the criminal courts. In addition, the fines were small and did not benefit either performer or record company. For many years performers and record companies were unsuccessful.[1] In 1987, however, the Court of Appeal in the *Peter Sellers* case held that the Acts did confer civil rights of action. In order fully to understand the decision in the *Peter Sellers* case it is necessary to see how the law had developed from 1925 to that point.

The *Blackmail* Case

A2.02   The first and only case under the 1925 Act on the question was *Musical Performers' Protection Association Ltd v British International Pictures Ltd* [2] in which it was held that the 1925 Act did not confer any civil right of action. That case arose out of the making of the Alfred Hitchcock film *Blackmail*. The defendant was the production company. It hired musicians to provide incidental music for the film. Although the musicians were paid, they were not asked to nor did they consent in writing to the use of their performances in the film. Five of the musicians later assigned their rights under the 1925 Act to the plaintiff association which brought proceedings. McCardie J began with the proposition that the Court would not grant an injunction to restrain the commission of a criminal offence in the absence of actual or

---

1   Discounting those out of the flurry of cases in the late 1970s and early 1980s – roughly the period from *Ex Parte Island Records* [1978] Ch 122 to *RCA Corp. v Pollard* [1983] Ch 135 – in which the performers succeeded. See paras. A2.07–09.
2   (1930) 46 TLR 485.

prospective injury to property.[3] He then considered whether the 1925 Act conferred any right of property:

> A consideration of the Act shows that there are no words providing it is to be read as one with the Copyright Acts. Nay, more, as I have already pointed out, the Copyright Acts are not mentioned in any way. The Act does not provide for 'penalties'; it provides for a 'fine' on summary conviction for an offence. The fine does not go to the performers; it goes to the Crown, and the performers get no share. Nowhere in the Act is there any indication of an intention to give the performers any 'right of property' in the performance of works. The prohibitions of the Act apply as much to non-copyright works as to copyright works. Any member of the public may commence a prosecution.
>
> Upon considering the Act, I come to the conclusion that the Legislature did not, by any inadvertence, omit to give a right of property to the performers, but that they deliberately so worded the Act as to preclude any notion that a right of property was conferred. Nothing would have been easier than to confer a right of property if such was the wish of Parliament. The Act, however, is most significant alike in its wording and in its omissions.[4]

He was fortified in this view by the consideration that otherwise there would be 100 separate rights of property in a performance by an orchestra of 100 performers. It does not appear to have been argued that the plaintiff could sue for breach of statutory duty imposed by the Act, although the concept was well known by that time.[5]

The Gregory Report and the Copyright Act 1956

A2.03 In 1952 the Gregory Committee in its Report on the reform of copyright stated (although without referring to the *Blackmail* case) that the 1925 Act did not give civil rights to performers.[6] Furthermore the Committee rejected a proposal by the Musicians' Union, Equity and the Variety Artistes' Federation that performers should be given a 'performers' right' in the nature of copyright.[7] Accordingly, the Copyright Act 1956, which was passed following the Gregory Committee's Report, did not provide for any such right. On the contrary, section 45 and the Sixth Schedule of the 1956 Act amended the 1925 Act by extending it to films but without changing the principle that breach was only a matter for the criminal courts. The Dramatic and Musical Performers' Protection Act 1958 was, as its long title said, an Act to consolidate the 1925 Act and the amendments made by the 1956 Act.

---

3 Relying upon Turner LJ in *Emperor of Austria v Day* 3 De GF&J 217, 253.
4 (1930) 46 TLR 485, 488.
5 The classic decision in favour of an apparently criminal statute imposing a civil duty being *Groves v Lord Wimborne* [1898] 2 QB 402.
6 Cmnd 8662 at para. 172.
7 *Ibid.*, at para. 180.

The 1963 Act

A2.04   The Performers' Protection Act 1963 was, in the words of its long title,

> An Act to amend the law relating to the protection of performers so as to enable effect to be given to a Convention entered into at Rome on 26 October 1961.

The Convention in question was the International Convention for the Protection of Performers, Producers of Phonograms and Broadcasting Organisations.[8] Again, the protection afforded by the Acts was somewhat extended, in particular by enlarging the categories of performance to which the Acts applied, but the basic structure was left unchanged.

The *Beatles* Case

A2.05   The next attempt to bring civil proceedings under the Performers' Protection Acts was *Apple Corps Ltd v Lingasong Ltd.*[9] This case concerned a tape recording of a concert by the Beatles at the Star Club in Hamburg in 1961 or 1962. The Beatles and their record company sought to restrain the making of records from the tape without their written consent. It was argued on behalf of the plaintiffs that a breach of the Performers' Protection Acts was actionable on the basis of breach of statutory duty, and it was pointed out that this argument had not been advanced in *MPPA v BIP*. Sir Robert Megarry V-C applied the earlier decision, however, observing:

> Whatever might have been the position under the Acts of 1925 and 1958 if they had stood alone, I think that it would be quite wrong to construe them as if no Copyright Acts had ever existed. The concept of copyright has been with us for a very long time, and when Parliament came to enact the Act of 1925 it cannot have failed to know that there was such a thing as copyright. The Copyright Act 1956, indeed, amended the Act of 1925 (see section 45 of and Schedule 6 to the Act of 1956); and the Act of 1958 consolidated the Act of 1925 as amended. Side by side with the individual rights of property given by the Copyright Act 1956 and its predecesors, Parliament enacted the limited remedies laid down by the Acts of 1925 and 1958, and abstained from conferring any copyright in a performance. What I think [counsel for the plaintiffs] is seeking to do is to bring into being a right of action in tort for breach of statutory duty which will confer something of the effect of a copyright on something that Parliament has refrained from making the subject of copyright.[10]

A2.06   The Vice-Chancellor also rejected an argument that the position had been altered by the giving of effect to the Rome Convention by the 1963 Act:

---

8   See below paras. A2.12–15.
9   [1977] FSR 345.
10   *Ibid.*, p. 349.

[Counsel for the plaintiffs] emphasised the words 'protection of performers' in the long title of the Act of 1963, and the words 'the protection provided for performers' in Article 7 of the Convention.[11] Such expressions, he said, made it plain that the purpose of this legislation was to protect performers, and this protection could not be provided to the requisite extent unless there was a right of civil action. In my judgment the inference to be drawn is the opposite. Let the protection of performers be duly emphasised; yet what does Parliament do? It carries out the Convention by making certain changes in the Act of 1958, but leaves its structure and operation just as they were; in particular, the only remedy provided still remains a prosecution.[12]

The *Island Records* Case

A2.07   The next case was *Ex parte Island Records Ltd*[13] in which various performers and their record companies applied for an Anton Piller[14] order against a bootlegger. Walton J held that there was no jurisdiction to make the order. The plaintiffs appealed, arguing first that a civil action lay for breach of statutory duty under the Performers' Protection Acts, and secondly that where a business or trade or interest in the nature of property was caused damage by criminal acts over and above that suffered by the public at large a civil action could be brought without requiring the relation of the Attorney-General.[15] Shaw and Waller LJJ rejected the first argument, Shaw LJ expressly approving the *MPPA v BIP* and *Apple v Lingasong* cases, while Lord Denning MR declined to decide the point. The reasoning of both Shaw and Waller LJJ was that, while the statute was arguably for the benefit of a particular class of persons, it did not impose any defined duty. Waller LJ observed:

> The words 'if a person knowingly . . . makes a record . . . or sells . . . he shall be guilty of an offence' do not impose a duty. All the cases in which it has been held that there is a duty imposed which can be made the subject of a private action are cases where a clear duty is stated. For example, the 'roof and sides of every . . . working place shall be made secure': section 49 of the Coal Mines Act 1911. Dangerous parts of machinery 'shall be securely fenced': see *Groves v Lord Wimborne* [1898] 2 QB 402 . . . We were referred to a number of other cases, but there is no case so far as counsel could discover where phraseology similar to that in the section we are considering has been held to impose a duty on which an action can be framed.[16]

---

11   See para. A2.15.
12   [1977] FSR 345, 350.
13   [1978] Ch 122.
14   *Anton Piller KG v Manufacturing Processes Ltd* [1976] Ch 55.
15   [1978] Ch. 122, pp. 126G, 127G–H and 128A. It was stated that an attempt had previously been made to bring a relator action, but the Attorney-General had refused consent: pp. 125H, 136H.
16   *Ibid.*, p. 142F–H.

The appeal was allowed, however, by a majority (Lord Denning MR and Waller LJ, Shaw LJ dissenting) on the second ground. Both Lord Denning MR and Waller LJ held that the rights of the performers and the record companies under the contracts between them were rights in the nature of rights of property[17] damage to which by criminal acts gave rise to a civil cause of action.

The *Lonrho* Case

A2.08   The correctness of this decision came under scrunity in *Lonrho Ltd v Shell Petroleum Co. Ltd (No. 2)*[18] in which Lonrho were claiming damages for alleged breaches by Shell and BP of sanctions orders against Rhodesia after UDI. Lord Diplock began with the presumption laid down by Lord Tenterden CJ in *Doe d. Murray v Bridges*[19] that:

> ... where an Act creates an obligation, and enforces the performance in a specified manner ... that performance cannot be enforced in any other manner.

Where the only manner of enforcing performance provided by the Act was criminal prosecution for failure to perform the statutory obligation or for contravening the statutory prohibition, said Lord Diplock, there were two classes of exception:

> The first is where upon the true construction of the Act it is apparent that the obligation or prohibition was imposed for the benefit or protection of a particular class of individuals, as in the case of the Factories Acts and similar legislation ...
>   The second exception is where the statute creates a public right (that is, a right to be enjoyed by all those of Her Majesty's subjects who wish to avail themselves of it) and a particular member of the public suffers what Brett J in *Benjamin v Storr* (1874) LR 9 CP 400, 406 described as 'particular, direct and substantial' damage 'other and different from that which was common to all the rest of the public'.[20]

Lord Diplock rejected any wider basis of liability:

> ... I should mention two cases, one in the Court of Appeal of England, *Ex parte Island Records Ltd* [1978] Ch 122, and in the High Court of Australia, *Beaudesert Shire Council v Smith* (1966) 120 CLR 145, which counsel for Lonrho, as a last resort, relied upon as showing that some broader principle has of recent years replaced these long-established principles that I have just stated for determining whether a contravention of a particular statutory prohibition by one private individual makes him liable in tort to another private individual who can prove that he has suffered damage as a result of the contravention.
>   *Ex parte Island Records Ltd* was an unopposed application for an Anton Piller order ... against a defendant who, without the consent of the performers, had

---

17   *Ibid.*, pp. 137C–D and 144C–E respectively.
18   [1982] AC 173.
19   (1831) 1 B & Ad 847, 859.
20   [1982] AC 173, 185D,G.

made records of musical performances for the purposes of trade. This was an offence, punishable by a relatively small penalty under the Dramatic and Musical Performers' Protection Act 1958. The application for the Anton Piller order was made by performers whose performances had been 'bootlegged' by the defendant without their consent and also by record companies with whom the performers had entered into exclusive contracts. *So far as the application by performers was concerned, it could have been granted for entirely orthodox reasons. The Act was passed for the protection of a particular class of individuals, dramatic and musical performers; even the short title said so.* Whether the record companies would have been entitled to obtain the order in a civil action to which the performers whose performances had been bootlegged were not parties is a matter which for present purposes it is not necessary to decide. Lord Denning MR, however, with whom Waller LJ agreed (Shaw LJ dissenting) appears to enunciate a wider general rule, which does not depend upon the scope and language of the statute by which a criminal offence is committed, that whenever a lawful business carried on by one individual in fact suffers damage as a consequence of a contravention by another individual of any statutory prohibition the former has a civil right of action against the latter for such damage.

My Lords, with respect, I am unable to accept that this is the law . . .[21]
[emphasis added]

The Post-*Lonrho* Cases

A2.09   It is clear that Lord Diplock (with whom the other members of the House of Lords agreed) was disapproving the ruling of Lord Denning MR and Waller LJ on the second argument.[22] Whether he was also, in the sentences italicised above, disapproving the ruling of Shaw and Waller LJJ on the first argument so far as performers were concerned gave rise to a difference of judicial opinion in a series of cases which followed. The first was *Warner Bros Records Inc. v Parr*,[23] in which Julian Jeffs QC held that he was bound by the judgments of Shaw and Waller LJJ on the issue of breach of statutory duty under the Performers' Protection Acts not only with respect to record companies,[24] but also with respect to performers.[25] Two months later Vinelott J in *RCA Corp. v Pollard*[26] took the view that, as regards performers, *Lonrho*

---

21   *Ibid.*, p. 187B–F.
22   It having been argued on behalf of Lonrho that *Ex Parte Island Records Ltd* was directly applicable since in both cases the only rights which had been damaged were contractual rights: *ibid.*, p. 180A–C. See also the judgment of Lawton LJ in *RCA Corp. v Pollard* [1983] Ch 135, 146C–147B and 147B–148C.
23   [1982] FSR 383.
24   *Ibid.*, p. 394. He nevertheless granted the plaintiff record companies relief on the same ground as Lord Denning MR and Waller LJ, taking the view that Lord Diplock had not intended to disapprove their ruling but merely some of Lord Denning's wider *dicta*.
25   *Ibid.*, p. 395.
26   [1982] FSR 369.

v Shell had effectively overruled *Island Records*.[27] Shortly after that Peter Gibson J in *Ekland v Scripglow Ltd*[28] agreed with Vinelott J. When the *RCA* case came to the Court of Appeal later the same year,[29] Oliver LJ held that as regards performers the decision of Shaw and Waller LJJ had *not* been overruled by *Lonrho v Shell* and so was binding,[30] while Lawton and Slade LJJ[31] expressed no view on this point.[32] Finally, Harman J in *Shelley v Cunane*[33] declined to follow Vinelott and Peter Gibson JJ and applied the decision of Shaw and Waller LJJ in *Island Records*.

The *Peter Sellers* Case: Judgment of Hobhouse J

A2.10   The score at this stage, then, was that in the space of 12 months two judges had said that performers could sue for breach of statutory duty, three had said they could not and two had refrained from expressing an opinion. This was still the state of the authorities at the time of the *Peter Sellers* case. At first instance in that case, Hobhouse J held that the relevant law to be applied was contained in the speech of Lord Diplock in the *Lonrho* case. As to the principles enunciated by Lord Diplock, Hobhouse J made four points:

> The first is that Lord Diplock does not treat any particular statutory formulation of the criminal offence as being conclusive. Secondly, he expressly refers not only to the performance of a statutory obligation but also to the contravention of a statutory prohibition. Thus he rejects any argument that there must be an obligation stated in the statute and specifically recognises that statutory prohibitions can give rise to civil remedies as well. The third point is that Lord Diplock specifically recognises two classes of exception to the rule, the first of which he identifies as being 'where upon the true construction of the Act it is apparent that the obligation or prohibition was imposed for the benefit or protection of a particular class of individuals.'
>
> This exception then depends upon examining the purpose of the legislation. If it is legislation for the protection of a particular class . . . then *prima facie* the statute should be construed as giving a right to a civil remedy to the members of that class. This is a *prima facie* position because, of course, the construction of any statute has

---

27   As regards record companies, he held that it was arguable that they had a cause of action for unlawful interference with contractual relations apart from the Performers' Protection Acts.

28   [1982] FSR 431.

29   [1983] Ch 135.

30   *Ibid.*, p. 150D–G.

31   Hobhouse J suggested in the *Peter Sellers* case that Slade LJ used language which was open to the inference that he disagreed with Oliver LJ: [1986] FSR 502, 516 referring to [1983] Ch 135, 157. It is submitted, however, that the single sentence relied upon for this is too fragile to bear the weight.

32   So far as recording companies were concerned, all three members of the Court of Appeal agreed that the decision of Shaw and Waller LJJ in *Island Records* was binding on the issue of breach of statutory duty, but that the decision of Lord Denning MR and Waller LJ on the issue of damage to contractual rights had been overruled by *Lonrho v Shell*.

33   [1983] FSR 390.

to take into account all the terms of the statute and all the relevant aids to construction. (See for example the *McCall* case.[34]) Lastly the second exception stated by Lord Diplock contains two aspects, the first of which involves a consideration of when a private individual can sue without the intervention of the Attorney General; this aspect really turns upon considerations of the *locus standi* of a plaintiff in a particular situation. In contrast the second aspect clearly depends upon a specific question of statutory interpretation because Lord Diplock says:

> It has first to be shown that the statute having regard to its scope and language does fall within that class of statutes which creates a legal right to be enjoyed by all ... A mere prohibition upon members of the public generally from doing what it would otherwise be lawful for them to do is not enough.

In this connection therefore one can see that Lord Diplock draws a distinction between language which creates a legal right and language which creates a mere prohibition. It is at this point in his formulation and at this point alone that the type of criterion to which Shaw LJ referred in the *McCall* case[35] enters the analysis. It does not enter the analysis under the first class of exception which Lord Diplock formulated.[36]

The significance of all this, as the judge pointed out, was that Lord Diplock had effectively disapproved the reasoning of Shaw and Waller LJJ in *Island Records*:

> In the *Island Records* case two members of the Court of Appeal, Waller LJ and Shaw LJ, specifically rejected an argument that performers ... were entitled to relief on the basis that the 1958 Act fell within the equivalent of the first class of exception formulated by Lord Diplock ... With regard to the 1958 Act, their reasoning was in essence that formulated by Shaw LJ in the *McCall* case. Thus Shaw LJ himself ... looked for a defined duty for the benefit of a particular class and said that the 1958 Act contained no 'definition in terms of a such duty'. He refused to 'distil from the language of the section a specific duty to performers'. ... Lord Denning was not willing to agree with that approach either in the *Island Records* case itself nor in the Court of Appeal in the *Lonrho* case. It is clear that Lord Diplock did not agree with it either and formulated his statement of the law in terms which are inconsistent with the reasoning of Shaw LJ and Waller LJ.[37]

Not only had Lord Diplock disapproved the reasoning of Shaw and Waller LJJ, but in the view of Hobhouse J he had also disapproved their conclusion. Having quoted the passage italicised above, Hobhouse J said this:

> There can be no doubt that in *Lonrho*, Lord Diplock was intending to hold that as regards the 1958 Act, it fell within his first class of exception and he was leaving it open whether or not it could also be construed as an Act passed for the protection of record companies.[38]

---

34   *McCall v Abelesz* [1976] 1 QB 585.
35   *Ibid.*, p. 600.
36   *Rickless v United Artists Corp.* [1986] FSR 502, 513.
37   *Ibid.*, pp. 514–5.
38   *Ibid.*, p. 514.

Considering for himself whether there were any reasons why the 1958 Act should not be construed as implicitly conferring a right to civil remedies, Hobhouse J thought not. On the contrary, he was of the view that 'a coherent scheme of protection' would be established.[39]

Judgment of the Vice-Chancellor – the 1958 Act

A2.11   On appeal, Sir Nicolas Browne-Wilkinson V-C (with whom the other members of the Court of Appeal agreed) began by considering the matter apart from authority. In the Vice-Chancellor's view the fact that the Performers' Protection Acts were passed for the protection of perfomers was 'a very strong pointer' in favour of civil liability under Lord Diplock's first class of exception, but not decisive. Against civil liability were four 'formidable' arguments: the wording of sections 1 and 2 of the 1958 Act, which simply created offences; the decision in *MPPA v BIP*, which Parliament had to be presumed to have known of when it enacted the Copyright Act 1956 and the 1958 Act; the contents of the Gregory Report, which formed the basis for the 1956 Act; and that the result would be to give performers a right of perpetual duration and without any of the limitations on copyright for example, as to fair dealing. Nevertheless, the Vice-Chancellor found himself unable to get away from the fact that the Act was in terms one for the protection of performers.[40]

Judgment of the Vice-Chancellor – the Rome Convention

A2.12   As to Parliament's intention, the Vice-Chancellor found assistance in the manner in which the 1963 Act implemented the Rome Convention:[41]

> [Under the Rome Convention] the contracting states (of which the United Kingdom was one) undertook to protect, *inter alia*, 'the rights of performers' on records. Article 7(1) of the Convention provides that 'the protection provided for performers by this Convention shall include the possibility of preventing' the broadcasting, fixation or reproduction of the fixation of the performance without the consent of the performers. Two things seem to be clear. First, under the Convention the performer himself was to have 'rights'. Secondly, the performer's rights were to include something which, in some circumstances, would make it possible to *prevent* unauthorised reproduction, i.e. a *quia timet* injunction. Therefore, compliance with the Rome Convention required that there should be an English Act of Parliament which enabled the performer to obtain an injunction to

---

39   *Ibid.*, p. 517.
40   *Rickless v United Artists Corp.* [1988] QB 40, 51E–52E.
41   As to which, see generally Stewart, *International Copyright and Neighbouring Rights*, 2nd edition (Butterworths 1989), Ch. 8 and Masouyé and Wallace, *WIPO Guide to the Rome Convention* (WIPO).

prevent unauthorised reproduction on records. The Performers' Protection Act 1963 was passed expressly 'to enable effect to be given to' the Rome Convention. The Act of 1963 merely altered the class of acts which infringe sections 1 and 2 of the Act, i.e. the Act continued on its face as one imposing criminal sanctions only. In my judgment Parliament must have considered that the Performers' Protection Act 1963 gave rise to civil rights to obtain an injunction, since otherwise Parliament would not have been carrying out its declared intention of giving effect to the Convention.[42]

It does not appear from the report that this point was argued before the Court of Appeal; nor was *Apple v Lingasong*, in which the Vice-Chancellor's predecessor had rejected the same argument,[43] cited.

A2.13 Although the Vice-Chancellor's interpretation of the Rome Convention appears convincing, it is less so if Article 7 is compared with other Articles of the Convention. Like the Berne Convention, the Rome Convention lays down minimum standards of protection for certain persons – authors and composers in the case of the Berne Convention, performers, phonogram producers and broadcasting organisations in the case of the Rome Convention. Unlike the Berne Convention, however, the Rome Convention was not drawn up solely to harmonise national laws and enable reciprocity: its purpose was in large measure to provide for rights to be granted to persons who under many national laws had not previously enjoyed rights. Most countries therefore had to legislate to create the minimum rights stipulated before they could ratify the Convention – including the United Kingdom. The rights thus pioneered were the 'neighbouring rights' (to author's rights, that is).[44] The new right owners were those whose authorship was derivative from another's work in that by their contribution (performance, recording, broadcast) they converted the original work into a new form. The closest analogies in the Berne Convention are the rights of translators and arrangers. In both cases the rationale is the same: that the contribution of the derivative 'author' is worthy of protection because it provides a new object for consumption. The impulse for the extention to performers, producers and broadcasters came, of course, from technology. When it became possible to fix and reproduce such contributions, it became necessary to protect their originators.

---

42 *Ibid.*, pp. 52F–53A.
43 See para. A2.06.
44 The expression originates from the phrase *droits voisins* contained in a *voeu* adopted by the Brussels Conference for the Revision of the Berne Convention in 1948. The terms 'connected rights' (from the Italian, *diritti conessi*) and 'related rights' (from the German, *verwandte Schutzrechte*) are also used. As well as the narrow sense of performers', producers' and broadcasters' rights, 'neighbouring rights' is also used with a wider meaning, namely rights similar to, but lesser than, full copyright. This is because Continental copyright systems based on the natural law concept of *droit d'auteur* were traditionally reluctant to accord full copyright where the owner was, as with record producers and broadcasting organisations, a corporation. See Stewart, Note 41 above, Ch. 7 and Ch. 8, paras. 8.01–02. See also Sterling, 'Harmonisation of Usage of the Terms "Copyright", "Author's Right" and "Neighbouring Right"' [1989] EIPR 14.

A2.14   Because performing, recording and broadcasting are so interconnected, it was recognised that a single convention should deal with the creation of these rights and that it should strike a balance between the three different right owners. This balancing process seems to have worked to the relative disadvantage of performers. The reasons for this were mainly political. Authors' representatives feared that an absolute performers' right would compete with authors' rights; broadcasters feared that it would give performers' unions too powerful a weapon; and an absolute right was opposed by countries like the United Kingdom which already had legislation protecting performers by way of criminal penalties.[45] The result was that performers were given a different right to phonogram producers and broadcasters.

A2.15   This can be seen by comparing Article 7 clause 1 with Articles 10 and 13:

> Article 7.1   The protection provided for performers by this Convention shall include *the possibility of preventing* [broadcasting, fixation and the reproduction of fixations without consent].

> Article 10   Producers of phonograms shall enjoy *the right to authorise or prohibit* the direct or indirect reproduction of their phonograms.

> Article 13   Broadcasting organisations shall enjoy *the right to authorise or prohibit* [rebroadcasting, fixation and the reproduction of fixations of their broadcasts]. [emphases added]

Although the wording is notably unhappy, it is clear that the absolute 'right to authorise or prohibit' granted to producers and broadcasters is meant to be different from the 'possibility of preventing' accorded to performers. It might be argued that the latter is intended to be a greater right than the former, and not a lower. It is clear, however, that the intention was to grant phonogram producers and broadcasters an absolute right; and so the 'possibility of preventing' must be a lesser right. The position may be contrasted with that under the Model Law Concerning Protection of Performers, Producers of Phonograms and Broadcasting Organisations promulgated by ILO, WIPO and UNESCO in 1974 which provides in section 2(1) that 'without the authorisation of the performers, no person shall do any of the following acts . . .', the form of words being the same as that in section 4 relating to producers and in section 6 relating to broadcasters. Thus although to an English reader the use of the word 'prevent' in Article 7 of the Rome Convention suggests a right to an injunction, it seems that the intention was that the provision by national laws of something less than a performers' copyright – such as protection through the criminal law – should be permissible. In short, it is respectfully submitted that the Vice-Chancellor's interpretation of Parliament's intention when enacting the 1963 Act is mistaken, and that his predecessor's view is to be preferred.

---

45   Stewart, Note 41 above, Ch. 8 para. 8.16.

Judgment of the Vice-Chancellor – the Authorities

A2.16   Having given his view apart from authority, the Vice-Chancellor turned to the authorities. Here he was faced with the argument that the Court of Appeal was bound by its previous decision in *Island Records* to hold that the 1958 Act did not confer any right to civil remedies. The problem was that this could not have been overruled by *Lonrho*, since Lord Diplock's *dicta* concerning the position of performers under the 1958 Act were plainly *obiter*. The Vice-Chancellor's elegant solution to this dilemma was to point out that the Court was only bound by *ratio decidendi* of the previous case, and that the *ratio decidendi* was the reason given by the Court for making the order actually made. Thus the Court was not bound by reasons given, on an independant issue, for *not* making the order. Thus the reasons of Shaw and Waller LJJ were *obiter*. That being the case, the Court of Appeal was free to apply the higher source of persuasive authority, namely the *dicta* of Lord Diplock in *Lonrho*.[46]

Conclusion

A2.17   The author's view is that the argument based upon breach of statutory duty, if it had been run in *MPPA v BIP*, ought to have succeeded (although the plaintiff might well have failed on other grounds) for the reasons given later by Lord Diplock in *Lonrho* and applied by Hobhouse J and the Court of Appeal in *Rickless*. After the passing of the 1958 Act, however, it was too late. Sir Robert Megarry V-C's analysis of the statutory history of the Performers' Protection Acts and the conclusions he drew from that history cannot be faulted. It is, in the end, significant that Lord Diplock's remarks in *Lonrho* were *obiter*. The House of Lords had not had a full argument on the Performers' Protection Acts addressed to it. If Lord Diplock had had the benefit of reading *Apple v Lingasong*, he might well have expressed himself differently.

A2.18   That the Court of Appeal in the *Peter Sellers* case was somewhat uncertain about the conclusion it had reached is demonstrated by the fact that the defendants were granted leave to appeal to the House of Lords limited to the Performers' Protection Acts point. The defendants did not pursue the matter, however, presumably because it was thought that they would not succeed in the House of Lords on the other issue. By that time, too, it would have been apparent that the point was not worth pursuing simply to establish a precedent, for the 1986 White Paper[47] showed that the Government would give statutory endorsement to the Court of Appeal's decision.

---

46   [1988] QB 40, 55F–56B.
47   Cmnd. 9712, para. 14.4.

Appendix 3

Dramatic and Musical Performers' Protection Act 1925 (15 & 16 Geo. 5 c. 46)

An Act to prevent unauthorised reproductions of dramatic and musical performances   [31 July 1925]

Be it enacted by the King's most Excellent Majesty, by and with the advice and consent of the Lords Spiritual and Temporal, and Commons, in this present Parliament assembled, and by the authority of the same, as follows:

1. Penalties for making, etc., records without consent of performers

If any person knowingly:

(a) makes any record, directly or indirectly, from or by any means of the performance of any dramatic or musical work without the consent in writing of the performers; or
(b) sells or lets for hire, or distributes for the purposes of trade, or by way of trade exposes or offers for sale or hire, any record made in contravention of this Act; or
(c) uses for the purpose of a public performance any record made in contravention of this Act,

he shall be guilty of an offence under this Act, and shall be liable, on summary conviction, to a fine not exceeding forty shillings for each record in respect of which an offence is proved, but not exceeding fifty pounds in respect of any one transaction: Provided that it shall be a defence to any proceedings in respect of an alleged offence under the foregoing paragraph (a) if the defendant proves that the record in respect of which the offence is alleged was not made for purposes of trade.

2. Penalties for making or having plates, etc., for making records in contravension of Act

If any person makes, or has in his possession, any plate or similar contrivance for the purpose of making records in contravention of this Act, he shall be guilty of an offence under this Act, and shall be liable, on summary conviction, to a fine not exceeding fifty pounds for each plate or similar contrivance in respect of which an offence is proved.

3.   Power to order destruction of records, etc., contravening Act

The Court before which any proceedings are taken under this Act may, on conviction of the offender, order that all records or plates or similar contrivances in the possession of the offender which appear to the Court to have been made in contravention of this Act, or to be adapted for the making of records in contravention of this Act, and in respect of which the offender has been convicted, be destroyed, or otherwise dealt with as the Court may think fit.

4.   Interpretation

In this Act, unless the context otherwise requires,

– The expression 'record' means any record or similar contrivance for reproducing sound;
– The expression 'performance of any dramatic or musical work' includes any performance, mechanical or otherwise, of any such work which performance is rendered or intended to be rendered audible by mechanical or electrical means;
– The expression 'performers' in the case of a mechanical performance means the persons whose performance is mechanically reproduced.

5.   Short title

(1) This Act may be cited as the Dramatic and Musical Performers' Protection Act, 1925.
(2) This Act shall extend to Northern Ireland.

Appendix 4

Statutes in Force on 31 July 1989 (Part I)

Dramatic and Musical Performers' Protection Act 1958 (as amended) (6 & 7 Eliz. 2 c. 44)

Arrangement of sections

An Act to consolidate the Dramatic and Musical Performers' Protection Act 1925 and the provisions of the Copyright Act 1956 amending it [23 July 1958]

1. Penalization of making, etc., records without consent of performers

Subject to the provisions of this Act, if a person knowingly:

(a) makes a record, directly or indirectly from or by means of the performance of a dramatic or musical work without the consent in writing of the performers, or

(b) sells or lets for hire, or distributes for the purposes of trade, or by way of trade exposes or offers for sale or hire, a record made in contravention of this Act, or

(c) uses for the purposes of a public performance a record so made,

he shall be guilty of an offence under this Act, and shall be liable, on summary conviction, to a fine not exceeding *forty shillings [£20] for each record in respect of which an offence is proved, but not exceeding fifty pounds [£400] in respect of any one transaction* [the prescribed sum] [or, on conviction on indictment, to imprisonment for a term not exceeding two years, or to a fine, or to both]:

Provided that, where a person is charged with an offence under paragraph (a) of this section, it shall be a defence to prove that the record was made for his private and domestic use only.

Note
As amended, firstly by substitution of the figures in italicised square brackets by the Performers Protection Act 1972, section 1 and Schedule and by addition of the words in the second pair of square brackets by the Performers' Protection Act 1972, section 2; and secondly by substitution of the words in the first pair of square brackets by the Magistrates' Courts Act 1980, section 32(2).

2. Penalization of making, etc., cinematograph films without consent of performers

Subject to the provisions of this Act, if a person knowingly:

(a) makes a cinematograph film, directly or indirectly from or by means of the performance of a dramatic or musical work without the consent in writing of the performers, or
(b) sells or lets for hire, or distributes for the purposes of trade, or by way of trade exposes or offers for sale or hire, a cinematograph film made in contravention of this Act, or
(c) uses for the purposes of exhibition to the public a cinematograph film so made,

he shall be guilty of an offence under this Act, and shall be liable, on summary conviction, to a fine not exceeding *fifty pounds [£400]* [level 5 on the standard scale]:

Provided that, where a person is charged with an offence under paragraph (a) of this section, it shall be a defence to prove that the cinematograph film was made for his private and domestic use only.

Note
As amended, firstly by substitution of the figure in italicised square brackets by the Performers' Protection Act 1972, section 1 and Schedule; and secondly by substitution of the words in square brackets by the Criminal Justice Act 1981, sections 38 and 46.

3. Penalization of broadcasting without consent of performers

Subject to the provisions of this Act, a person who, otherwise than by the use of a record or cinematograph film, knowingly broadcasts a performance of a dramatic or musical work, or any part of such a performance, without the consent in writing of the performers, shall be guilty of an offence under this Act, and shall be liable, on summary conviction, to a fine not exceeding *fifty pounds [£400]* [level 5 on the standard scale].

Note

As amended, firstly by substitution of the figure in italicised square brackets by the Performers' Protection Act 1972, section 1 and Schedule; and secondly by substitution of the words in square brackets by the Criminal Justice Act 1981, sections 38 and 46.

4. Penalization of making or having plates, etc., for making records in contravention of Act

If a person makes, or has in his possession, a plate or similar contrivance for the purpose of making records in contravention of this Act, he shall be guilty of an offence under this Act, and shall be liable, on summary conviction, to a fine not exceeding *fifty pounds [£400]* [level 5 on the standard scale] for each plate or similar contrivance in respect of which an offence is proved.

Note

As amended, firstly by substitution of the figure in italicised square brackets by the Performers' Protection Act 1972, section 1 and Schedule; and secondly by substitution of the words in square brackets by the Criminal Justice Act 1981, sections 38 and 46.

5. Power of Court to order destruction of records, etc., contravening Act

The court before which any proceedings are taken under this Act may, on conviction of the offender, order that all records, cinematograph films, plates or similar contrivances in the possession of the offender which appear to the court to have been made in contravention of this Act, or to be adapted for the making of records in contravention of this Act, and in respect of which the offender has been convicted, be destroyed, or otherwise dealt with as the court may think fit.

6. Special defences

Notwithstanding anything in the preceding provisions of this Act, it shall be a defence to any proceedings under this Act to prove:

(a) that the record, cinematograph film *or broadcast* [broadcast or] *[transmission]* [cable programme] to which the proceedings relate was made [or included] only for the purpose of reporting current events, or
(b) that the inclusion of the performance in question in the record, cinematograph film *or broadcast* [broadcast or] *[transmission]* [cable programme] to which the proceedings relate was only by way of background or was otherwise only incidental to the principal matters com-

prised or represented in the record, film *or broadcast* [broadcast or] *[transmission]* [cable programme].

Note

As amended, firstly by substitution of the words 'broadcast or transmission' for the words 'or broadcast' by the Performers Protection Act 1963, section 3(3); and secondly by substitution of the words 'cable programme' for the word 'transmission' and addition of the words 'or included' by the Cable and Broadcasting Act 1984, section 57(1) and Schedule 5, para. 7(1).

7. Consent on behalf of performers

Where in any proceedings under this Act it is proved:

(a) that the record, cinematograph film *or broadcast* [broadcast or] *[transmission]* [cable programme] to which the proceedings relate was made [or included] with the consent in writing of a person who, at the time of giving the consent, represented that he was authorised by the performers to give it on their behalf, and

(b) that the person making [or including] the record, film *or broadcast* [broadcast or] *[transmission]* [cable programme] had no reasonable grounds for believing that the person giving the consent was not so authorised,

the provisions of this Act shall apply as if it had been proved that the performers had themselves consented in writing to the making [or including] of the record, film *or broadcast* [broadcast or] *[transmission]* [cable programme].

Note

As amended, firstly by substitution of the words 'broadcast or transmission' for the words 'or broadcast' by the Performers Protection Act 1963, section 3(3); and secondly by substitution of the words 'cable programme' for the word 'transmission' and addition of the words 'or included' by the Cable and Broadcasting Act 1984, section 57(1) and Schedule 5, para. 7(2).

8. Interpretation

(1) In this Act, unless the context otherwise requires, the following expressions have the meanings hereby respectively assigned to them, that is to say:

– 'broadcast' means broadcast by wireless telegraphy (within the meaning of the Wireless Telegraphy Act 1949), whether by way of sound broadcasting or of television;

– ['cable programme' means a programme included in a cable programme service, and references to the inclusion of a cable programme shall be construed accordingly;

– 'cable programme service' means a cable programme service within the meaning of the Cable and Broadcasting Act 1984 or a service provided outside the United Kingdom which would be such a service if subsection (7) of section 2 of that Act and references in subsection (1) of that section to the United Kingdom were omitted;]

— 'cinematograph film' means any print, negative, tape or other article on which a performance of a dramatic or musical work or part thereof is recorded for the purposes of visual reproduction;

— 'performance of a dramatic or musical work' includes any performance, mechanical or otherwise, of any such work, being a performance rendered or intended to be rendered audible by mechanical or electrical means;

— 'performers', in the case of a mechanical performance, means the persons whose performance is mechanically reproduced;

— ['programme', in relation to a cable programme service, includes any item included in that service;]

— 'record' means any record or similar contrivance for reproducing sound, including the sound-track of a cinematograph film.

(2) Any reference in this Act to the making of a cinematograph film is a reference to the carrying out of any process whereby the performance of a dramatic or musical work or part thereof is recorded for the purposes of visual reproduction.

[(3) Section 48(3) of the Copyright Act 1956 (which explains the meaning of references in that Act to the inclusion of a programme in a cable programme service) shall apply for the purposes of this Act as it applies for the purposes of that Act.]

Note
As amended, by addition of the words in square brackets by the Cable and Broadcasting Act 1984, section 57(1) and Schedule 5, para. 7(3)–(5).

9. Short title, extent, repeal and commencement

(1) This Act may be cited as the Dramatic and Musical Performers' Protection Act 1958.

(2) It is hereby declared that this Act extends to Northern Ireland.

(3) *The Dramatic and Musical Performers Protection Act 1925, and section 45 of, and the Sixth Schedule to, the Copyright Act 1956, are hereby repealed.*

(4) This Act shall come into operation at the expiration of one month beginning with the date of its passing.

Note
Subsection (3) was repealed by the Statute Law (Repeals) Act 1974.

Performers' Protection Act 1963 (as amended) (1963 c. 53)

Arrangement of sections

An Act to amend the law relating to the protection of performers so as to enable effect to be given to a Convention entered into at Rome on 26th October 1961   [31 July 1963]

Whereas, with a view to the ratification by Her Majesty of the International Convention for the Protection of Performers, Producers of Phonograms and Broadcasting Organisations entered into at Rome on 26th October 1961, it is expedient to amend and supplement the Dramatic and Musical Performers' Protection Act 1958 (in this Act referred to as 'the principal Act'):

1.   Performances to which Principal Act applies

(1) The principal Act shall have effect as if for references therein to the performance of a dramatic or musical work there were substituted references to the performance of any actors, singers, musicians, dancers or other persons who act, sing, deliver, declaim, play in or otherwise perform literary, dramatic, musical or artistic works, and the definition contained in section 8(1) of that Act of the expression 'performance of a dramatic or musical work' (by which that expression is made to include a performance rendered or intended to be rendered audible by mechanical or electrical means) shall be construed accordingly.

(2) For the avoidance of doubt it is hereby declared that the principal Act' applies as respects anything done in relation to a performance notwithstanding that the performance took place outside the United Kingdom, but this shall not cause anything done out of the United Kingdom to be treated as an offence.

2.   Sales etc. of records made abroad

For the purposes of paragraphs (b) and (c) of section 1 of the principal Act (by which sales of, and other dealing with, records made in contravention of the Act are rendered punishable) a record made in a country outside the United Kingdom directly or indirectly from or by means of a performance to which the principal Act applies shall, where the civil or criminal law of that country contains a provision for the protection of performers under which the consent of any person to the making of the record was required, be deemed to have been made in contravention of the principal Act if, whether knowingly or not, it was made without the consent in writing of the performers.

3.   Relaying of performances

(1) A person who, otherwise that by the use of a record or cinematograph film or the reception [and immediate re-transmission] of a broadcast, knowingly *causes a performance to which the principal Act applies, or any part of such a performance, to be transmitted without the consent in writing of the performers:*

> *(a) to subscribers to a diffusion service; or*
> *(b) over wires or other paths provided by a material substance so as to be seen or heard in public,*

[includes a performance to which the principal Act applies, or any part of such performance, in a cable programme without the consent in writing of the performers] shall be guilty of an offence, and shall be liable, on summary conviction, to a fine not exceeding *fifty pounds [£400]* [level 5 on the standard scale].

(2) Section 48(3) of the Copyright Act 1956 (which explains the meaning of references in that Act to the transmission of a work or other subject-matter to subscribers to a diffusion service) shall apply for the purposes of the preceding subsection as it applies for the purposes of that Act.

(3) Section 6 of the principal Act (which provides for special defences) shall have effect as if the preceding subsections were inserted immediately before that section, and that section and section 7 of the principal Act (which provides for the giving of consent on behalf of performers) shall have effect as if for the words 'or broadcast' in each place where they occur there were substituted the words 'broadcast or transmission'.

Note
As amended, firstly by substitution of the figure in italicised square brackets by the Performers' Protection Act 1972, section 1 and Schedule; secondly by substitution of the words in the third pair of square brackets by the Criminal Justice Act 1982, sections 38 and 46; and thirdly by addition of the words in the first pair of square brackets and substitution of the words in the second pair of square brackets by the Cable and Broadcasting Act 1984, section 57(1) and Schedule 5, para. 13(1). Subsection (2) was repealed by the Cable and Broadcasting Act 1984, section 57(2) and Schedule 6.

4. Giving of consent without authority

(1) Where:

(a) a record, cinematograph film, *broadcast or transmission is made* [or broadcast is made or cable programme is included] with the consent in writing of a person who, at the time of giving the consent, represented that he was authorised by the performers to give it on their behalf when to his knowledge he was not so authorised, and

(b) if proceedings were brought against the person to whom the consent was given, the consent would by virtue of section 7 of the principal Act afford a defence to those proceedings,

the person giving the consent shall be guilty of an offence, and shall be liable, on summary conviction, to a fine not exceeding *fifty pounds [£400]* [level 5 on the standard scale].

(2) The said section 7 shall not apply to proceedings under this section.

Note
As amended, firstly by substitution of the figure in italicised square brackets by the Performers' Protection Act 1972, section 1 and Schedule; secondly by substitution of the words in the second pair of square brackets by the Criminal Justice Act 1982, sections 38 and 46; and thirdly by substitution of the words in the first pair of square brackets by the Cable and Broadcasting Act 1984, section 57(1) and Schedule 5, para. 13(2).

[4A. Offences by bodies corporate

Where an offence under the principal Act or this Act committed by a body corporate is proved to have been committed with the consent or connivance of, or to be attributable to any neglect on the part of, any director, manager, secretary or other similar officer of the body corporate or any person who was purporting to act in any such capacity, he, as well as the body corporate, shall be guilty of that offence and shall be liable to be proceeded against and punished accordingly.]

Note
This section was added by the Performers' Protection Act 1972, section 3.

5. Citation, construction, commencement and extent

(1) This Act may be cited as the Performers' Protection Act 1963, and the principal Act and this Act may be cited together as the Performers' Protection Acts 1958 and 1963.

(2) This Act shall be construed as one with the principal Act.

(3) This Act shall come into operation at the expiration of the period of one

month beginning with the date of its passing, and shall apply only in relation to performances taking place after its commencement.

(4) It is hereby declared that this Act extends to Northern Ireland.

Performers' Protection Act 1972 (1972 c. 32)

Arrangement of sections

Section
1. Increase of fines under Performers' Protection Acts 1958 and 1963
2. Amendment of section 1 of Dramatic and Musical Performers' Protection Act 1958
3. Amendment of Performers' Protection Act 1963
4. Citation, construction, commencement and extent

SCHEDULE – Increase in fines

An Act to amend the Performers' Protection Acts 1958 and 1963 [29 June 1972]

1.   Increase of fines under Performers' Protection Acts 1958 and 1963

The enactments specified in column 1 of the Schedule to this Act (being enactments creating the offences under the Performers' Protection Acts 1958 and 1963 broadly described in column 2 of that Schedule) shall each have effect as if the maximum fine which may be imposed on summary conviction of any offence specified in that enactment were a fine not exceeding the amount specified in column 4 of that Schedule instead of a fine not exceeding the amount specified in column 3 of that Schedule.

Note
This has been superseded. See *ante*.

2.   Amendment of Section 1 of Dramatic and Musical Performers' Protection Act 1958

Section 1 of the Dramatic and Musical Performers' Protection Act 1958 (by which the making of records without the consent of the performers and sales of, and other dealings with, such records are rendered punishable) shall have effect as if after the word 'transaction' there were inserted the words 'or, on conviction on indictment, to imprisonment for a term not exceeding two years, or to a fine, or to both'.

SCHEDULE

Section 1
Increase of fines

(1) *Enactment*	(2) *Description of Offence*	(3) *Old Maximum Fine*	(4) *New Maximum Fine*
The Dramatic and Musical Performers' Protection Act 1958			
Section 1	Making, etc., records without consent of performers	£2 for each record in respect of which an offence is proved subject to a limit of £50 in respect of any one transaction	£20 for each record in respect of which an offence is proved subject to a limit of £400 in respect of any one transaction
Section 2	Making, etc., cinematograph films without consent of performers	£50	£400
Section 3	Broadcasting without consent of performers	£50	£400
Section 4	Making or having plates, etc., for making records in contravention of Act	£50	£400
The Performers' Protection Act 1963			
Section 3(1)	Relaying performances without consent of performers	£50	£400
Section 4(1)	Giving consent without authority	£50	£400

3.   Amendment of Performers' Protection Act 1963

In the Performers' Protection Act 1963 there shall be inserted after section 4 the following section:

4A. Offences by bodies corporate
Where an offence under the principal Act or this Act committed by a body corporate is proved to have been committed with the consent or connivance of, or to be attributable to any neglect on the part of, any director, manager, secretary or other similar officer of the body corporate or any person who was purporting to act in any such capacity, he, as well as the body corporate, shall be guilty of that offence and shall be liable to be proceeded against and punished accordingly.

4.   Citation, construction, commencement and extent

(1) This Act may be cited as the Performers' Protection Act 1972, and the Performers' Protection Acts 1958 and 1963 and this Act may be cited together as the Performers' Protection Acts 1958 to 1972.

(2) This Act shall come into operation at the expiration of the period of one month beginning with the date of its passing, but nothing in this Act shall affect the punishment for an offence committed before the commencement of this Act.

(3) It is hereby declared that this Act extends to Northern Ireland.

Appendix 5

Statute in Force from 1 August 1989

Copyright, Designs and Patents Act 1988 (c. 48)

Arrangement of sections

PART II RIGHTS IN PERFORMANCES

Remedies for infringement
194. Infringement actionable as breach of statutory duty
195. Order for delivery up
196. Right to seize illicit recordings
197. Meaning of 'illicit recording'

Offences
198. Criminal liability for making, dealing with or using illicit recordings
199. Order for delivery up in criminal proceedings
200. Search warrants
201. False representation of authority to give consent
202. Offence by body corporate: liability of officers

Supplementary provisions with respect to delivery up and seizure
203. Period after which remedy of delivery up not available
204. Order as to disposal of illicit recording
205. Jurisdiction of county court and sheriff court

Qualification for protection and extent
206. Qualifying countries, individuals and persons
207. Countries to which this Part extends
208. Countries enjoying reciprocal protection
209. Territorial waters and the continental shelf
210. British ships, aircraft and hovercraft

Interpretation
211. Expressions having same meaning as in copyright provisions
212. Index of defined expressions
SCHEDULE 2 – Permitted acts

PART II RIGHTS IN PERFORMANCES

Introductory

180. **Rights conferred on performers and persons having recording rights**

(1) This Part confers rights:

> (a) on a performer, by requiring his consent to the exploitation of his performances (see sections 181 to 184), and
> (b) on a person having recording rights in relation to a performance, in relation to recordings made without his consent or that of the performer (see sections 185 to 188),

and creates offences in relation to dealing with or using illicit recordings and certain other related acts (see sections 198 and 201).

(2) In this Part 'performance' means:

(a) a dramatic performance (which includes dance and mime),
(b) a musical performance,
(c) a reading or recitation of a literary work, or
(d) a performance of a variety act or any similar presentation,

which is, or so far as it is, a live performance given by one or more individuals; and 'recording', in relation to a performance, means a film or sound recording:

(a) made directly from the live performance,
(b) made from a broadcast of, or cable programme including, the performance, or
(c) made, directly or indirectly, from another recording of the performance.

(3) The rights conferred by this Part apply in relation to performances taking place before the commencement of this Part; but no act done before commencement, or in pursuance of arrangements made before commencement, shall be regarded as infringing those rights.

(4) The rights conferred by this Part are independent of:

(a) any copyright in, or moral rights relating to, any work performed or any film or sound recording of, or broadcast or cable programme including, the performance, and
(b) any other right or obligation arising otherwise than under this Part.

Performers' rights

181. Qualifying performances

A performance is a qualifying performance for the purposes of the provisions of this Part relating to performers' rights if it is given by a qualifying individual (as defined in section 206) or takes place in a qualifying country (as so defined).

182. Consent required for recording or live transmission of performance

(1) A performer's rights are infringed by a person who, without his consent:

(a) makes, otherwise than for his private and domestic use, a recording of the whole or any substantial part of a qualifying performance, or
(b) broadcasts live, or includes live in a cable programme service, the whole or any substantial part of a qualifying performance.

(2) In an action for infringement of a performer's rights brought by virtue of this section damages shall not be awarded against a defendant who shows that

at the time of the infringement he believed on reasonable grounds that consent had been given.

183.   Infringement of performer's rights by use of recording made without consent

A performer's rights are infringed by a person who, without his consent:

(a) shows or plays in public the whole or any substantial part of a qualifying performance, or
(b) broadcasts or includes in a cable programme service the whole or any substantial part of a qualifying performance,

by means of a recording which was, and which that person knows or has reason to believe was, made without the performer's consent.

184.   Infringement of performer's rights by importing, possessing or dealing with illicit recording

(1) A performer's rights are infringed by a person who, without his consent:

(a) imports into the United Kingdom otherwise than for his private and domestic use, or
(b) in the course of a business possesses, sells or lets for hire, offers or exposes for sale or hire, or distributes,

a recording of a qualifying performance which is, and which that person knows or has reason to believe is, an illicit recording.

(2) Where in an action for infringement of a performer's rights brought by virtue of this section a defendant shows that the illicit recording was innocently acquired by him or a predecessor in title of his, the only remedy available against him in respect of the infringement is damages not exceeding a reasonable payment in respect of the act complained of.

(3) In subsection (2) 'innocently acquired' means that the person acquiring the recording did not know and had no reason to believe that it was an illicit recording.

Rights of person having recording rights

185.   Exclusive recording contracts and persons having recording rights

(1) In this Part an 'exclusive recording contract' means a contract between a performer and another person under which that person is entitled to the exclusion of all other persons (including the performer) to make recordings of one or more of his performances with a view to their commercial exploitation.

(2) References in this Part to a 'person having recording rights', in relation to a performance, are (subject to subsection (3)) to a person:

(a) who is party to and has the benefit of an exclusive recording contract to which the performance is subject, or

(b) to whom the benefit of such a contract has been assigned,

and who is a qualifying person.

(3) If a performance is subject to an exclusive recording contract but the person mentioned in subsection (2) is not a qualifying person, references in this Part to a 'person having recording rights' in relation to the performance are to any person:

(a) who is licensed by such a person to make recordings of the performance with a view to their commercial exploitation, or

(b) to whom the benefit of such a licence has been assigned,

and who is a qualifying person.

(4) In this section 'with a view to commercial exploitation' means with a view to the recordings being sold or let for hire, or shown or played in public.

186. Consent required for recording of performance subject to exclusive contract

(1) A person infringes the rights of a person having recording rights in relation to a performance who, without his consent or that of the performer, makes a recording of the whole or any substantial part of the performance, otherwise than for his private and domestic use.

(2) In an action for infringement of those rights brought by virtue of this section damages shall not be awarded against a defendant who shows that at the time of the infringement he believed on reasonable grounds that consent had been given.

187. Infringement of recording rights by use of recording made without consent

(1) A person infringes the rights of a person having recording rights in relation to a performance who, without his consent or, in the case of a qualifying performance, that of the performer:

(a) shows or plays in public the whole or any substantial part of the performance, or

(b) broadcasts or includes in a cable programme service the whole or any substantial part of the performance,

by means of a recording which was, and which that person knows or has reason to believe was, made without the appropriate consent.

(2) The reference in subsection (1) to 'the appropriate consent' is to the consent of:

(a) the performer, or

(b) the person who at the time the consent was given had recording rights in relation to the performance (or, if there was more than one such person, of all of them).

188.   Infringement of recording rights by importing, possessing or dealing with illicit recording

(1) A person infringes the rights of a person having recording rights in relation to a performance who, without his consent or, in the case of a qualifying performance, that of the performer:

(a) imports into the United Kingdom otherwise than for his private and domestic use, or

(b) in the course of a business possesses, sells or lets for hire, offers or exposes for sale or hire, or distributes,

a recording of the performance which is, and which that person knows or has reason to believe is, an illicit recording.

(2) Where in an action for infringement of those rights brought by virtue of this section a defendant shows that the illicit recording was innocently acquired by him or a predecessor in title of his, the only remedy available against him in respect of the infringement is damages not exceeding a reasonable payment in respect of the act complained of.

(3) In subsection (2) 'innocently acquired' means that the person acquiring the recording did not know and had no reason to believe that it was an illicit recording.

Exceptions to rights conferred

189.   Acts permitted notwithstanding rights conferred by this Part

The provisions of Schedule 2 specify acts which may be done notwithstanding the rights conferred by this Part, being acts which correspond broadly to certain of those specified in Chapter III of Part I (acts permitted notwithstanding copyright).

190.   Power of Tribunal to give consent on behalf of performer in certain cases

(1) The Copyright Tribunal may, on the application of a person wishing to make a recording from a previous recording of a performance, give consent in a case where:

(a) the identity or whereabouts of a performer cannot be ascertained by reasonable inquiry, or

(b) a performer unreasonably withholds his consent.

(2) Consent given by the Tribunal has effect as consent of the performer for the purposes of:

(a) the provisions of this Part relating to performers' rights, and
(b) section 198(3)(a) (criminal liability: sufficient consent in relation to qualifying performances),

and may be given subject to any conditions specified in the Tribunal's order.

(3) The Tribunal shall not give consent under subsection (1)(a) except after the service or publication of such notices as may be required by rules made under section 150 (general procedural rules) or as the Tribunal may in any particular case direct.

(4) The Tribunal shall not give consent under subsection (1)(b) unless satisfied that the performer's reasons for withholding consent do not include the protection of any legitimate interest of his; but it shall be for the performer to show what his reasons are for withholding consent, and in default of evidence as to his reasons the Tribunal may draw such inferences as it thinks fit.

(5) In any case the Tribunal shall take into account the following factors:

(a) whether the original recording was made with the performer's consent and is lawfully in the possession or control of the person proposing to make the further recording;
(b) whether the making of the further recording is consistent with the obligations of the parties to the arrangements under which, or is otherwise consistent with the purposes for which, the original recording was made.

(6) Where the Tribunal gives consent under this section it shall, in default of agreement between the applicant and the performer, make such order as it thinks fit as to the payment to be made to the performer in consideration of consent being given.

Duration and transmission of rights; consent

191. Duration of rights

The rights conferred by this Part continue to subsist in relation to a performance until the end of the period of 50 years from the end of the calendar year in which the performance takes place.

192. Transmission of rights

(1) The rights conferred by this Part are not assignable or transmissible, except to the extent that performers' rights are transmissible in accordance with the following provisions.

(2) On the death of a person entitled to performer's rights:

(a) the rights pass to such person as he may by testamentary disposition specifically direct, and

(b) if or to the extent that there is no such direction, the rights are exercisable by his personal representatives;

and references in this Part to the performer, in the context of the person having performers' rights, shall be construed as references to the person for the time being entitled to exercise those rights.

(3) Where by virtue of subsection (2)(a) a right becomes exercisable by more than one person, it is exercisable by each of them independently of the other or others.

(4) The above provisions do not affect section 185(2)(b) or (3)(b), so far as those provisions confer rights under this Part on a person to whom the benefit of a contract or licence is assigned.

(5) Any damages recovered by personal representatives by virtue of this section in respect of an infringement after a person's death shall devolve as part of his estate as if the right of action had subsisted and been vested in him immediately before his death.

193.   Consent

(1) Consent for the purposes of this Part may be given in relation to a specific performance, a specified description of performances or performances generally, and may relate to past or future performances.

(2) A person having recording rights in a performance is bound by any consent given by a person through whom he derives his rights under the exclusive recording contract or licence in question, in the same way as if the consent had been given by him.

(3) Where a right conferred by this Part passes to another person, any consent binding on the person previously entitled binds the person to whom the right passes in the same way as if the consent had been given by him.

Remedies for infringement

194.   Infringement actionable as breach of statutory duty

An infringement of any of the rights conferred by this Part is actionable by the person entitled to the right as a breach of statutory duty.

195.   Order for delivery up

(1) Where a person has in his possession, custody or control in the course of a business an illicit recording of a performance, a person having performer's

rights or recording rights in relation to the performance under this Part may apply to the court for an order that the recording be delivered up to him or to such other person as the court may direct.

(2) An application shall not be made after the end of the period specified in section 203; and no order shall be made unless the court also makes, or it appears to the court that there are grounds for making, an order under section 204 (order as to disposal of illicit recording).

(3) A person to whom a recording is delivered up in pursuance of an order under the section shall, if an order under section 204 is not made, retain it pending the making of an order, or the decision not to make an order, under that section.

(4) Nothing in this section affects any other power of the court.

196. Right to seize illicit recordings

(1) An illicit recording of a performance which is found exposed or otherwise immediately available for sale or hire, and in respect of which a person would be entitled to apply for an order under section 195, may be seized and detained by him or a person authorised by him.

The right to seize and detain is exercisable subject to the following conditions and is subject to any decision of the court under section 204 (order as to disposal of illicit recording).

(2) Before anything is seized under this section notice of the time and place of the proposed seizure must be given to a local police station.

(3) A person may for the purpose of exercising the right conferred by this section enter premises to which the public have access but may not seize anything in the possession, custody or control of a person at a permanent or regular place of business of his and may not use any force.

(4) At the time when anything is seized under this section there shall be left at the place where it was seized a notice in the prescribed form containing the prescribed particulars as to the person by whom or on whose authority the seizure is made and the grounds on which it is made.

(5) In this section:

– 'premises' includes land, buildings, fixed or moveable structures, vehicles, vessels, aircraft and hovercraft; and
– 'prescribed' means prescribed by order of the Secretary of State.

(6) An order of the Secretary of State under this section shall be made by statutory instrument which shall be subject to annulment in pursuance of a resolution of either House of Parliament.

197.   Meaning of 'illicit recording'

(1) In this Part 'illicit recording', in relation to a performance, shall be construed in accordance with this section.

(2) For the purpose of a performer's rights, a recording of the whole or any substantial part of a performance of his is an illicit recording if it is made, otherwise than for private purposes, without his consent.

(3) For the purposes of the rights of a person having recording rights, a recording of the whole or any substantial part of a performance subject to the exclusive recording contract is an illicit recording if it is made, otherwise than for private purposes, without his consent or that of the performer.

(4) For the purposes of sections 198 and 199 (offences and orders for delivery up in criminal proceedings), a recording is an illicit recording if it is an illicit recording for the purposes mentioned in subsection (2) or subsection (3).

(5) In this Part 'illicit recording' includes a recording falling to be treated as an illicit recording by virtue of any of the following provisions of Schedule 2:

  – paragraph 4(3) (recordings made for purposes of instruction or examination),
  – paragraph 6(2) (recordings made by educational establishments for educational purposes),
  – paragraph 12(2) (recordings of performance in electronic form retained on transfer of principal recording), or
  – paragraph 16(3) (recordings made for purposes of broadcast or cable programme),

but otherwise does not include a recording made in accordance with any of the provisions of that Schedule.

(6) It is immaterial for the purposes of this section where the recording was made.

Offences

198.   Criminal liability for making, dealing with or using illicit recordings

(1) A person commits an offence who without sufficient consent:

  (a) makes for sale or hire, or
  (b) imports into the United Kingdom otherwise than for his private and domestic use, or
  (c) possesses in the course of a business with a view to committing any act infringing the rights conferred by this Part, or
  (d) in the course of a business:
      (i) sells or lets for hire, or

(ii) offers or exposes for sale or hire, or
(iii) distributes,

a recording which is, and which he knows or has reason to believe is, an illicit recording.

(2) A person commits an offence who causes a recording of a performance made without sufficient consent to be:

(a) shown or played in public, or
(b) broadcast or included in a cable programme service,

thereby infringing any of the rights conferred by this Part, if he knows or has reason to believe that those rights are thereby infringed.

(3) In subsections (1) and (2) 'sufficient consent' means:

(a) in the case of a qualifying performance, the consent of the performer, and
(b) in the case of a non-qualifying performance subject to an exclusive recording contract:
(i) for the purposes of subsection (1)(a) (making of recording), the consent of the performer or the person having recording rights, and
(ii) for the purposes of subsection (1)(b), (c) and (d) and subsection (2) (dealing with or using recording), the consent of the person having recording rights.

The references in this subsection to the person having recording rights are to the person having those rights at the time the consent is given or, if there is more than one such person, to all of them.

(4) No offence is committed under subsection (1) or (2) by the commission of an act which by virtue of any provision of Schedule 2 may be done without infringing the rights conferred by this Part.

(5) A person guilty of an offence under subsection (1)(a), (b) or (d)(iii) is liable:

(a) on summary conviction to imprisonment for a term not exceeding six months or a fine not exceeding the statutory maximum, or both;
(b) on conviction on indictment to a fine or imprisonment for a term not exceeding two years, or both.

(6) A person guilty of any other offence under this section is liable on summary conviction to a fine not exceeding level 5 on the standard scale or imprisonment for a term not exceeding six months, or both.

199. Order for delivery up in criminal proceedings

(1) The Court before which proceedings are brought against a person for an offence under section 198 may, if satisfied that at the time of his arrest or charge he had in his possession, custody or control in the course of a business

an illicit recording of a performance, order that it be delivered up to a person having performers' rights or recording rights in relation to the performance or to such other person as the court may direct.

(2) For this purpose a person shall be treated as charged with an offence:

(a) in England, Wales and Northern Ireland, when he is orally charged or is served with a summons or indictment;

(b) in Scotland, when he is cautioned, charged or served with a complaint or indictment.

(3) An order may be made by the court of its own motion or on the application of the prosecutor (or, in Scotland, the Lord Advocate or procurator-fiscal), and may be made whether or not the person is convicted of the offence, but shall not be made:

(a) after the end of the period specified in section 203 (period after which remedy of delivery up not available), or

(b) if it appears to the court unlikely that any order will be made under section 204 (order as to disposal of illicit recording).

(4) An appeal lies from an order made under this section by a magistrates' court.

(a) in England and Wales, to the Crown Court, and

(b) in Northern Ireland, to the county court;

and in Scotland, where an order has been made under this section, the person from whose possession, custody or control the illicit recording has been removed may, without prejudice to any other form of appeal under any rule of law, appeal against that order in the same manner as against sentence.

(5) A person to whom an illicit recording is delivered up in pursuance of an order under this section shall retain it pending the making of an order, or the decision not to make an order, under section 204.

(6) Nothing in this section affects the powers of the court under section 43 of the Powers of Criminal Courts Act 1973, section 223 or 436 of the Criminal Procedure (Scotland) Act 1975 or Article 7 of the Criminal Justice (Northern Ireland) Order 1980 (general provisions as to forfeiture in criminal proceedings).

200. Search warrants

(1) Where a justice of the peace (in Scotland, a sheriff or justice of the peace) is satisfied by information on oath given by a constable (in Scotland, by evidence on oath) that there are reasonable grounds for believing:

(a) that an offence under section 198(1)(a) (b) or (d)(iii) (offences of making, importing or distributing illicit recordings) has been or is about to be committed in any premises, and

(b) that evidence that such an offence has been or is about to be committed is in those premises,

he may issue a warrant authorising a constable to enter and search the premises, using such reasonable force as is necessary.

(2) The power conferred by subsection (1) does not, in England and Wales, extend to authorising a search for material of the kinds mentioned in section 9(2) of the Police and Criminal Evidence Act 1984 (certain classes of personal or confidential material).

(3) A warrant under subsection (1):

(a) may authorise persons to accompany any constable executing the warrant, and
(b) remains in force for 28 days from the date of its issue.

(4) In this section 'premises' includes land, buildings, fixed or moveable structures, vehicles, vessels, aircraft and hovercraft.

201.   False representation of authority to give consent

(1) It is an offence for a person to represent falsely that he is authorised by any person to give consent for the purposes of this Part in relation to a performance, unless he believes on reasonable grounds that he is so authorised.

(2) A person guilty of an offence under this section is liable on summary conviction to imprisonment for a term not exceeding six months or a fine not exceeding level 5 on the standard scale or both.

202.   Offence by body corporate: liability of officers

(1) Where an offence under this Part committed by a body corporate is proved to have been committed with the consent or connivance of a director, manager, secretary or other similar officer of the body, or a person purporting to act in any such capacity, he as well as the body corporate is guilty of the offence and liable to be proceeded against and punished accordingly.

(2) In relation to a body corporate whose affairs are managed by its members 'director' means a member of the body corporate.

Supplementary provisions with respect to delivery up and seizure

203.   Period after which remedy of delivery up not available

(1) An application for an order under section 195 (order for delivery up in civil proceedings) may not be made after the end of the period of six years from the date on which the illicit recording in question was made, subject to the following provisions.

(2) If during the whole or any part of that period a person entitled to apply for an order:

(a) is under a disability, or
(b) is prevented by fraud or concealment from discovering the facts entitling him to apply,

an application may be made by him at any time before the end of the period of six years from the date on which he ceased to be under a disability or, as the case may be, could with reasonable diligence have discovered those facts.

(3) In subsection (2) 'disability':

(a) in England and Wales, has the same meaning as in the Limitation Act 1980;
(b) in Scotland, means legal disability within the meaning of the Prescription and Limitations (Scotland) Act 1973;
(c) in Northern Ireland, has the same meaning as in the Statute of Limitation (Northern Ireland) 1958.

(4) An order under section 199 (order for delivery up in criminal proceedings) shall not, in any case, be made after the end of the period of six years from the date on which the illicit recording in question was made.

204.   Order as to disposal of illicit recording

(1) An application may be made to the court for an order that an illicit recording of a performance delivered up in pursuance of an order under section 195 or 199, or seized and detained in pursuance of the right conferred by section 196, shall be:

(a) forfeited to such person having performer's rights or recording rights in relation to the performance as the court may direct, or
(b) destroyed or otherwise dealt with as the court may think fit,

or for a decision that no such order should be made.

(2) In considering what order (if any) should be made, the court shall consider whether other remedies available in an action for infringement of the rights conferred by this Part would be adequate to compensate the person or persons entitled to the rights and to protect their interests.

(3) Provision shall be made by rules of court as to the service of notice on persons having an interest in the recording, and any such person is entitled:

(a) to appear in proceedings for an order under this section, whether or not he was served with notice, and
(b) to appeal against any order made, whether or not he appeared;

and an order shall not take effect until the end of the period within which notice of an appeal may be given or, if before the end of that period notice of appeal is duly given, until the final determination or abandonment of the proceedings on the appeal.

(4) Where there is more than one person interested in a recording, the court shall make such order as it thinks just and may (in particular) direct that the recording be sold, or otherwise dealt with, and the proceeds divided.

(5) If the court decides that no order should be made under this section, the person in whose possession, custody or control the recording was before being delivered up or seized is entitled to its return.

(6) References in this section to a person having an interest in a recording include any person in whose favour an order could be made in respect of the recording under this section or under section 114 or 231 of this Act or section 58C of the Trade Marks Act 1938 (which make similar provision in relation to infringement of copyright, design right and trade marks).

205. Jurisdiction of county court and sheriff court

(1) In England, Wales and Northern Ireland a county court may entertain proceedings under:

- section 195 (order for delivery up of illicit recording), or
- section 204 (order as to disposal of illicit recording),

where the value of the illicit recordings in question does not exceed the county court limit for actions in tort.

(2) In Scotland proceedings for an order under either of those provisions may be brought in the sheriff court.

(3) Nothing in this section shall be construed as affecting the jurisdiction of the High Court or, in Scotland, the Court of Session.

Qualification for protection and extent

206. Qualifying countries, individuals and persons

(1) In this Part:

- 'qualifying country' means:

    (a) the United Kingdom,
    (b) another member State of the European Economic Community, or
    (c) to the extent that an Order under section 208 so provides, a country designated under that section as enjoying reciprocal protection;

- 'qualifying individual' means a citizen or subject of, or an individual resident in, a qualifying country; and

— 'qualifying person' means a qualifying individual or a body corporate or other body having legal personality which:

(a) is formed under the law of a part of the United Kingdom or another qualifying country, and

(b) has in any qualifying country a place of business at which substantial business activity is carried on.

(2) The reference in the definition of 'qualifying individual' to a person's being a citizen or subject of a qualifying country shall be construed:

(a) in relation to the United Kingdom, as a reference to his being a British citizen, and

(b) in relation to a colony of the United Kingdom, as a reference to his being a British Dependent Territories' citizen by connection with that colony.

(3) In determining for the purpose of the definition of 'qualifying person' whether substantial business activity is carried on at a place of business in any country, no account shall be taken of dealings in goods which are at all material times outside that country.

207.   Countries to which this Part extends

This Part extends to England and Wales, Scotland and Northern Ireland.

208.   Countries enjoying reciprocal protection

(1) Her Majesty may by Order in Council designate as enjoying reciprocal protection under this Part:

(a) a Convention country, or

(b) a country as to which Her Majesty is satisfied that provision has been or will be made under its law giving adequate protection for British performances.

(2) A 'Convention country' means a country which is a party to a Convention relating to performers' rights to which the United Kingdom is also a party.

(3) A 'British performance' means a performance:

(a) given by an individual who is a British citizen or resident in the United Kingdom, or

(b) taking place in the United Kingdom.

(4) If the law of that country provides adequate protection only for certain descriptions of performance, an Order under subsection (1)(b) designating that country shall contain provision limiting to a corresponding extent the protection afforded by this Part in relation to performances connected with that country.

(5) The power conferred by subsection (1)(b) is exercisable in relation to any of the Channel Islands, the Isle of Man or any colony of the United Kingdom, as in relation to a foreign country.

(6) A statutory instrument containing an Order in Council under this section shall be subject to annulment in pursuance of a resolution of either House of Parliament.

209.   Territorial waters and the continental shelf

(1) For the purposes of this Part the territorial waters of the United Kingdom shall be treated as part of the United Kingdom.

(2) This Part applies to things done in the United Kingdom sector of the continental shelf on a structure or vessel which is present there for purposes directly connected with the exploration of the sea bed or subsoil or the exploitation of their natural resources as it applies to things done in the United Kingdom.

(3) The United Kingdom sector of the continental shelf means the areas designated by order under section (17) of the Continental Shelf Act 1964.

210.   British ships, aircraft and hovercraft

(1) This Part applies to things done on a British ship, aircraft or hovercraft as it applies to things done in the United Kingdom.

(2) In this section:

– 'British ship' means a ship which is a British ship for the purposes of the Merchant Shipping Acts (see section 2 of the Merchant Shipping Act 1988) otherwise than by virtue of registration in a country outside the United Kingdom; and
– 'British aircraft' and 'British hovercraft' mean an aircraft or hovercraft registered in the United Kingdom.

Interpretation

211.   Expressions having same meaning as in copyright provisions

(1) The following expressions have the same meaning in this Part as in Part I (copyright):

– broadcast,
– business,
– cable programme,
– cable programme service,
– country,
– defendant (in Scotland),

- delivery up (in Scotland),
- film,
- literary work,
- published, and
- sound recording.

(2) The provisions of section 6(3) to (5), section 7(5) and 19(4) (supplementary provisions relating to broadcasting and cable programme services) apply for the purposes of this Part, and in relation to an infringement of the rights conferred by this Part, as they apply for the purposes of Part I and in relation to an infringement of copyright.

212. Index of defined expressions

The following Table shows provisions defining or otherwise explaining expressions used in this Part (other than provisions defining or explaining an expression used only in the same section):

broadcast (and related expressions)	section 211 (and section 6)
business	section 211(1) (and section 178)
cable programme, cable programme service (and related expressions)	section 211 (and section 7)
country	section 211(1) (and section 178)
defendant (in Scotland)	section 211(1) (and section 177)
delivery up (in Scotland)	section 211(1) (and section 177)
exclusive recording contract	section 185(1)
film	section 211(1) (and section 5)
illicit recording	section 197
literary work	section 211(1) (and section 3(1))
performance	section 180(2)
published	section 211(1) (and section 175)
qualifying country	section 206(1)
qualifying individual	section 206(1) and (2)
qualifying performance	section 181
qualifying person	section 206(1) and (3)
recording (of a performance)	section 180(2)
recording rights (person having)	section 185(2) and (3)
sound recording	section 211(1) (and section 5)

SCHEDULE 2

RIGHTS IN PERFORMANCES: PERMITTED ACTS

Introductory

1. (1) The provisions of this Schedule specify acts which may be done in relation to a performance or recording notwithstanding the rights conferred by Part II; they relate only to the question of infringement of those rights and do

not affect any other right or obligation restricting the doing of any of the specified acts.

(2) No inference shall be drawn from the description of any act which may by virtue of this Schedule be done without infringing the rights conferred by Part II as to the scope of those rights.

(3) The provisions of this Schedule are to be construed independently of each other, so that the fact that an act does not fall within one provision does not mean that it is not covered by another provision.

Criticism, reviews and news reporting
2. (1) Fair dealing with a performance or recording:

(a) for the purpose of criticism or review, of that or another performance or recording, or of a work, or
(b) for the purpose of reporting current events,

does not infringe any of the rights conferred by Part II.

(2) Expressions used in this paragraph have the same meaning as in section 30.

Incidental inclusion of performance or recording
3. (1) The rights conferred by Part II are not infringed by the incidental inclusion of a performance or recording in a sound recording, film, broadcast or cable programme.

(2) Nor are those rights infringed by anything done in relation to copies of, or the playing, showing, broadcasting or inclusion in a cable programme service of, anything whose making was, by virtue of sub-paragraph (1), not an infringement of those rights.

(3) A performance or recording so far as it consists of music, or words spoken or sung with music, shall not be regarded as incidentally included in a sound recording, broadcast or cable programme if it is deliberately included.

(4) Expressions used in this paragraph have the same meaning as in section 31.

Things done for purposes of instruction or examination
4. (1) The rights conferred by Part II are not infringed by the copying of a recording of a performance in the course of instruction, or of preparation for instruction, in the making of films or film sound-tracks, provided the copying is done by a person giving or receiving instruction.

(2) The rights conferred by Part II are not infringed:

(a) by the copying of a recording of a performance for the purposes of setting or answering the questions in an examination, or
(b) by anything done for the purposes of an examination by way of communicating the questions to the candidates.

(3) Where a recording which would otherwise be an illicit recording is made in

accordance with this paragraph but is subsequently dealt with, it shall be treated as an illicit recording for the purposes of that dealing, and if that dealing infringes any right conferred by Part II for all subsequent purposes.

For this purpose 'dealt with' means sold or let for hire, or offered or exposed for sale or hire.

(4) Expressions used in this paragraph have the same meaning as in section 32.

Playing or showing sound recording, film, broadcast or cable programme at educational establishment
5. (1) The playing or showing of a sound recording, film, broadcast or cable programme at an educational establishment for the purposes of instruction before an audience consisting of teachers and pupils at the establishment and other persons directly connected with the activities of the establishment is not a playing or showing of a performance in public for the purposes of infringement of the rights conferred by Part II.

(2) A person is not for this purpose directly connected with the activities of the educational establishment simply because he is the parent of a pupil at the establishment.

(3) Expressions used in this paragraph have the same meaning as in section 34 and any provision made under section 174(2) with respect to the application of that section also applies for the purposes of this paragraph.

Recording of broadcasts and cable programmes by educational establishments
6. (1) A recording of a broadcast or cable programme, or a copy of such a recording, may be made by or on behalf of an educational establishment for the educational purposes of that establishment without thereby infringing any of the rights conferred by Part II in relation to any performance or recording included in it.

(2) Where a recording which would otherwise be an illicit recording is made in accordance with this paragraph but is subsequently dealt with, it shall be treated as an illicit recording for the purposes of that dealing, and if that dealing infringes any right conferred by Part II for all subsequent purposes.

For this purpose 'dealt with' means sold or let for hire, or offered or exposed for sale or hire.

(3) Expressions used in this paragraph have the same meaning as in section 35 and any provision made under section 174(2) with respect to the application of that section also applies for the purposes of this paragraph.

Copy of work required to be made as condition of export
7. (1) If an article of cultural or historical importance or interest cannot lawfully be exported from the United Kingdom unless a copy of it is made and deposited in an appropriate library or archive, it is not an infringement of any right conferred by Part II to make that copy.

(2) Expressions used in this paragraph have the same meaning as in section 44.

Parliamentary and judicial proceedings

8. (1) The rights conferred by Part II are not infringed by anything done for the purposes of parliamentary or judicial proceedings or for the purpose of reporting such proceedings.

(2) Expressions used in this paragraph have the same meaning as in section 45.

Royal Commissions and statutory inquiries

9. (1) The rights conferred by Part II are not infringed by anything done for the purposes of the procedings of a Royal Commission or statutory inquiry or for the purpose of reporting any such proceedings held in public.

(2) Expressions used in this paragraph have the same meaning as in section 46.

Public records

10. (1) Material which is comprised in public records within the meaning of the Public Records Act 1958, the Public Records (Scotland) Act 1937 or the Public Records Act (Northern Ireland) 1923 which are open to public inspection in pursuance of that Act, may be copied, and a copy may be supplied to any person, by or with the authority of any officer appointed under that Act, without infringing any right conferred by Part II.

(2) Expressions used in this paragraph have the same meaning as in section 49.

Acts done under statutory authority

11. (1) Where the doing of a particular act is specifically authorised by an Act of Parliament, whenever passed, then, unless the Act provides otherwise, the doing of that act does not infringe the rights conferred by Part II.

(2) Sub-paragraph (1) applies in relation to an enactment contained in Northern Ireland legislation as it applies to an Act of Parliament.

(3) Nothing in this paragraph shall be construed as excluding any defence of statutory authority otherwise available under or by virtue of any enactment.

(4) Expressions used in this paragraph have the same meaning as in section 50.

Transfer of copies of works in electronic form

12. (1) This paragraph applies where a recording of a performance in electronic form has been purchased on terms which, expressly or impliedly or by virtue of any rule of law, allow the purchaser to make further recordings in connection with his use of the recording.

(2) If there are no express terms:

> (a) prohibiting the transfer of the recording by the purchaser, imposing obligations which continue after a transfer, prohibiting the assignment of any consent or terminating any consent on a transfer, or
> (b) providing for the terms on which a transferee may do the things which the purchaser was permitted to do,

anything which the purchaser was allowed to do may also be done by a transferee without infringement of the rights conferred by this Part, but any recording made by the purchaser which is not also transferred shall be treated as an illicit recording for all purposes after the transfer.

(3) The same applies where the original purchased recording is no longer usable and what is transferred is a further copy used in its place.

(4) The above provisions also apply on a subsequent transfer, with the substitution for references in sub-paragraph (2) to the purchaser of references to the subsequent transferor.

(5) This paragraph does not apply in relation to a recording purchased before the commencement of Part II.

(6) Expressions used in this paragraph have the same meaning as in section 56.

Use of recordings of spoken works in certain cases

13. (1) Where a recording of the reading or recitation of a literary work is made for the purpose:

(a) of reporting current events, or
(b) of broadcasting or including in a cable programme service the whole or part of the reading or recitation,

it is not an infringement of the rights conferred by Part II to use the recording (or to copy the recording and use the copy) for that purpose, provided the following conditions are met.

(2) The conditions are that:

(a) the recording is a direct recording of the reading or recitation and is not taken from a previous recording or from a broadcast or cable programme;
(b) the making of the recording was not prohibited by or on behalf of the person giving the reading or recitation;
(c) the use made of the recording is not of a kind prohibited by or on behalf of that person before the recording was made; and
(d) the use is by or with the authority of a person who is lawfully in possession of the recording.

(3) Expressions used in this paragraph have the same meaning as in section 58.

Recordings of folksongs

14. (1) A recording of a performance of a song may be made for the purpose of including it in an archive maintained by a designated body without infringing any of the rights conferred by Part II, provided the conditions in sub-paragraph (2) below are met.

(2) The conditions are that:

(a) the words are unpublished and of unknown authorship at the time the recording is made,

(b) the making of the recording does not infringe any copyright, and

(c) its making is not prohibited by any performer.

(3) Copies of a recording made in reliance on sub-paragraph (1) and included in an archive maintained by a designated body may, if the prescribed conditions are met, be made and supplied by the archivist without infringing any of the rights conferred by Part II.

(4) In this paragraph:

– 'designated body' means a body designated for the purposes of section 61, and

– 'the prescribed conditions' means the conditions prescribed for the purposes of subsection (3) of that section;

and other expressions used in this paragraph have the same meaning as in that section.

Playing of sound recordings for purposes of club, society, etc.

15. (1) It is not an infringement of any right conferred by Part II to play a sound recording as part of the activities of, or for the benefit of, a club, society or other organisation if the following conditions are met.

(2) The conditions are:

(a) that the organisation is not established or conducted for profit and its main objects are charitable or are otherwise concerned with the advancement of religion, education or social welfare, and

(b) that the proceeds of any charge for admission to the place where the recording is to be heard are applied solely for the purposes of the organisation.

(3) Expressions used in this paragraph have the same meaning as in section 67.

Incidental recording for purposes of broadcast or cable programme

16. (1) A person who proposes to broadcast a recording of a performance, or include a recording of a performance in a cable programme service, in circumstances not infringing the rights conferred by Part II shall be treated as having consent for the purposes of that Part for the making of a further recording for the purposes of the broadcast or cable programme.

(2) That consent is subject to the condition that the further recording:

(a) shall not be used for any other purpose, and

(b) shall be destroyed within 28 days of being first used for broadcasting the performance or including it in a cable programme service.

(3) A recording made in accordance with this paragraph shall be treated as an illicit recording:

(a) for the purposes of any use in breach of the condition mentioned in sub-paragraph (2)(a), and

(b) for all purposes after that condition or the condition mentioned in sub-paragraph (2)(b) is broken.

(4) Expressions used in this paragraph have the same meaning as in section 68.

Recordings for purposes of supervision and control of broadcasts and cable programmes

17. (1) The rights conferred by Part II are not infringed by the making or use by the British Broadcasting Corporation, for the purpose of maintaining supervision and control over programmes broadcast by them, of recordings of those programmes.

(2) The rights conferred by Part II are not infringed by:

(a) the making or use of recordings by the Independent Broadcasting Authority for the purposes mentioned in section 4(7) of the Broadcasting Act 1981 (maintenance of supervision and control over programmes and advertisements); or

(b) anything done under or in pursuance of provision included in a contract between a programme contractor and the Authority in accordance with section 21 of that Act.

(3) The rights conferred by Part II are not infringed by:

(a) the making by or with the authority of the Cable Authority, or the use by that Authority, for the purpose of maintaining supervision and control over programmes included in services listed under Part I of the Cable and Broadcasting Act 1984, of recordings of those programmes; or

(b) anything done under or in pursuance of:

(i) a notice or direction given under section 16 of the Cable and Broadcasting Act 1984 (power of Cable Authority to require production of recordings); or

(ii) a condition included in a licence by virtue of section 35 of that Act (duty of Authority to secure that recordings are available for certain purposes).

(4) Expressions used in this paragraph have the same meaning as in section 69.

Free public showing or playing of broadcast or cable programme

18. (1) The showing or playing in public of a broadcast or cable programme to an audience who have not paid for admission to the place where the broadcast or programme is to be seen or heard does not infringe any right conferred by Part II in relation to a performance or recording included in:

(a) the broadcast or cable programme, or

(b) any sound recording or film which is played or shown in public by reception of the broadcast or cable programme.

(2) The audience shall be treated as having paid for admission to a place:

(a) if they have paid for admission to a place of which that place forms part; or

(b) if goods or services are supplied at that place (or a place of which it forms part):

(i) at prices which are substantially attributable to the facilities afforded for seeing or hearing the broadcast or programme, or

(ii) at prices exceeding those usually charged there and which are partly attributable to those facilities.

(3) The following shall not be regarded as having paid for admission to a place:

(a) persons admitted as residents or inmates of the place;

(b) persons admitted as members of a club or society where the payment is only for membership of the club or society and the provision of facilities for seeing or hearing broadcasts or programmes is only incidental to the main purposes of the club or society.

(4) Where the making of the broadcast or inclusion of the programme in a cable programme service was an infringement of the rights conferred by Part II in relation to a performance or recording, the fact that it was heard or seen in public by the reception of the broadcast or programme shall be taken into account in assessing the damages for that infringement.

(5) Expressions used in this paragraph have the same meaning as in section 72.

Reception and re-transmission of broadcast in cable programme service

19. (1) This paragraph applies where a broadcast made from a place in the United Kingdom is, by reception and immediate re-transmission, included in a cable programme service.

(2) The rights conferred by Part II in relation to a performance or recording included in the broadcast are not infringed:

(a) if the inclusion of the broadcast in the cable programme service is in pursuance of a requirement imposed under section 13(1) of the Cable and Broadcasting Act 1984 (duty of Cable Authority to secure inclusion in cable service of certain programmes), or

(b) if and to the extent that the broadcast is made for reception in the area in which the cable programme service is provided;

but where the making of the broadcast was an infringement of those rights, the fact that the broadcast was re-transmitted as a programme in a cable programme service shall be taken into account in assessing the damages for that infringement.

(3) Expressions used in this paragraph have the same meaning as in section 73.

Provision of sub-titled copies of broadcast or cable programme

20. (1) A designated body may, for the purpose of providing people who are deaf or hard of hearing, or physically or mentally handicapped in other ways,

with copies which are sub-titled or otherwise modified for their special needs, make recordings of television broadcasts or cable programmes without infringing any right conferred by Part II in relation to a performance or recording included in the broadcast or cable programme.

(2) In this paragraph 'designated body' means a body designated for the purposes of section 74 and other expressions used in this paragraph have the same meaning as in that section.

Recording of broadcast or cable programme for archival purposes
21. (1) A recording of a broadcast or cable programme of a designated class, or a copy of such a recording, may be made for the purpose of being placed in an archive maintained by a designated body without thereby infringing any right conferred by Part II in relation to a performance or recording included in the broadcast or cable programme.

(2) In this paragraph 'designated class' and 'designated body' means a class or body designated for the purposes of section 75 and other expressions used in this paragraph have the same meaning as in that section.

Appendix 6

Secondary Legislation in Force from 1 August 1989

The Copyright Tribunal Rules 1989 (S.I. 1989 No. 1129) (Extracts)

Made	4th July 1989
Laid before Parliament	10th July 1989
Coming into force	1st August 1989

Arrangement of Rules

44. Intervener's application
45. Effect of suspension of order

Miscellaneous and general
46. Application of Arbitration Acts
47. Enforcement of Tribunal's order in Scotland
48. Costs
49. Fees
50. Service of documents
51. Time
52. Office hours
53. Failure to comply with directions
54. Power of Tribunal to regulate procedure
55. Transitional provision and revocation of previous Rules

SCHEDULE 3 – Forms

References and applications with respect to licensing schemes
Amendment of statement of case and answer
10. (1) Subject to paragraph (3) of this rule, a party may at any time amend his statement of case or answer by serving on the Secretary the amended statement or answer.

(2) On being served with an amended statement of case or answer, the Secretary shall as soon as practicable serve a copy thereof on every other party.

(3) No amended statement of case or answer shall, without the leave of the Chairman, be served after such date as the Chairman may direct under rule 11(2)(iii).

Chairman's directions
11. (1) Upon the expiration of the time specified by rule 9(2) for the service on the Secretary of a statement of case or answer, the Chairman shall appoint a date and place for the attendance of the parties for the purpose of his giving directions as to the further conduct of the proceedings, and the Secretary shall serve on every party and every person whose application under rule 7(1) has not been determined not less than 21 days' notice of such date and place.

(2) On the appointed day, the Chairman shall afford every party attending the appointment an opportunity of being heard and, after considering any representations made orally or in writing, give such directions as he thinks fit with a view to the just, expeditious and economical disposition of the proceedings and, without prejudice to the generality of the foregoing, may give directions as to:

    (i) the date and place of any oral hearing requested by any party or which the Chairman for any reason considers necessary, and the procedure (including the number of representatives each party may appoint for the purpose of such hearing) and the timetable (including the allocation of time for the making of representations by each party) to be followed at such a hearing;

(ii) the procedure to be followed with regard to the submission and exchange of written arguments;

(iii) the date after which no amended statement of case or answer may be served without leave;

(iv) the preparation and service by each party, or any one party if all other parties agree, of a schedule setting out the issues to be determined by the Tribunal and brief particulars of the contentions of each party in relation thereto;

(v) the admission of any facts or documents, and the discovery and inspection of the documents

(vi) the giving of evidence on affidavit; and

(vii) the consideration by the Tribunal of whether any objection made to an intervener's credentials under rule 8 shall operate as a stay of the proceedings.

(3) The Chairman may postpone or adjourn to a later date to be appointed by him the giving of any directions under this rule and, at any time after directions have been given under this rule the Chairman may, whether or not any application on that behalf has been made under rule 12, give such further directions as he may think fit.

(4) If any party fails to comply with any direction given or order made under this rule or rule 12, the Chairman may, without prejudice to the making of any order under rule 53, give such consequential directions as may be necessary and may order such a party to pay any costs occasioned by his default.

Application for directions
12. (1) A party may, at any stage of the proceedings, apply to the Tribunal for directions with respect to any issue or other matter in the proceedings and, except where the Tribunal (whether generally or in any particular case) otherwise directs or these Rules otherwise provide, every such application shall be disposed of by the Chairman.

(2) The application shall be made by the service of a notice on the Secretary (stating the grounds upon which it is made) and, unless the notice is accompanied by the written consent of all parties to the proceedings, the party making the application shall serve a copy of the application on every other party to the proceedings and inform the Secretary of the date of such service.

(3) Any party who objects to the application may, within 7 days after being served with the copy thereof, serve a notice of application (stating the grounds of objection) on the Secretary and he shall serve a copy of the same on the applicant and any other party to the proceedings and inform the Secretary of the date of such service.

(4) After considering the application and any objection thereto and, if he considers necessary, after having given all parties concerned an opportunity of being heard, the Chairman may make such order in the matter as he thinks fit and give such consequential directions as may be necessary.

Consolidation of proceedings

13. Where there is pending before the Tribunal more than one reference under section 118, 119, or 120 of the Act, or more than one application under section 121 or 122 of the Act relating to the same licensing scheme, the Chairman may if he thinks fit, either of his own motion or on an application made under rule 12, order that some or all of the references or applications, as the case may be, shall be considered together, and may give such consequential directions as may be necessary:

Provided that the Chairman shall not make an order under this rule of his own motion without giving all parties concerned a reasonable opportunity of objecting to the proposed order.

Procedure and evidence at hearing

14. (1) Every party to a reference or application which is considered at an oral hearing before the Tribunal shall be entitled to attend the hearing, to address the Tribunal, to give evidence and call witnesses.

(2) Except where the Tribunal or the Chairman otherwise orders in the case of an application for directions under rule 12, the hearing shall be in public.

(3) Evidence before the Tribunal shall be given orally or, if the parties so agree or the Tribunal or the Chairman so orders, by affidavit, but the Tribunal may at any stage of the proceedings require the personal attendance of any deponent for examination and cross-examination.

Representation and rights of audience

15. (1) Subject to paragraph (5) of this rule, a party may at any stage of the proceedings appoint some other person to act as agent for him in the proceedings.

(2) The appointment of an agent shall be made in writing and shall not be effective until notice thereof has been served on the Secretary, and a copy of the same has been served on every other party and the Secretary informed of the date of such service.

(3) Only one agent shall be appointed to act for a party at any one time.

(4) For the purpose of service on a party of any document, or the taking of any step required or authorised by these Rules, an agent appointed by a party shall be deemed to continue to have authority to act for such a party until the Secretary and every other party has received notice of the termination of his appointment.

(5) A party or an agent appointed by him under paragraph (1) of this rule may be represented at any hearing, whether before the Tribunal or the Chairman,

by a barrister, or in Scotland an advocate, or a solicitor, or by any other person allowed by the Tribunal or the Chairman to appear on his behalf or may, save in the case of a corporation or unincorporated body, appear in person.

Withdrawal of reference or application

16. (1) The applicant may withdraw his reference or application made under rule 3 at any time before it has been finally disposed of by serving a notice thereof on the Secretary, but such withdrawal shall be without prejudice to the Tribunal's power to make an order as to the payment of costs incurred up to the time of service of the notice. The applicant shall serve a copy of the notice on every other party to the proceedings and inform the Secretary of the date of such service.

(2) Any party to the proceedings upon whom a copy of the notice of withdrawal is served under this rule may, within 14 days of such service, apply to the Tribunal for an order that, notwithstanding such withdrawal, such reference or application should proceed to be determined by the Tribunal, and if the Tribunal decides, at its discretion, to proceed with such reference or application it may for that purpose substitute such party as to the applicant to the proceedings and give such consequential directions as may be necessary.

Publication of decision

18. The Secretary shall cause a copy of the Tribunal's decision to be made available at the office for public inspection during office hours and, if the Chairman so directs, shall cause to be advertised, in such manner as the Chairman thinks fit, short particulars of the decision.

Effective date of order

19. Except where the operation of the order is suspended under rule 42 or 43, the order of the Tribunal shall take effect from such date, and shall remain in force for such period, as shall be specified in the order.

References and applications with respect to licensing by licensing bodies

Intervener's application (Forms 5 & 6)

23. (1) A person or organisation who claims to have a substantial interest in proceedings in respect of a reference of an application under rule 20 may apply to the Tribunal to be made a party to that reference or application by serving on the Secretary a notice of intervention in Form 5, together with a statement of his interest.

(2) As soon as practicable after receipt of a notice under this rule the Secretary shall:

(a) serve a copy of the notice on every other party to the proceedings, and
(b) serve on the intervener a copy of the applicant's reference or application and statement of case, together with any other notice of intervention which has been served on him.

(3) Within 14 days of the service upon him of the notice, a party intending to

object to an intervener's credentials shall serve on the Secretary a notice of objection in Form 6 and shall serve a copy of the same on the intervener and inform the Secretary of the date of such service.

(4) The Tribunal, after considering the intervener's application and any objection to his credentials and, if it considers necessary, after having given the intervener and any party who has served a notice of objection an opportunity of being heard, shall, if satisfied of the substantial interest of the intervener, grant the application and may thereupon give such directions or further directions as to the taking of any steps required or authorised under these Rules or as to any further matters as may be necessary to enable the intervener to participate in the proceedings as a party.

(5) Subject to any direction to the contrary that the Chairman may give under rule 11(2)(vii) an objection to an intervener's credentials shall not operate as a stay of proceedings and shall be considered by the Tribunal at the same time as the reference or application in question.

Application for Tribunal's consent on behalf of performer

Commencement of proceedings (Form 14)
34. Proceedings under section 190 of the Act for the Tribunal's consent on behalf of the performer to the making of a recording from a previous recording of a performance shall be commenced by the service by the applicant on the Secretary of a notice in Form 14 together with a statement:

> (a) Where the identity or whereabouts of the performer cannot be ascertained, of the inquiries made by him in that respect and the result of those inquiries, or
> (b) where the identity or whereabouts of the performer are known, of the grounds on which the applicant considers that the performer's withholding of consent is unreasonable, and by serving a copy thereof on the performer.

Inquiries by Tribunal
35. (1) Where a notice has been served in accordance with rule 34(a), the Tribunal shall, after requiring of the applicant such further particulars as it may consider necessary, cause to be served on such persons as it considers are likely to have relevant information with regard to the identity or the whereabouts of the performer a notice seeking such information, and at the same time cause to be published, in such publications as it considers appropriate and at such intervals as it may determine, a notice setting out brief particulars of the application and requesting information on the identity or whereabouts of the performer.

(2) On the expiration of 28 days from the date of the publication of the notice, or the date of publication of the last such notice, the Tribunal may, on being satisfied that the identity or whereabouts of the performer cannot be ascertained, make an order giving its consent on such terms as it thinks fit.

Procedure and decision of Tribunal

36. (1) Within 21 days of the service of the notice under rule 34(b), the performer may serve on the Secretary his answer setting out his case and of the grounds for his withholding of consent, and shall serve a copy of the same on the applicant and inform the Secretary of the date of such service.

(2) Rules 10 to 16 shall apply to proceedings in respect of an application under rule 34(b) as they apply to proceedings in respect of an application under rule 3.

(3) The final decision of the Tribunal on an application under rule 34 shall be given in writing and shall include a statement of the Tribunal's reasons and where the Tribunal has, in default of an agreement between the application and the performer, made an order as to the payment to be made to the performer in consideration of the consent given on his behalf by the Tribunal, there shall be annexed to the decision a copy of that order; and the Secretary shall, as soon as practicable serve on every party to the proceedings a copy of the Tribunal's decision. Rules 18 and 19 shall apply with regard to the publication and the effective date of the decision.

Intervener's application (Forms 5 & 6)

37. A person or organisation who claims to have a substantial interest in proceedings in respect of an application under rule 34 may, in accordance with rule 23, apply to the Tribunal to be made a party, and that rule shall apply to proceedings in respect of such an application as it applies to proceedings in respect of an application under rule 20.

Appeal to the Court from decision of Tribunal and suspension of Tribunal's orders

Notice of appeal (Form 17)

42. (1) An appeal to the High Court or, in the case of proceedings of the Tribunal in Scotland, to the Court of Session under section 152 of the Act on a point of law arising from a decision of the Tribunal shall be brought within 28 days of the date of the decision of the Tribunal or within such further period as the court may, on an application to it, allow.

(2) A party so appealing to the court on a point of law shall as soon as may be practicable serve on the Secretary a notice in Form 17 of such an appeal, and shall serve a copy thereof on every person who was a party to the proceedings giving rise to that decision.

(3) Where an appeal has been lodged with the court, the Tribunal shall not make any further order on the reference or application which is the subject of the appeal until the court has given its decision thereon.

(4) On receipt of the notice of appeal by the Secretary the Tribunal may of its own motion suspend the operation of any order contained in its decision, and shall, if an order is so suspended, cause notice of the same to be served on every

person affected by the suspension and may, if it thinks fit, cause notice of the suspension to be published in such manner as it may direct.

Application for suspension of order (Form 18)

43. (1) A party to the proceedings may, pending the determination of an appeal under rule 42, apply to the Tribunal to suspend the operation of an order made by it by serving on the Secretary a notice in Form 18 within 7 days of the receipt of the decision of the Tribunal together with a statement of the grounds for suspension, and he shall serve a copy of the same on every person who was a party to the proceedings giving rise to that decision and inform the Secretary of the date of such service.

(2) Within 14 days of the service of the notice under paragraph (1) above a party may serve on the Secretary a statement setting out the grounds of his objection to the applicant's case, and shall serve a copy of the same on every person who was a party to the proceedings giving rise to the decision and inform the Secretary of the date of such service.

(3) Rules 10 to 16 shall apply in proceedings in respect of an application under this rule as they apply to proceedings in respect of an application under rule 3.

(4) Where the Tribunal, after consideration of the application and any representations, refuses an application to suspend the operation of its order, the Secretary shall as soon as practicable serve on every party to the proceedings a copy of the Tribunal's decision together with a statement of the Tribunal's reasons for refusal.

(5) Where any order of the Tribunal has been suspended upon the application of a party to the proceedings or by the court the Secretary shall serve notice of the suspension on all parties to the proceedings, and if particulars of the order have been advertised shall cause notice of the suspension to be advertised in the same manner, and rule 18 shall apply with regard to the publication of the decision.

Intervener's application (Forms 5 & 6)

44. A person or organisation who claims to have a substantial interest in proceedings in respect of an application under rule 43 may, in accordance with rule 23, apply to the Tribunal to be made a party, and that rule shall apply to proceedings in respect of such an application as it applies to proceedings in respect of an application under rule 20.

Effect of suspension of order

45. If the operation of any order is suspended under rule 42 or 43, then, while the order remains suspended, sections 123 and 128 of the Act shall not have effect in relation to the order.

Miscellaneous and general

Appliction of Arbitration Acts

46. The provisions of sections 12, 14, 17 and 26 of the Arbitration Act 1950

(which are set out in Part 1 of Schedule 2), shall apply in the case of proceedings before the Tribunal in England and Wales, and the provisions of sections 13, 14, 16, 21 and 24 of, and paragraphs 4, 5 and 8 of Schedule 1 to, the Arbitration Act (Northern Ireland) 1937 (which are set out in Part 2 of Schedule 2), shall apply in the case of proceedings before the Tribunal in Northern Ireland, as those provisions respectively apply to an arbitration where no contrary intention is expressed in the arbitration agreement.

Enforcement of Tribunal's orders in Scotland
47. Any decision of the Tribunal may be enforced in Scotland in like manner as a recorded decree arbitral.

Costs
48. (1) The Tribunal may, at its discretion, at any stage of the proceedings make any order it thinks fit in relation to the payment of costs by one party to another in respect of the whole or part of the proceedings.

(2) Any party against whom an order for costs is made shall, if the Tribunal so directs, pay to any other party a lump sum by way of costs, or such proportion of the costs as may be just, and in the last mentioned case the Tribunal may assess the sum to be paid or may direct that it be assessed by the Chairman, or taxed by a taxing officer of the Supreme Court or the Supreme Court of Northern Ireland or by the Auditor of the Court of Session.

Fees
49. The fees specified in Schedule 1 shall be payable in respect of the matters therein mentioned.

Service of documents
50. (1) Any notice or other document required by these Rules to be served on any person may be sent to him by pre-paid post at his address for service, or, where no address for service has been given, at his registered office, principal place of business or last known address, and every notice or other document required to be served on the Secretary may be sent by pre-paid post to the Secretary at the office.

(2) Service of any notice or document on a successor in title or successor in interest of a party to any proceedings shall be effective if served or sent to him in accordance with this rule.

(3) Any notice or other document required to be served on a licensing body or organisation which is not a body corporate may be sent to the secretary, manager or other similar officer.

(4) The Tribunal or the Chairman may direct that service of any notice or other document be dispensed with or effected otherwise than in the manner provided by these Rules.

(5) Service of any notice or document on a party's solicitor or agent shall be deemed to be service on such party, and service on a solicitor or agent for more

than one partyy shall be deemed to be service on every party for whom such a solicitor or agent acts.

Time
51. (12) Except in the case of the time limit imposed under rule 42(1), the time for doing any act may (whether it has already expired or not) be extended:

> (a) with the leave of the Tribunal or the Chairman, or
> (b) by the consent in writing of all parties, except where the Tribunal or Chairman has fixed the time by order or, if the time is prescribed by these Rules, has directed that it may not be extended or further extended without leave.

(2) A party in whose favour time is extended by consent under paragraph (1)(b) above shall, as soon as may be practicable after the necessary consents have been obtained, serve notice thereof on the Secretary.

(3) Where the last day for the doing of any act falls on a day on which the office is closed and by reason thereof the act cannot be done on that day, it may be done on the next day on which the office is open.

Office hours
52. The office shall be open between 10.00am and 4.00pm Monday to Friday, excluding Good Friday, Christmas Day and any day specified or proclaimed to be a bank holiday under section 1 of the Banking and Financial Dealings Act 1971.

Failure to comply with directions
53. If any party fails to comply with any direction given, in accordance with these Rules, by the Tribunal or the Chairman, the Tribunal may, if it considers that the justice of the case so requires, order that such party be debarred from taking any further part in the proceedings without leave of the Tribunal.

Power of Tribunal to regulate procedure
54. Subject to the provisions of the Act and these Rules, the Tribunal shall have power to regulate its own procedure.

Transitional provisions and revocation of previous Rules
55. (1) In relation to any proceedings which are pending under Part IV of the Copyright Act 1956 when these Rules come into force, these Rules shall apply subject to such modifications as the Tribunal or the Chairman may, in the circumstances, consider appropriate.

(2) The Performing Right Tribunal Rules 1965 and the Performing Right Tribunal (Amendment) Rules 1971 are hereby revoked, but without prejudice to anything done thereunder.

SCHEDULE 3

FORM 5   Rules 7(1), 23(1), 26, 30
33, 37, 41 and 44

COPYRIGHT, DESIGNS AND PATENTS ACT 1988
COPYRIGHT TRIBUNAL

Notice of Intervention

To,

The Secretary to the Tribunal

1. TAKE NOTICE that [name and address of intervener] ('the Intervener') wishes to be made a party to the proceedings commenced by notice of *reference/application/appeal dated ....

*[which was advertised in [name of publication and date of issue]].

2. The Intervener has a substantial interest in the matter for the following reasons [state reasons].

3. All communications about this reference should be address to

*[the Intervener at the address shown above]
*[name and address of Intervener's solicitor/agent].

Signed ....

Status of signatory .... [Intervener,
an officer of Intervener, solicitor or agent]

Date ....

*Delete whichever is inappropriate

FORM 6   Rules 8(1), 23(3), 26, 30
33, 37, 41 and 44

COPYRIGHT, DESIGNS AND PATENTS ACT 1988
COPYRIGHT TRIBUNAL

Notice of Objection to Intervener's Credentials

To,

The Secretary to the Tribunal

1. TAKE NOTICE that in connection with *proceedings commenced by notice of *reference/application dated .... served by [name of Applicant], and with the notice of intervention given by [name of Intervener] dated .... [name and address of party making objection] ('the Objector'), being

*[the Applicant]

*[the licensing body named in the notice of 8reference/application]

*[*a person/an organisation on whom the notice of 8reference/application was served]

*[an intervener in the proceedings by virtue of a notice of intervention served on [date of service]]

objects to the Intervener's credentials.

2. The Objector's grounds for objection are as follows [state grounds].

3. All communications about this reference should be addressed to

*[the Objector at the address shown above]
*[name and address of Objector's solicitor/agent].

Signed ....

Status of signatory .... [Objector,
an officer of Objector, solicitor or agent]

Date ....

*Delete whichever is inappropriate

FORM 14   Rule 34

COPYRIGHT, DESIGNS AND PATENTS ACT 1988
COPYRIGHT TRIBUNAL

Notice of Application for Tribunal's Consent on behalf of Performer under Section 190

To the Secretary to the Tribunal

1. TAKE NOTICE that [name and address of applicant] ('the Applicant') wishes to make a recording from a previous recording of [specify performance]

*[the identity or whereabouts of the performer(s) of which cannot be ascertained by reasonable inquiry]
*[the performer(s) of which unreasonably withhold his/their consent]

hereby applies to the Tribunal for its consent to the recording.

2. There is delivered herewith a statement setting out –

*[the inquiries made by the Applicant as to the identity or whereabouts of the performer(s) and the result of those inquiries]
*[the grounds on which the Applicant considers that the withholding of consent is unreasonable].

*3. [A copy of the Applicant's statement *has been/will be served on [date of service] on the performer(s) [state name(s) and address(es) of performer(s)]].

4. All communications about this reference should be addressed to

   *[the Applicant at the address shown above]
   *[name and address of Applicant's solicitor/agent].

Signed ....

Status of signatory .... [Applicant,
                              an officer of Applicant, solicitor or agent]

Date ....

*Delete whichever is inappropriate

FORM 17   Rules 42(2)

COPYRIGHT, DESIGNS AND PATENTS ACT 1988
COPYRIGHT TRIBUNAL

Notice of Appeal on Point of Law under Section 152

To,
      The Secretary to the Tribunal

1. TAKE NOTICE that [name and address of appellant] ('the Appellant'), being a party
to the proceedings on the *reference/application/appeal intends to appeal to the *High
Court/Court of Session against the decision of the Tribunal dated .... and bearing
the reference number .... on the following point(s) of law—

   [state point(s) of law].

2. A copy of this Notice *has been/will be served on [date of service] on every person or
organisation who was a party to the proceedings, namely [specify names and addresses
of parties].

3. All communications about this appeal should be addressed to

   *[the Appellant at the address shown above]
   *[name and address of Appellant's solicitor/agent].

Signed ....

Status of signatory .... [Appellant,
                              an officer of Appellant, solicitor or agent]

Date ....

*Delete whichever is inappropriate

FORM 18   Rules 43(1)

COPYRIGHT, DESIGNS AND PATENTS ACT 1988
COPYRIGHT TRIBUNAL

Notice of Application to Suspend Order of Tribunal

To,

The Secretary to the Tribunal

1. TAKE NOTICE that [name and address of applicant] ('the Applicant'), being a party to the proceedings on the *reference/application/appeal [specify the proceedings] hereby applies to the Tribunal for the suspension of the operation of the Order of the Tribunal dated .... and bearing the reference number ....

2. There is delivered herewith a statement setting out the grounds for suspension-

[state grounds for suspension].

3. A copy of this Notice, together with the statement, *has been/will be served on [date of service] on every person or organisation who was a party to the proceedings, namely [specify names and addresses of parties].

4. All communications about this application should be addressed to

*[the Applicant at the address shown above]
*[name and address of Applicant's solicitor/agent].

Signed ....

Status of signatory .... [Applicant,
an officer of Applicant, solicitor or agent]

Date ....

*Delete whichever is inappropriate

THE COPYRIGHT AND RIGHTS IN PERFORMANCES
(NOTICE OF SEIZURE) ORDER 1989 (S.I. 1989 No. 1006)

Made	13th June 1989
Laid before Parliament	26th June 1989
Coming into force	1st August 1989

The Secretary of State, in exercise of the powers conferred upon him by section 100(4) and (5) and section 196(4) and (5) of the Copyright, Designs and Patents Act 1988(a) ('the Act'), hereby makes the following Order:

1. This Order may be cited as the Copyright and Rights in Performances (Notice of Seizure) Order 1989 and shall come into force on 1st August 1989.

2. The form set out in the Schedule to this Order is hereby prescribed for the notice required under section 100(4) and section 196(4), respectively, of the Act.

SCHEDULE   Article 2

THE COPYRIGHT AND RIGHTS IN PERFORMANCES (NOTICE OF SEIZURE) ORDER 1989

NOTICE OF SEIZURE

To Whom it May Concern

1. Goods in which you were trading have been seized. This notice tells you who carried out the seizure, the legal grounds on which this has been done and the goods which have been seized and detained. As required by the Copyright, Designs and Patents Act 1988, notice of the proposed seizure was given to the police station at (state address).

Person carrying out seizure

2. (State name and address)
*acting on the authority of (state name and address).

Legal grounds for seizure and detention

3. This action has been taken under *section 100/section 196 of the Act which (subject to certain conditions) permits a copyright owner, or a person having performing rights or recording rights, to seize and detain infringing copies or illicit recordings found exposed or immediately available for sale or hire, or to authorise such seizure. The right to seize and detain is subject to a decision of the court under *section 114/section 204 of the Act (order as to disposal of goods seized and detained).

Nature of the goods seized and detained

*4. Infringing copies of works (within the meaning of section 27 of the Act) – (specify all articles seized)

   Illicit recordings (within the meaning of section 197 of the Act) – (specify all articles seized)

Signed .... Date ....

---

* Delete as necessary

Appendix 7

International Agreements

International Convention for the Protection of Performers, Producers of Phonograms and Broadcasting Organisations (Rome, 26 October 1961)

The Contracting States, moved by the desire to protect the rights of performers, producers of phonograms, and broadcasting organisations,
Have agreed as follows:

Article 1
Protection granted under this Convention shall leave intact and shall in no way affect the protection of copyright in literary and artistic works. Consequently, no provision of this Convention may be interpreted as prejudicing such protection.

Article 2
1. For the purposes of this Convention, national treatment shall mean the treatment accorded by the domestic law of the Contracting State in which protection is claimed:

(a) to performers who are its nationals, as regards performance taking place, broadcast, or first fixed, on its territory;
(b) to producers of phonograms who are its nationals, as regards phonograms first fixed or first published on its territory;
(c) to broadcasting organisations which have their headquarters on its territory, as regards broadcasts transmitted from transmitters situated on its territory.

2. National treatment shall be subject to the protection specifically guaranteed, and the limitations specifically provided for, in this Convention.

Article 3
For the purposes of this Convention:

(a) 'Performers' means actors, singers, musicians, dancers, and other persons who act, sing, deliver, declaim, play in, or otherwise perform literary or artistic works;
(b) 'Phonogram' means any exclusively aural fixation of sounds of a performance or of other sounds;

(c) 'Producer of phonograms' means the person who, or the legal entity which, first fixes the sounds of a performance or other sounds;

(d) 'Publication' means the offering of copies of a phonogram to the public in reasonable quantity;

(e) 'Reproduction' means the making of a copy or copies of a fixation;

(f) 'Broadcasting' means the transmission by wireless means for public reception of sounds or of images and sounds;

(g) 'Rebroadcasting' means the simultaneous broadcasting by one broadcasting organisation of the broadcast of another broadcasting organisation.

Article 4

Each Contracting State shall grant national treatment to performers if any of the following conditions is met:

(a) the performance takes place in another Contracting State;

(b) the performance is incorporated in a phonogram which is protected under Article 5 of this Convention;

(c) the performance, not being fixed on a phonogram, is carried by a broadcast which is protected by Article 6 of this Convention.

Article 5

1. Each Contracting State shall grant national treatment to producers of phonograms if any of the following conditions is met:

(a) the producer of the phonogram is a national of another Contracting State (criterion of nationality);

(b) the first fixation of the sound was made in another Contracting State (criterion of fixation);

(c) the phonogram was first published in another Contracting State (criterion of publication).

2. If a phonogram was first published in a non-Contracting State but if it was also published, within thirty days of its first publication, in a Contracting State (simultaneous publication), it shall be considered as first published in the Contracting State.

3. By means of a notification deposited with the Secretary-General of the United Nations, any Contracting State may declare that it will not apply the criterion of publication or, alternatively, the criterion of fixation. Such notification may be deposited at the time of ratification, acceptance or accession, or at any time thereafter; in the last case, it shall become effective six months after it has been deposited.

Article 6

1. Each Contracting State shall grant national treatment to broadcasting organisations if either of the following conditions is met:

(a) the headquarters of the broadcasting organisation is situated in another Contracting State;

(b) the broadcast was transmitted from a transmitter situated in another Contracting State.

2. By means of a notification deposited with the Secretary-General of the United Nations, any Contracting State may declare that it will protect broadcasts only if the headquarters of the broadcasting organisation is situated in another Contracting State and the broadcast was transmitted from a transmitter situated in the same Contracting State. Such notification may be deposited at the time of ratification, acceptance or accession, or at any time thereafter; in the last case, it shall become effective six months after it has been deposited.

Article 7

1. The protection provided for performers by this Convention shall include the possibility of preventing:

(a) the broadcasting and the communication to the public, without their consent, of their performance, except where the performance used in the broadcasting or of the public communication is itself already a broadcast performance or is made from a fixation;
(b) the fixation, without their consent, of their unfixed performance;
(c) the reproduction, without their consent, of a fixation of their performance:

(i) if the original fixation itself was made without their consent;
(ii) if the reproduction is made for purposes different from those for which the performers gave their consent;
(iii) if the original fixation was made in accordance with the provisions of Article 15, and the reproduction is made for purposes different from those referred to in those provisions.

2. (1) If broadcasting was consented to by the performers it shall be a matter for the domestic law of the Contracting State where protection is claimed to regulate the protection against rebroadcasting, fixation for broadcasting purposes, and the reproduction of such fixation for broadcasting purposes.

(2) The terms and conditions governing the use by broadcasting organisations of fixations made for broadcasting purposes shall be determined in accordance with the doemstic law of the Contracting State where protection is claimed.

(3) However, the domestic law referred to in sub-paragraphs (1) and (2) of this paragraph shall not operate to deprive performers of the ability to control, by contract, their relations with broadcasting organisations.

Article 8

Any Contracting State may, by its domestic laws and regulations, specify the manner in which performers will be represented in connexion with the exercise of their rights if several of them participate in the same performance.

Article 9
Any Contracting State may, by its domestic laws and regulations extend the protection provided for in this Convention to artistes who do not perform literary or artistic works.

Article 10
Producers of phonograms shall enjoy the right to authorise or prohibit the direct or indirect reproduction of their phonograms.

Article 11
If, as a condition of protecting the rights of producers of phonograms, or of performers, or both, in relation to phonograms, a Contracting State, under its domestic law, requires compliance with formalities, there shall be considered as fulfilled if all the copies in commerce of the published phonogram or their containers bear a notice consisting of the symbol ℗, accompanied by the year date of the first publication, placed in such a manner as to give reasonable notice of claim of protection; and if the copies or their containers do not identify the producer or the licensee of the producer (by carrying his name, trade mark or other appropriate designation), the notice shall also include the name of the owner of the rights of the producer; and, furthermore, if the copies or their containers do not identify the principal performers the notice shall also include the name of the person who, in the country in which the fixation was effected, owns the rights of such performers.

Article 12
If a phonogram published for commercial purposes, or a reproduction of such phonogram, is used directly for broadcasting or for any communication to the public, a single equitable remuneration shall be paid by the user to the performers, or to the producers of the phonograms, or to both. Domestic law may, in the absence of agreement between these parties, lay down the conditions as to the sharing of this remuneration.

Article 13
Broadcasting organisations shall enjoy the right to authorise or prohibit:

    (a) the rebroadcasting of their broadcasts;
    (b) the fixation of their broadcasts;
    (c) the reproduction:
        (i) of fixations, made without their consent, of their broadcasts;
        (ii) of fixations, made in accordance with the provisions of Article 15, of their broadcasts if the reproduction is made for purposes different from those referred to in those provisions;
    (d) the communication to the public of their television broadcasts if such communication is made in places accessible to the public against payment of an entrance fee; it shall be a matter for the domestic law of the State where protection of this right is claimed to determine the conditions under which it may be exercised.

Article 14

The term of protection to be granted under this Convention shall last at least until the end of a period of twenty years computed from the end of the year in which:

(a) the fixation was made – for phonograms and for performances incorporated therein;
(b) the performance took place – for performances not incorporated in phonograms;
(c) the broadcast took place – for broadcasts.

Article 15

1. Any Contracting State may, in its domestic laws and regulations, provide for exceptions to the protection guaranteed by this Convention as regards:

(a) private use;
(b) use of short excerpts in connexion with the reporting of current events;
(c) ephemeral fixation by a broadcasting organisation by means of its own facilities and for its own broadcasts;
(d) use solely for the purposes of teaching or scientific research.

2. Irrespective of paragraph 1 of this Article, any Contracting State may, in its domestic laws and regulations, provide for the same kinds of limitations with regard to the protection of performers, producers and phonograms and broadcasting organisations as it provides for, in its domestic laws and regulations, in connexion with the protection of copyright in literary and artistic works. However, compulsory licences may be provided for only to the extent to which they are compatible with this Convention.

Article 16

1. Any State, upon becoming party to this Convention, shall be bound by all the obligations and shall enjoy all the benefits thereof. However a State may at any time, in a notification deposited with the Secretary-General of the United Nations, declare that:

(a) as regards Article 12:
(i) it will not apply the provisions of that Article;
(ii) it will not apply the provisions of that Article in respect of certain uses;
(iii) as regards phonograms the producer of which is not a national of another Contracting State, it will not apply that Article;
(iv) as regards phonograms the producer of which is a national of another Contracting State, it will limit the protection provided for by that Article to the extent to which, and to the term for which, the latter State grants protection to phonograms first fixed by a national of the State making the declaration; however, the fact that the Contracting State of which the producer is a national does not grant the protection to the same beneficiary or beneficiaries as the State making the

declaration shall not be considered as a difference in the extent of the protection;

(b) as regards Article 13, it will not apply item (d) of that Article, if a Contracting State makes such a declaration, the other Contracting States shall not be obliged to grant the right referred to in Article 13, item (d), to broadcasting organisations whose headquarters are in that State.

2. If the notification referred to in paragraph 1 of this Article is made after the date of the deposit of the instrument of ratification, acceptance or accession, the declaration will become effective six months after it has been deposited.

Article 17

Any State which, on 26 October 1961, grants protection to producers of phonograms solely on the basis of the criterion of fixation may, by a notification deposited with the Secretary-General of the United Nations at the time of ratification, acceptance or accession, declare that it will apply, for the purposes of Article 5, the criterion of fixation alone and, for the purposes of paragraph 1(a)(iii) and (iv) of Article 16, the criterion of fixation instead of the criterion of nationality.

Article 18

Any State which has deposited a notification under paragraph 3 of Article 5, paragraph 2 of Article 6, paragraph 1 of Article 16 or Article 17, may, by a further notification deposited with the Secretary-General of the United Nations, reduce its scope or withdraw it.

Article 19

Notwithstanding anything in this Convention, once a performer has consented to the incorporation of his performance in a visual or audio-visual fixation, Article 7 shall have no further application.

Article 20

1. This Convention shall not prejudice rights acquired in any Contracting State before the date of coming into force of this Convention for that State.

2. No Contracting State shall be bound to apply the provisions of this Convention to performances or broadcasts which took place, or to phonograms which were fixed, before the date of coming into force of this Convention for that State.

Article 21

The protection provided for in this Convention shall not prejudice any protection otherwise secured to performers, producers of phonograms and broadcasting organisations.

Article 22

Contracting States reserve the right to enter into special agreements among themselves in so far as such agreements grant to performers, producers of phonograms or broadcasting organisations more extensive rights than those granted by this Convention or contain other provisions not contrary to this Convention.

Article 27

1. Any State may, at the time of ratification, acceptance or accession, or at any time thereafter, declare by notification addressed to the Secretary-General of the United Nations that this Convention shall extend to all or any of the territories for whose international relations it is responsible, provided that the Universal Copyright Convention or the International Convention for the Protection of Literary and Artistic Works applies to the territory or territories concerned. This notification shall take effect three months after the date of its receipt.

2. The notifications referred to in paragraph 3 of Article 5, paragraph 2 of Article 6, paragraph 2 of Article 16 and Articles 17 and 18, may be extended to cover all or any of the territories referred to in paragraph 1 of this Article.

Article 33

1. The present Convention is drawn up in English, French and Spanish, the three texts being equally authentic.

2. In addition, official texts of the present Convention shall be drawn up in German, Italian and Portuguese.

Note

Cmnd. 2425. Ratified by the United Kingdom 30 October 1963. Entered into force 18 May 1964. The United Kingdom ratification was accompanied by the following declaration:

(1) in respect of Article 5(1)(b) and in accordance with Article 5(3) of the Convention, the United Kingdom will not apply, in respect of phonograms, the criterion of fixation;

(2) in respect of Article 6(1) and in accordance with Article 6(2) of the Convention, the United Kingdom will protect broadcasts only if the headquarters of the broadcasting organisation is situated in another Contracting State and the broadcast was transmitted from a transmitter situated in the same Contracting State;

(3) in respect of Article 12 and in accordance with Article 16(1) of the Convention,

    (a) the United Kingdom will not apply the provisions of Article 12 in respect of the following uses:

        (i) the causing of a phonogram to be heard in public at any premises where persons reside or sleep, as part of the amenities provided exclusively or mainly for residents or inmates therein except where a special charge is made for admission to the part of the premises where the phonogram is to be heard,

        (ii) the causing of a phonogram to be heard in public as part of the activities of, or for the benefit of, a club, society or other organisation which is not established or conducted for profit and whose main objects are charitable or are otherwise concerned with the advancement of religion, education or social welfare, except where a charge is made for admission to the place where the phonogram is to be heard, and any of the proceeds of the charge are applied otherwise than for the purpose of the organisation;

    (b) as regards phonograms the producer of which is not a national of another

Contracting State or as regards phonograms the producer of which is a national of a Contracting State which has made a dceclaration under Article 16(1)(a)(i) stating that it will not apply the provisions of Article 12, the United Kingdom will not grant the protection provided for by Article 12, unless, in either event, the phonogram has been first published in a Contracting State which has made no such declaration.

Treaty of Rome (Extracts)

From Part Two ('Foundation of the Community'), Title 1 ('Free movement of goods'), Chapter 2 ('Elimination of Quantitative Restrictions between Member States')

Article 30
Quantitative restrictions on imports and all measures having equivalent effect shall, without prejudice to the following provisions, be prohibited between Member States.

Article 34
1. Quantitative restrictions on exports, and all measures having equivalent effect, shall be prohibited between Member States.

2. Member States shall, by the end of the first stage at the latest, abolish all quantitative restrictions on exports and any measures having equivalent effect which are in existence when this Treaty enters into force.

Article 36
The provisions of Articles 30 to 34 shall not preclude prohibitions or restrictions on imports, exports or goods in transit justified on grounds of public morality, public policy or public security; the protection of health and life of humans, animals or plants; the protection of national treasures possessing artistic, historic or archaeological value; or the protection of industrial and commercial property. Such prohibitions or restrictions shall not, however, constitute a means of arbitrary discrimination or a disguised restriction on trade between Member States.

From Part Three ('Policy of the Community'), Title 1 ('Common Rules') Chapter 1 ('Rules on Competition')

Article 85
1. The following shall be prohibited as incompatible with the common market: all agreements between undertakings, decision by associations of undertakings and concerted practices which may affect trade between Member States and which have as their object or effect the prevention, restriction or distortion of competition within the common market, and in particular those which:

  (a) directly or indirectly fix purchase or selling prices or any other trading conditions;

(b) limit or control production, markets, technical development, or investment;

(c) share markets or sources of supply;

(d) apply dissimilar conditions to equivalent transactions with other trading parties, thereby placing them at a competitive disadvantage;

(e) make the conclusion of contracts subject to acceptance by the other parties of supplementary obligations which, by their nature or according to commercial usage, have no connection with the subject of such contracts.

2. Any agreements or decisions prohibited pursuant to this Article shall be automatically void.

3. The provision of paragraph 2 may, however, be declared inapplicable in the case of:

— any agreement or category of agreements between undertakings;
— any decision or category of decisions by associations of undertakings;
— any concerted practice or category of concerted practices;

which contributes to improving the production or distribution of goods or to promoting technical or economic progress, while allowing consumers a fair share of the resulting benefit, and which does not:

(a) impose on the undertakings concerned restrictions which are not indispensable to the attainment of these objectives;

(b) afford such undertakings the possibility of eliminating competition in respect of a substantial part of the products in question.

Article 86

Any abuse by one or more undertakings of a dominant position within the common market or in a substantial part of it shall be prohibited as incompatible with the common market in so far as it may affect trade between Member States. Such abuse may, in particular, consist in:

(a) directly or indirectly imposing unfair purchase or selling prices or other unfair trading conditions;

(b) limiting production, markets or technical development to the prejudice of consumers;

(c) applying dissimilar conditions to equivalent transactions with other trading parties, thereby placing them at a competitive disadvantage;

(d) making the conclusion of contracts subject to acceptance by the other parties of supplementary obligations which, by their nature or according to commercial usage, have no connection with the subject of such contracts.

Index